War and Occupation in Iraqi Fiction

Edinburgh Studies in Modern Arabic Literature
Series Editor: Rasheed El-Enany

Writing Beirut: Mappings of the City in the Modern Arabic Novel
Samira Aghacy

Autobiographical Identities in Contemporary Arab Literature
Valerie Anishchenkova

The Iraqi Novel: Key Writers, Key Texts
Fabio Caiani and Catherine Cobham

Sufism in the Contemporary Arabic Novel
Ziad Elmarsafy

Gender, Nation, and the Arabic Novel: Egypt 1892–2008
Hoda Elsadda

Post-War Anglophone Lebanese Fiction: Home Matters in the Diaspora
Syrine Hout

War and Occupation in Iraqi Fiction
Ikram Masmoudi

The Arab Nahdah*: The Making of the Intellectual and Humanist Movement*
Abdulrazzak Patel

www.euppublishing.com/series/smal

War and Occupation in Iraqi Fiction

Ikram Masmoudi

EDINBURGH
University Press

To Noureddine, my father . . . whose voice is still with me . . .

Edinburgh University Press Ltd
The Tun – Holyrood Road
12 (2f) Jackson's Entry
Edinburgh EH8 8PJ
www.euppublishing.com

Typeset in 11/15 Adobe Garamond by
Servis Filmsetting Ltd, Stockport, Cheshire

A CIP record for this book is available from the British Library

ISBN 978 0 7486 9655 0 (hardback)
ISBN 978 0 7486 9656 7 (webready PDF)
ISBN 978 1 4744 0352 8 (epub)

Contents

Series Editor's Foreword vi

Acknowledgements ix

Introduction 1

1 The Iran–Iraq War and the Bare Life of the War Deserter 28

2 Postmodern War, the Gulf War and the Iraqi Soldier 85

3 Bare Life in the 'New Iraq' 134

4 Bare Life in the Camp 184

Conclusion 215

Bibliography 220

Index 228

Series Editor's Foreword

The Edinburgh Studies in Modern Arabic Literature is a new and unique series which will, it is hoped, fill in a glaring gap in scholarship in the field of modern Arabic literature. Its dedication to Arabic literature in the modern period, that is, from the nineteenth century onwards, is what makes it unique among series undertaken by academic publishers in the English-speaking world. Individual books on modern Arabic literature in general or aspects of it have been and continue to be published sporadically. Series on Islamic studies and Arab/Islamic thought and civilisation are not in short supply either in the academic world, but these are far removed from the study of Arabic literature qua literature, that is, imaginative, creative literature as we understand the term when, for instance, we speak of English literature or French literature, etc. Even series labelled 'Arabic/Middle Eastern Literature' make no period distinction, extending their purview from the sixth century to the present, and often including non-Arabic literatures of the region. This series aims to redress the situation by focusing on the Arabic literature and criticism of today, stretching its interest to the earliest beginnings of Arab modernity in the nineteenth century.

The need for such a dedicated series, and generally for the redoubling of scholarly endeavour in researching and introducing modern Arabic literature to the Western reader has never been stronger. The significant growth in the last decades of the translation of contemporary Arab authors from all genres, especially fiction, into English; the higher profile of Arabic literature internationally since the award of the Nobel Prize for Literature to Naguib Mahfouz in 1988; the growing number of Arab authors living in the Western diaspora and writing both in English and in Arabic; the adoption of such authors and others by mainstream, high-circulation publishers, as opposed to the academic publishers of the past; the establishment of prestigious prizes, such as the International Prize for Arabic Fiction (the Arabic Booker), run by the Man Booker Foundation, which brings huge publicity to the shortlist and winner every year, as well as translation contracts into English and other languages – all this and very recently the events of the Arab Spring have heightened public, let alone academic, interest in all things Arab, and not least Arabic literature. It is therefore part of the ambition of this series that it will increasingly address a wider reading public beyond its natural territory of students and researchers in Arabic and world literature. Nor indeed is the academic readership of the series expected to be confined to specialists in literature in the light of the growing trend for interdisciplinarity, which increasingly sees scholars crossing field boundaries in their research tools and coming up with findings that equally cross discipline borders in their appeal.

Iraq's history during the last fifty-odd years has been turbulent and often bloody: coups, violent struggles for power, ethnic and religious coercion, major prolonged wars, UN sanctions – all of which occurred mostly under the brutal dictatorship of the Baᶜath Party and Saddam Hussein, who ruled the country from 1979 until his overthrow after the Anglo-American invasion of 2003. As is the norm in totalitarian regimes, the iron grip of authority in Iraq was not limited to high affairs of the state – politics, economy, security and so on – but extended to all aspects of intellectual and cultural life. Censorship was total and so effective through sheer terror that in effect there was nothing to censor: writers did not dare in the first place to write something that would have needed to be censored by the regime's cultural agents. Nor was exile a licence for free expression: fear of the regime's long arm abroad or reprisals against family at home did the censor's job efficiently and comprehensively. So brutal was the regime that there came a time when it was dangerous to be a known writer and be silent. Silence was prone to be construed as disapproval: as a writer you had to speak out in support of the regime and in praise of the leader, or face the consequences.

As a result, and since the fall of Saddam Hussein, Iraqi writers, experiencing a measure of freedom of expression hitherto impossible for them, have been hugely engaged in a process of reassessment of their contemporary history, especially in fiction. A substantial number of novels by Iraqi writers has come out in the last ten years, eagerly asking the questions they could not ask before and looking for answers. A great amount of soul-searching is going on at present in Iraqi fiction, trying to understand and reinterpret not only the Saddam era, but the run-up to it since the independence of Iraq from British rule, and indeed the decade since the fall of Saddam Hussein, which ironically brought about not freedom and dignity but a brutal foreign occupation, collapse of law and order, violent sectarianism, ethnic strife and the daily reality of car bombs, suicide attacks and random death, which continues unabated until today.

This surge in literary output has been running fast ahead of Western scholarship. Indeed the Iraqi novel as a whole, let alone its latest trends in the post-Saddam era, has largely found little favour with Western academia, where the focus has traditionally been on the more-established Egyptian and Syro-Lebanese scenes.

And it is exactly this that makes the current monograph, *War and Occupation in Iraqi Fiction*, a welcome and timely publication. It will, as if by design, pick up the narrative where it was dropped by an earlier volume of this series, Fabio Caiani and Catherine Cobham's *The Iraqi Novel: Key Writers, Key Texts*. The study, utilising Giorgio Agamben's notions of the 'homo sacer' and 'state of exceptions', has a contemporary relevance and immediacy that is self-evident and I imagine that it will have an appeal beyond literary scholarship, for example to scholars of Iraqi history as well as social and political scientists with interest in Iraq and the region as a whole. The author examines a wide range of authors and texts revolving around the central theme of 'war and occupation', mostly previously unstudied in English, though a few have already appeared in translation.

Rasheed El-Enany
Emeritus Professor, University of Exeter

Acknowledgements

My interest in Iraqi fiction started with the 2003 US-led invasion and subsequent occupation of Iraq. In 2005–6, I attended Professor Muhsin al-Musawi's seminar 'Culture and Power in Iraq' at Columbia University which fuelled my enthusiasm for Iraqi culture and literature. The idea for this book started in 2009 after I read a novel written by an Iraqi soldier who participated in the 1991 Gulf War. I would like to thank the Iraqi author Ali Badr who connected me with different authors living in Iraq and abroad, among whom are Nasīf Falak, 'Abd al-Karīm al-'Ubaydī and Ahmad al-Sa'dāwī. My thanks go to these authors and to Shākir Nūrī; they shared their works with me in electronic format and were generous with their time answering the many questions I had.

This work would not have been possible without the academic and financial support of the University of Delaware in the form of a General University Research Grant and the International Research Award; and I would like to thank the former chair of the Department of Foreign Languages and Literatures at the University of Delaware, Richard Zipser, for his continuous support and encouragement. All my gratitude goes to Professor Monika Shafi for her time, moral support and valuable advice.

My deep thanks go to Professor miriam cooke for her constant encouragement and to Professors Ron Martin, Roger Allen and Salih Altoma for reading this manuscript and making valuable suggestions. I am very grateful to Professor Rasheed El-Enany, the editor of Edinburgh Studies in Modern Arabic Literature, for his help and advice. I also would like to thank Tom McCone and Aaron Ward at the University of Delaware for their help with the technology. Finally, I am deeply indebted to Hassan Dargham, Cecily Harmon and my family for their love and encouragement and, in particular my wonderful brother Khalil Masmoudi for his moral support and help throughout the years of our life in exile.

Introduction

Since 2003, as a result of the overthrow of Saddam Hussein's regime, the occupation of Iraq by American forces and the internal political strife, interest has increased in Western countries in Iraq in general and Iraqi society, culture and literature in particular. At home and in exile, Iraqi authors have been prolific, unleashing an unprecedented number of novels and short stories about the years under dictatorship and the successive wars their country has witnessed.

I found myself drawn to this compelling literature because it represents a missing piece in the puzzle of knowledge of and relationship to contemporary Iraqi society and culture. The world's relationship to Iraq has been dominated by the West's own military, political and academic discourses on Iraq; there remains a significant gap in this knowledge that can be filled by the testimony of Iraqi writers, told in their own voices, and, to date, only in their own language, offering their own perspectives on the events that have shaped their history and changed their lives.

The character of the past three decades in Iraqi history can be summarised as 'dictatorship and war' and 'war and occupation'. Years under a stifling dictatorship were replaced by military occupation following a long period of sanctions and a 'pure war' that used ultramodern technology and was marked by the absence of 'symbolic exchange', as Jean Baudrillard would put it. In the context of the concomitant fear, doubts, and uncertainty, what does the Iraqi combined narrative of these years tell us? How does fiction explore these times of war? How does the novel portray Iraqi individuals in their relation to war and sovereign power? From what perspectives do Iraqi authors choose to record the historical content? How do they represent the postmodern war in their novels? And how does the 'new Iraq' look in the recent writings?

This book explores how recent novels portray the struggles of the Iraqi individual in a landscape where violence and death proliferate, focusing specifically on the tangible experiences of the soldier, the war deserter, the suicide bomber and the camp detainee.

In this introduction, I define the theoretical framework within which I analyse and discuss the condition and the relations of the Iraqi subject to war and sovereign power, and I establish the literary, historical and political background to account for the situation of the Iraqi novel from its beginning, through the era of the Baᶜath – Saddam's ruling political party – up to the eve of the fall of the dictatorship and during the first decade of the American occupation of the country. I give an overview of the beginning of Iraqi fiction and the developments of the novel in Iraq and its main tenets as a creative genre. I stress how, with the arrival of the Baᶜath and the beginning of the Iran–Iraq War, intellectuals and fiction writers were collectively co-opted and silenced and were condemned either to glorify the regime and its senseless wars or to say nothing in print or in public.

Theoretical Framework

Looking at some of the titles of recent Iraqi fiction published in the past ten years, one is struck by the references to death, killing, madness and loss, all in connection with Iraq itself – for example, *Amwāt Baghdad* (The dead of Baghdad),[1] *Mashraḥat Baghdad* (The morgue of Baghdad),[2] *Frānkinshtāyn fī Baghdad* (Frankenstein in Baghdad),[3] *Majānīn Būkā* (The madmen of Camp Bucca),[4] *al-Minṭaqa al-Khaḍrā*ᵓ (The Green Zone),[5] *Qatala* (Killers),[6] *Ḍayā*ᶜ *fī Ḥafr al-Bāṭin* (Loss in Ḥafr al-Bāṭin)[7] and many others. From these titles, Iraq and especially Baghdad appear to be a death world where thanatopolitics, war and killing are omnipresent. One might advance the argument that the Iraqi novel has become a representation of the manifestation of sovereign power, examining how the individual Iraqi has coped with and withstood the subjugation of life to the power of death and killing during three decades of raw power, murderous wars and, more recently, a war of occupation within the context of the war on terror.

This obvious political dimension in recent Iraqi fiction and its focus on the ways the individual Iraqi wrestles with the manifestations of sovereign power and war invite us to use the best theoretical tools for addressing the problematic of sovereign power and describing the ways the Iraqi is entangled with it. In this regard, perhaps Michel Foucault's focus on the structures of modern power – whether disciplinary power (focused on the control of the individual body) or biopower (focused on the life of the species and the control of the population) – would seem to shed some light on the complexities of the relations between the population and the state in Iraq. In his studies of sexuality, security and governmentality, Foucault focuses on the bodily aspects of politics, inaugurating the concept of 'biopolitics'. However, as some scholars have pointed out, in his analysis of the problematic and technologies of modern power he neglects to address the structure of totalitarian states of the twentieth century or modern genocides such as the Holocaust during the Second World War.

Building on Foucault's heritage and his concept of biopolitics, however, Giorgio Agamben's work focuses more on the connections between the two forms of power – sovereign power and biopolitics. Agamben has pushed Foucauldian thought and the connections between the political and the biological further by locating the beginnings of sovereign administration of 'bare life' in ancient Roman law, in particular in the figure of the *homo sacer*, an idea he develops in his book *Homo Sacer: Sovereign Power and Bare Life.*[8] The main thesis of his account is built on the fundamental axis of sovereign power, the state of exception and the production of 'bare life'. Drawing on a group of European thinkers such as Walter Benjamin, Michel Foucault and Carl Schmitt and on a series of reflections and argumentations from classical, medieval and modern law, Agamben revives and contemporises a figure from archaic Roman law: the *homo sacer*, sacred man – a figure defined by a double exclusion from both divine law and human law. Archaic Roman law conferred this position upon those who could not be sacrificed according to ritual because their deaths were without worth to the gods but who could be killed with impunity because their lives were of no value to their contemporaries. Agamben projects this figure into the present and makes it a bearer of what he calls 'bare life'. This condition or form of life, Agamben argues, emerges in the state of exception when the sovereign suspends the law, thus excluding and abandoning the natural life of the citizen to sovereign and political violence. Bare life is then a distinct modality of existence where *zoe*, the natural or biological life, is politicised through abandonment and exposure to sovereign violence. There are four categories of 'life' in Agamben's book *Homo Sacer: zoe, bios*, naked or bare life and form-of-life. Agamben recalls the Aristotelian distinction between *zoe*, basic natural life or the simple fact of biological life that is common to all living beings, and *bios*, a qualified life or 'a certain way of living proper to an individual or a group'.[9] In the classical age, *zoe* was excluded from the polis and kept separate from politics. However, as Foucault demonstrates in *The History of Sexuality*, the transition to political modernity was marked by the inclusion of *zoe* into the center of strategies and calculations of state power, thus inaugurating a new era for politics to become 'biopolitics': 'For millennia man remained what he was for Aristotle: a living animal with the additional capacity for political existence; modern man is an animal whose politics calls his existence into question'.[10] When *zoe*, biological or natural life, 'is included in the juridical order solely in the form of its exclusion from the polis (that is, of its capacity to be killed)' [11]– that is, abandoned (the original act of sovereignty) – naked life or bare life is produced.[12] Bare life is a life exposed and abandoned to violence.[13] Peter Fitzpatrick clarifies the 'bare' condition of the *homo sacer*: 'What is bare about the life of *homo sacer* is that it can be taken by anyone and that this is to be done without sacrificing that life'.[14] By exploring the ancient figure of the *homo sacer* and completing Foucault, Agamben demonstrates how the inclusion of *zoe* in the political realm antedates the passage to modernity and how its inclusion persists today not only in totalitarian states but also in Western democracies. It is this subjection of biological life to the immediate control and the right of death and life exercised by the sovereign power that is contained within the concept of *homo sacer*.

Drawing on original sources, Agamben elucidates the condition of *sacratio*, whose two main traits are 'the unpunishability of killing and the exclusion from sacrifice', as an exception to human law and at the same time an exclusion from divine law: '*Homo sacer* is he who because of his crime is set outside human jurisdiction without being brought into the realm of divine law'.[15] Agamben's overall effort is to split the concept of the sacred in *homo sacer* from notions of sacrifice, holiness and religious experience and to reveal the concept as a primordial political exercise, a setting apart.[16] The sacredness of this man is not to be understood as a positive thing that contradicts the permissibility of killing him; on the contrary, as Agamben has pointed out, 'the sacred is necessarily an ambiguous and circular concept. (In Latin, *sacer* means vile, ignominious, and also august, reserved for the gods; both the law and he who violates it are sacred.)' [17] Agamben dismisses as 'hypocritical dogma' and empty declarations all rhetoric about the sacredness of human life. For him, 'the sacredness of life' precisely 'expresses life's subjection to a power over death and life's irreparable exposure in the relation of abandonment'.[18]

The exploration of the meaning of the Latin formula *sacer esto* might help us further understand the category of *homo sacer*. According to Harold Bennett, *sacer esto* refers to one of the earliest penalties of Roman law: 'Probably the earliest penalty of Roman criminal law was that of pronouncing a man *sacer*'.[19] One of the meanings of *sacer* is that 'it puts a man apart from his fellow citizens'. Bennett thinks that the formula reflects a stage where sacred and secular laws were not clearly distinct from one another: 'It would seem that religious obligation is invoked as justification for the taking of human life'. He concludes his explorations of the term by saying that, 'on account of the primitive association of law with religion, this penalty [the *sacer homo*] was at first regarded as a sacrifice and performed only by a magistrate invested with the right to have dealings with the gods'.[20]

W. Warde Fowler offers a more convincing explanation of the apparent contradiction. He argues that '*sacer esto* is in fact a curse, and the *homo sacer* on whom this curse falls is an outcast, a banned man, tabooed, dangerous'.[21] The 'holy' thing has nothing to do with the gods, but with the taboo aspect of this man. Being cursed, he is not valued by the gods, so anyone slaying him will not be committing a crime. In addition, because of his imperfection he is not fit to go through the ritual of the altar.

Thus, *homo sacer* finds himself excluded from both human (profane) law and religious (divine) law. It is this double exclusion, says Agamben, 'into which he is taken and the violence to which he is exposed – the unsanctionable killing that, in his case, anyone may commit' – that defines the status of this figure.[22] This violence is simply permitted and is considered neither sacrilege nor homicide. What justifies it are the sovereign decision and the sovereign sphere, where the law can be thus suspended and where a human victim can be captured: 'The sovereign sphere is the sphere in which it is permitted to kill without committing homicide and without celebrating a sacrifice, and sacred life – that is life that may be killed but not sacrificed – is the life that has been captured in this sphere'.[23] *Homo sacer* is then a particular form of life, according to Agamben, 'a life that is included in the political order in being exposed to an unconditional capacity to be killed'.[24]

Agamben uncovers and contemporises this ancient figure by demonstrating its relevance to the necropolitical context of our current condition. He argues that humans today, whether in totalitarian regimes or in Western liberal democracies, exist in the category *homines sacri* – that is, sacred people who occupy a space between life and death, deprived of universal human and political rights and living a virtual death whenever the sovereign suspends the law and calls for a 'state of exception', thus subjecting the biological life of citizens to its immediate control. Agamben calls this living death 'bare life', stripped of political life and rights and abandoned by the law.

Agamben argues that today sovereign states exempt themselves and make themselves exception to their laws against killing and torture and in the name of the state can kill people through capital punishment, death in detention, and death by torture or in war (and so, as noted, his theories apply just as much to Western democracies as to dictatorships). Today, the sovereign's wars give the sovereign the capacity to kill with immunity, so that the sovereign is not committing homicide and cannot be punished for a crime. The sovereign's actions create new forms of life where individuals are exposed, targeted and exterminated in camps, whether they find immediate death or linger in a space between life and death, a virtual death in a waiting zone, where they are less than human.

Agamben's theory and examples are drawn from European contexts, and he has condemned both modern democracies and totalitarian states for their convergence around the sovereign exception (life is valuable, and yet the state may except itself from the preservation of life and the saving of *zoe*). For my purposes here, his work and his approach are central and offer a framework within which to understand other instances of contemporary bare life: in particular in the context of war under totalitarian regimes, under occupation and more recently under the banner of the 'war on terror', where sovereign powers suspend normal law and exempt themselves from it, thus authorising in the name of the state all sorts of abuse and exactions.

According to Agamben, modern instances of this ancient figure of bare life, the *homines sacri* of our modern condition, include the refugee, the comatose, the death-row inmate, the prisoner and the camp detainee. Thus, this ancient category of Roman law functions in Agamben's analysis as a metaphor for any situation where human life is threatened. To these examples we can safely add the figure of the warrior, the war deserter and the prisoner of war as they are depicted in the space of the Iraqi novel – all of these are forms of bare life caught in the sovereign sphere and emerge in the context of a totalitarian regime and a police society at war or under military occupation and a war on terror.

The past few years have seen a rise in the use of Agamben's insights, especially as developed in his book *Homo Sacer: Sovereign Power and Bare Life*. A range of academic disciplines, from anthropology to history, sociology and legal theory has been permeated by the influence of his theoretical insights into the modern political realm. For my purposes here, within the Iraqi situation – a situation devoid of normalcy and in the context of a dictatorship, wars, economic sanctions and occupation, where sovereign power and its exceptionalisms are usually privileged and enacted – his analysis and its contemporary projections, his focus on sovereign power and the key concept of the *homo sacer* prove useful and illuminating for analysing Iraqi novels and the thanatopolitics that they reflect.

The Development of the Iraqi Novel: An Overview

Iraqi authors, critics and intellectuals tend to think of their political and literary experiences as being singular in the Arab world because of their country's unique political circumstances and the literary developments brought about as a result of the political situation.[25] Indeed, since the inception of modern Iraq in 1921, the country has witnessed bloody political struggles, armed opposition movements, military coups leading to a three-decade-long dictatorship, a succession of wars, a stifling economic siege, a war of invasion and a new occupation. This history has led to a sharp distinction in the nature of the literature produced by Iraqi authors: on the one hand, there is the literature written inside the country under the dictatorship of Saddam Hussein; on the other hand, there are the novels written outside Iraq, in the freedom of exile, by many Iraqi writers and intellectuals who fled the country in the 1970s and 1990s. In addition to this first distinction, another historical landmark is used in the categorisation of Iraqi literature – the occupation and the literature written after the American invasion – wherein a retrospective view is taken in which modern Iraqi history and literature are examined as a whole either from an inside angle or from the point of view of exiled writers.

In this book, I examine the main characteristics and preoccupations of the Iraqi novel, its changes over the decades and the major authors who have contributed to its development from its beginning in the 1920s to its recent growth after the occupation.

There is a consensus among critics and writers that from its beginnings Iraqi fiction, whether the novel or short story, has been closely connected to the history of Iraq and its violent political developments over the years.[26] It has been characterised predominantly by the realism of its orientation, its characters and its themes. 'The focus was on the problems of Iraqi society of the day', state Fabio Caiani and Catherine Cobham,[27] and most authors and intellectuals were predominantly secular in their outlook and believed in Marxist and socialist ideals.

The novel made its appearance relatively late in Iraq in comparison with poetry and the short story. We can trace the early development of Iraqi fiction from the publication in 1919 of Sulaymān Fayḍī's *al-Riwāya al-īqāẓiyya*, which set the stage for the publication of, among other early works of fiction, the novella *Jalāl Khālid* in 1928 by Maḥmūd Aḥmad al-Sayyid, which is 'regarded as more significant in the history of the Iraqi novel in that it is used to portray some of the events surrounding the Iraqi revolt against the British occupying forces in 1920',[28] and *al-Duktūr Ibrāhim* in 1939 by Dhū al-Nūn Ayyūb, who was an established and prolific short-story writer with an obvious sociopolitical intent.[29] It was not until 1966 that *al-Nakhla wa al-jīrān* (The palm tree and the neighbours), 'unanimously considered to be the true beginning of the artistically mature Iraqi novel',[30] was published by Ghāᵓib Tuᶜma Farmān (1927–90). This novel is considered to be 'a successful realist novel' as opposed to early experiments marked by sentimentality and journalistic style.[31] For almost a decade, the literary scene in Iraq was dominated by Farmān, writing and bearing witness to the troubles of his country from his exile in Moscow, with the publication of five major novels, from *al-Nakhla wa al-jīrān* to *al-Qurbān* (The offering) in 1975 and *al-Markab* (The boat) in 1989. A sophisticated and successful realist novel, *al-Nakhla wa al-jīrān* is about Baghdad and the poor people of its popular neighbourhoods during the Second World War. Farmān also published in 1967 *Khamsat aṣwāt* (Five voices'), which depicts the intellectual and political atmosphere in the Iraq of the 1950s and 'provides a realistic picture of the prerevolutionary period seen through the eyes of five characters drawn from the intellectual, bourgeois class'.[32] In most of his novels, Farmān adopts a multivoice structure, offering a comprehensive view of Iraqi society, negotiating between a documentary and fictional style, and using colloquial language in the dialogues.[33] It is important to note, however, that Farmān wrote most of his novels while in exile in Moscow, where he died in 1990.

Already before the publication of *al-Nakhla wa al-jīrān* in 1966, Iraq had undergone radical political transformations and had entered into a spiral of violent developments, starting with the coup by the Free Officers in 1958, which put an end to the monarchy and British occupation and included the killing of members of the royal family. This first coup was then followed by schisms and bloody disputes between the Communists and the Nationalists; the next ten years were to be marked by successive military coups and countercoups, killings, detention of members of the Communist Party and bloodbaths. This bloody period ended with the Baᶜath coup in 1968 and the official rise to power of the Baᶜath Party. Saddam Hussein's emergence as head of state in 1979 inaugurated a new era of successive wars (the Iran–Iraq War, the invasion of Kuwait in August 1990, and the 1991 Gulf War) and a further militarisation of life and society in Iraq. All of this brought about the steady disintegration of the fabric of Iraqi society and precipitated the country's decline, resulting in a new military occupation after the 2003 US-led invasion. It is against such an incessantly violent political and historical background that Iraqi fiction writers established and developed the foundations of the Iraqi novel.

According to the writer and critic Salām Ibrāhīm,

> This bloody history of the past three decades has made the Iraqi individual largely preoccupied with ways of saving himself from a death that lurks and threatens him, whether at the war fronts, in detention, or caught in the claws of hunger, during the years of economic siege.[34]

Many novelists of the 1950s found inspiration in the political strife and conflicts that shook the country, whether the revolution of 1958 or the subsequent coups. In this regard, ᶜAbd al-Raḥmān Majīd al-Rubayᶜī and the publication of his novel *al-Washm* (The tattoo) in 1972 are of particular note. This novel was critically acclaimed not only in Iraq but in the entire Arab world; it reflects the political struggles and prevalent confusion after the coup that was spearheaded by General ᶜAbd al-Karīm Qāsim: the main character, Karīm al-Nāṣirī, feels guilty after being imprisoned and giving in to the authorities; as punishment, he exiles himself. Some critics also give credit to the novel *al-Qalᶜa al-khāmisa* (The fifth fortress) by Fāḍil al-ᶜAzzāwī, also published in 1972, which tells the story of an employee from Kirkūk who comes to Baghdad for vacation but is arrested and imprisoned along with the Communists. According to Salām Ibrāhīm, this novel, despite its modest artistic structure and the limitations of its characters, inaugurated what would be known later as 'the biographical novel', which would be a main genre in the decades to follow.[35]

The publication in 1980 of Fuᵓād al-Takarlī's (1927–2008) masterpiece *al-Rajᶜ al-baᶜīd* (translated as *The Long Way Back*, 2001), 'widely recognized not only as one of the most successful Iraqi novels but also as an outstanding contribution to the Arabic novel as a whole',[36] is another important landmark in the history of the Iraqi novel. Focusing on the psychological portrait of the characters, who belong to a cultured environment and take part in the political struggle that is raging between Communist and Nationalist forces in the aftermath of the 1958 revolution, this novel is totally different from the novels and style of Ghāᵓib Tuᶜma Farmān in terms of both structure and artistic outlook. Al-Takarlī published more novels, such as *al-Masarrāt wa al-awjāᶜ* (Joys and sorrows) in 1998; he was not only a successful novelist but also a prolific short-story writer. Like Farmān, he spent most of his productive years living in exile, first in Tunis during the 1990s and then in Damascus and Amman, where he died in 2008.

Fiction Writers under the Baᶜath: Between Co-optation and Silence

It is important to note that most of the novels mentioned so far are focused on the political and social turning points of the 1960s. With the rise of Saddam Hussein as head of state in 1979 and the outbreak of the Iran–Iraq War in 1980, the literary scene in Iraq changed dramatically. Under the campaign of Baᶜathification of the entire society, which forced citizens to sign Article 200, requiring them to embrace the party and condemned to death anyone who practised political activities under any other party,[37] and in the context of the war, it became increasingly difficult for novelists and fiction writers to write. This difficulty led to the migration of a large number of intellectuals and fiction writers. By the mid-1970s, many authors had already fled the country, among them Fāḍil al-ᶜAzzāwī, Salām ᶜAbbūd, ᶜĀliya Mamdūḥ, Hayfāᵓ Zangana, Najm Wālī and Zuhayr al-Jazāᵓirī. Some authors were actually at the war front when they arranged their escape and joined the armed opposition in the mountains of Iraq, such as Jinān Jāsim Hillāwī, Shākir al-Anbārī and Salām Ibrāhīm. Others, such as Khuḍayyir Mīrī,[38] were captured in flight and had to suffer imprisonment; Mīrī affected madness and was committed to mental health hospitals for years.[39] Most of these authors were not yet established novelists when they fled the country.[40]

The Iraqi writer and critic Ḥamza al-Ḥasan likes to speak about the literary landscape in Iraq since the 1970s by using the metaphor of a party set on fire, those attending it trying to jump from whatever openings they can find to save themselves:

> Since the 1970s of the previous century, the literary landscape . . . is much like the sight of a party set on fire and where the people start leaping from the windows, the walls, the doors and through any kind of opening . . . and all those who escape from the fire take with them forever the print of the jump and the wound as an alternative identity.[41]

A second wave of migration took place after the invasion of Kuwait in 1990 and in the aftermath of the 1991 Gulf War, with more writers leaving the country: among them Hadiyya Hussein, ᶜAli Badr, ᶜAbd al-Sattār Nāṣir, Sinān Antūn and Fayṣal ᶜAbd al- Ḥusayn. Exile and its impact on Iraqi writers are perhaps what have produced the singular situation of Iraqi writers. As Caiani and Cobham put it,

> Exile has of course, not only been the fate of writers of the 1950's generation. In the succeeding decades, Iraqi writers left their country in increasing numbers, so that it has become almost inevitable for people to talk about two Iraqi literatures: one written by exiles and one by those remaining inside Iraq. To make a distinction between the two literatures is not always possible, nor is it useful to divide 'inside' and 'outside' writers in

the polemical tones sometimes used by Iraqi journalists, critics, and even writers themselves.[42]

Reflecting on this splitting of Iraqi writers and intellectuals, the Iraqi novelist ᶜAli Badr, who now lives in Brussels, finds it 'absurd' to be considered an insider one day and an outsider the next:

> I had now become one of the overseas intellectuals: I, who had been recognized just two years before as being one of 'the inside intellectuals'. It all seemed to be part of an absurd game of place – nothing more than that – a game that marginalized people by using the idea of place, temporarily dislodging them from their positions, and labeling them as insiders or outsiders. Thus this game being the result of war, it is the war to which I owe my endless skepticism.[43]

In the context of the war against Iran and the atmosphere of repression, there appeared two kinds of Iraqi novels, one that was written in Iraq under the dictatorship and sanctioned by the regime and another written in the freedom of exile, and each type had its distinctive characteristics and its intellectual and artistic features.

From the beginning of the war against Iran, Iraqi writers, artists and intellectuals still inside the country found themselves under pressure from the regime to rally behind the war effort. Literary competitions and prizes were established to entice writers into what was called the 'Qādisiyyat Saddam', in reference to the battle of Qādisiyya, where the Arabs triumphed over the Persian (Sassanian) army in 637.[44] Poets, novelists and short-story writers had no choice but to comply with the regime's wishes. The result of this campaign was that an extraordinary amount of work was published during the eight years of the war and beyond: 'Only one year into the war, two substantial volumes of short stories by Iraqi authors were published by the Iraqi Ministry of Culture and Information under the title *Qādisiyyat Saddam, Qiṣaṣ taḥta lahīb al-nār* (Saddam's Qādisiyya, stories under fire)'.[45] At the time, writers were not the only ones recruited to immortalise the predicted victory; critics also were asked to analyse and investigate this literature. Here we can mention the 1986 critical and analytical study by Muḥsin al-Mūsawī *al- Marʾī wa al-mutakhayyal* (The seen and the imagined). The novel, too, witnessed an immediate and surprising flourishing: 'The number of novels published in Iraq during the eight years of this war was possibly higher than the number of novels published in the whole previous history of Iraqi fiction'.[46] Jāsim al-Raṣīf was one of the most prominent and successful authors who participated in the literary push for the Qādisiyyat Saddam: he won the first prize twice. His novel *Khaṭṭ aḥmar* (Red line, 1985), in which he describes the devastation suffered by Basra during the war and the steadfastness of its people, was heralded for its artistic maturity and its documentation of the destruction caused by the war; it won the first prize in the literary competition of 1985.

Today, many Iraqi writers and critics look back at this war literature as propaganda that glorified war, death and a false sense of nationalism, without any artistic value.[47] Others, such as the writer Fuʾād al-Takarlī, who served as a judge in one of the regime's literary competitions, acknowledge the merit of some of these war novels, not least as testimonies from the front, for future generations.[48] Other critics, such as Jabrā Ibrāhīm Jabrā, heralded this war literature as making a substantial contribution to Arabic literature in general at the time (Jabrā's views are discussed more fully in Chapter 1).

Although many authors inside Iraq participated in the Qādisiyyat Saddam, others, such as Mahdī ᶜĪsā al-Ṣaqr – who was one of the leading writers from the 1950s and who, unlike many authors of his generation, never left Iraq – did not write about the war until the 1990s, taking the risk to critically note its devastating effects on social relationships and to call it 'a period of isolation and considerable material hardship in the country at large'.[49] Al-Ṣaqr wrote two novels portraying the human suffering caused by the war and dealing with soldiers' homecoming. Both novels were written in the 1990s, but only one, *Ṣurākh al-nawāris* (The cry of the seagulls), was published that decade, in 1997 in Beirut; the other, *Bayt ᶜalā nahr Dijla* (A house on the Tigris), had to wait until 2006 for publication because it was much more critical of the regime, and 'every line in it would have been enough to make the author disappear like his characters'.[50] Both novels have closely related subject matter, but it is developed in a more obscure and opaque way in the novel published in 1997 because of self-imposed censorship.

From this same fear and self-censorship, many other authors also wrote in an opaque and oblique fashion, resorting to myth and a symbolic language as it became increasingly difficult to write in a clear straightforward way if one opposed the war or Baᶜath politics. In this regard, of note are ᶜAbd al-Khāliq al-Rukābī's *Man yaftaḥ bāb al-ṭalṣam* (Who opens the talisman's door, 1982), Luṭfiyya al-Dulaymī's *Man yarith al-firdaws* (Who inherits paradise, 1989), and Muḥammad Khuḍayyir's evocative portrait of his city, Basra, in *Baṣrayātha* (1992), translated into English in 2006 as *Baṣrayātha: Portrait of a City*.

Describing the oppression suffered by authors inside Iraq and the consequences of censorship, Ibrāhīm states,

> Under the dictatorship, the novelist at the instant of writing suffered from the syndrome of self-censorship. Words might lead to assured death, as was the case with the novelists Maḫmūd Jandārī and Ḥasan Muṭlaq. All this made the novel weak, treating everything unessential in the experience, preoccupied with unimportant details, old history, regular social worries that had nothing to do with the daily confrontations of death . . . All this impacted the structure of the novel, which emerged weak, confused and immature.[51]

Liberating the Genie of Creation

In contrast with the atmosphere of repression and the lack of freedom suffered by the writers inside the country, Iraqi writers who left the country enjoyed the various levels of freedom offered by their different exiles and started writing and publishing prolifically beginning in the 1990s, their work becoming, according to some critics, an important literary phenomenon in need of study and exploration.[52] To date, however, not many studies have been dedicated to the examination of this body of Iraqi literature of exile, apart from a few articles and book reviews published in daily newspapers and literary magazines. The main characteristic of this literature of exile is that it addresses clearly and unequivocally the trials, ordeals and suffering of the Iraqi people in the face of daily death during the years of the dictatorship and throughout the different wars that it had brought upon the people. It was impossible for these kinds of novels to be published inside Iraq.[53] One of the first novels to be written about the Iran–Iraq War from a viewpoint other than that espoused by state-sponsored literature is *al-Ḥarb fi ḥayy al-ṭarab* (War in the neighbourhood of rapture, 1993) by Najm Wālī, who has lived in Berlin since 1980. It is important to note that this novel appeared first in Germany in a German translation in 1989, but not in the original Arabic until 1993, after many publishing houses rejected it. According to Ibrāhīm, many of these war novels written in exile privileged the style of the biographical novel, often telling through the main character the stories of the author himself, who had faced death and experienced detention, torture and war. In this way, they added new themes to Iraqi and Arabic literature and revised old themes – for example, the theme of war experience but from the point of view of the deserter or the theme of the soldier's experience during peace and war, but not from the mainstream point of view of the defence of the homeland. These biographical novels treat the experiences of a main character facing death on the war front or fleeing an assured death penalty after desertion. They dared not only to treat these themes but also to point to and condemn the ruthlessness of the military institution and its horrendous dehumanising practices. Among these novels is *Layl al-bilād* (The country's long night) by Jinān Jāsim Ḥillāwī, written in exile between 1993 and 1998 and published in 2002. This novel focuses on ᶜAbdallah, who is led by force to the front during the Iran–Iraq War and returns a maimed madman to Basra, his hometown, now reduced to a wasteland. In addition to ᶜAbdallah's war experience, this novel delves into the armed movements of the rebels in the north of the country and the Kurdish resistance, thus documenting in a fictional way movements that for many years posed a real challenge to Saddam Hussein's regime. Many other novels that focus on a male character's war experience based on the author's real life have been published in the past few years. For example, in Ḥamīd al-ᶜUqābī's novel *ᵓUṣghī ilā Ramādī* (I listen to my ashes, 2002) the narrator meditates on the experience of desertion from the Iran–Iraq War and on the meaning of a life made up of fear, flight and exile. Naṣīf Falak's first novel, *Khiḍr Qad wa al-ᶜaṣr al-zaytūnī* (Khiḍr Qad and the drab olive years), published in Iraq in 2006, is also another example of this type of biographical novel, wherein the main character's steadfastness and stubbornness lead him to desert during the war and to live his life in hiding until he encounters death in the Shiᶜa uprising in 1991. In ᶜAli Badr's novel *Asātidhat al-wahm* (The professors of illusion, 2011), the characters are poets, torn between their poetic aspirations and their obligations as conscripted soldiers who are forced to join the war's northern front. But the main character, the poet ᶜĪsā, ends up deserting and leading a bohemian life, experimenting with poetry and living in hiding and fear until he is finally captured and killed. Desertion during wartime is also depicted in the novel *Hubūṭ al-malāᵓika* (The descent of the angels, 2013) by Muḥammad Ḥasan, portraying and comparing the destinies of three different deserters. In Chapter 1, I focus on this experience of desertion during war as it is depicted in recent novels.

The Iraqi novel in exile goes beyond the bloody history of violence and oppression under the dictatorship of Saddam Hussein, however, to depict through the eyes of the Iraqi returnee a dark tableau of the situation after the occupation beginning in 2003, condemning the spread of violence, killing and kidnapping in occupied Baghdad and uncovering the corruption and moral bankruptcy of an entire society and its occupiers. These themes are well developed, for example, in Shākir al-Anbārī's recent novel *Najmat al-Battāwīn* (The star of al-Battāwīn, 2010), which draws a graphic portrait of decaying Baghdad during the occupation, focusing on the sectarian war, the daily kidnapping and killing between the years 2006 and 2008. ᶜAwwād ᶜAli depicts in his novel *Halīb al-mārinz* (The milk of the marines, 2008) the same disappointment and distress caused by the nightmarish image of the country after the occupation. These exiled authors dreamed of an imagined homeland, but, when they were finally able to return to Baghdad, they found that the dream had turned into a nightmare. The homeland was not only burning with the fire of the invasion and the occupation but also engulfed in sectarian violence and blind killing, as portrayed in the novel *Baghdad mālbūrū* (Baghdad Marlboro) by Najm Wālī. Published in 2012 and set in the context of the chaos of the occupation and the sectarian violence, this novel digs deep into the history of Iraq in the past three decades and depicts the phantasmagoric atmosphere in post-occupation Baghdad, where the narrator tirelessly attempts to escape the fatality of a single alternative: kill or be killed in a city in the grip of militias and sectarian war.

This spiral of violence and revenge killings is nowhere better described and dramatised than in *Frānkinshtāyn fī Baghdad* (Frankenstein in Baghdad, 2013), the third novel by Aḥmad Saᶜdāwī, who belongs to the young generation of Iraqi writers who still live and write in Baghdad. The main character in this novel is a junk recycler, Hādī al-ᶜAttāk, who lives in al- Battāwīn, the same popular neighbourhood where the characters of *Najmat al-Battāwīn* meet. One day Hādī al-ᶜAttāk starts collecting the remains of victims of terrorist explosions, recycling them into a new strange creation: a monster named in the novel 'al-shismah' (he whom I don't know the name of) who wakes up one day and takes revenge on the criminals responsible for the sectarian killings in Baghdad, thus reinforcing the ugly spiral of violence and death. The monster spreads more panic in the city and gets chased by the authorities. *Frānkishtāyn fī Baghdad* won the International Prize for Arabic Fiction (IPAF), popularly known as the Arabic Booker, in 2014.This atmosphere of fear and horror spread throughout Baghdad is also echoed in the novel *Mashraḥat Baghdad* (The morgue of Baghdad, 2012) by Burhān Shāwī, who had originally fled to Germany, returned to Iraq after 2003, and then went right back to his European exile. In this nightmarish novel, Baghdad is a morgue full of cadavers, and the main characters, all of whom are named Adam (for the males) and Eve (for the females), are the victims of daily killing. These cadavers wake up at night in the morgue to tell and share stories of the horrific circumstances of their killing. Through the corpses' confessions, the novel dissects the causes and consequences of an entire society's corrupt practices.

This landscape shaped by violence and killing, whether under Saddam's regime or the American occupation or the sectarian skirmishes, also features prominently in Sinān Antūn's novels, such as *Iᶜjām: An Iraqi Rhapsody* (2007),[54] examining life under the dictatorship of Saddam Hussein, and *The Corpse Washer* (2012),[55] where the Iraqi theatre of events becomes a washhouse for the dead fallen in sectarian killings in the exacerbated culture of violence and death that has seized Baghdad, cutting short the dreams of life and success for the young Jawād, who has to abandon his career as an artist and return to his ancestral work as a corpse washer when the corpses pile up.

In addition to these new ways of looking at the Iraqi experience, the authors in exile use their novels to treat new problematics, such as the question of identity and the predicament of life in exile.[56]

The Iraqi novelist and critic Ḥamza al-Ḥasan sees in the new generation of Iraqi fiction writers 'a promise, a prophecy and a hope':

> The new generation of Iraqi novelists that emerged from the rubble, wars and exiles of the inside and outside . . . is a promise, a prophecy and a hope.

> It is a promise because it has been long awaited in the country of storytelling, a prophecy because it came to us from unexpected times . . . and a hope because arrival from unexpected directions is like a bird alighting on an isolated tree in the middle of the desert, before a lonely traveller . . . The generation of Aḥmad Saᶜdāwī, Ṣalāḥ Ṣalāḥ, Ḍiyā al-Jubaylī, ᶜAwwād ᶜAli, Naṣīf Falak, Inaᶜām Kachāchī and so on.[57]

To these names we can add Nāẓum al-ᶜUbaydī, who published *Arḍ al-layālī* (The land of the nights, 2007); ᶜAbd al-Karīm al-ᶜUbaydī, who turned his Gulf War experience into the novel *Ḍayāᵓ fī Ḥafr al-Bāṭin* (Loss in Ḥafr al-Bāṭin, 2009); Luᵓay Ḥamza ᶜAbbās, a prolific novelist and short-story writer who published among other collections *al-Farīsa* (The prey, 2005), *Ṣadāqat al-nimr* (The tiger's friendship, 2004) and *Madīnat al-ṣuwar* (City of pictures, 2011); Ḥasan Blāsim a short-story writer and a filmmaker who published *Majnūn sāḥat al- ḥurriya* (*The Madman of Freedom Square*, 2009) and *al-Masīḥ al-ᶜirāqī* (*The Iraqi Christ*, 2013); and the young novelist Ḍiyāᵓ al-Khālidī, with one novel published so far, *Qatala* (Killers, 2012).

The first two decades of the twenty-first century have also witnessed the emergence of a new generation of Iraqi women writers, whose lives and works are equally marked by the trauma of war and the loss of exile. Their perspectives on and articulations of these realities demonstrate a radical shift from the writings of the 1980s generation, which were mostly male-dominated and commissioned by the Iraqi government.[58] In the context of ongoing wars, occupation, exile and dispossession, this new generation of women writers – 'the granddaughters of Scheherazade', as Inaᶜām Kachāchī calls them – uses fiction as an investigative tool to record women's unique experiences of war, trauma and exile; 'their narratives speak more truth than all the bulletins of the world', comments Kachāchī.[59] They explore the impact of dictatorship, successive wars, and sanctions on women's lives and illustrate the complexities of exile and its effects on the psyche of the exiled Iraqi woman. In these new writings, women are traumatised and haunted by the nightmarish history and geography of the space left behind, yet they have to speak out and bear witness to the horrors of wars and dictatorship. Not only are they obsessed by a traumatising past, but they are also tortured from the heart of their exile by new modern spectacles of devastation as new wars and new calamities keep befalling Iraq, to which women have to bear witness.

This literature testifies to the historical task and the cultural role Iraqi women play in the recording of intertwined histories: their own private histories and the modern history of their country. These new Iraqi voices include Luṭfiyya al-Dulaymī, ᶜĀliya Mamdūḥ, Inaᶜām Kachāchī, Hayfāᵓ Zangana, Iqbāl al-Qazwīnī, Hadiyya Hussein and Batūl Khudayrī, among others. Whether set in exile, as in Zangana's *Nisāᶜ ᵓalā safar* (2001, *Women on a Journey* (2007)) and al-Qazwīnī's *Mamarrāt al-sukūn* (2006, *Zubaida's Window* (2008)); during the war and the years of economic siege, as in Khudayrī's two novels *Kam badat al-samāᵓ qarība* (1999, *A Sky so Close* (2001)) and *Ghāᵓib* (2004, *Absent* (2005)) and Hadiyya Hussein's *Mā baᵓd al-ḥubb* (2003, *Beyond Love* (2012)); or in post-occupation Iraq, as in Kachāchī's *al-Ḥafīda al-Amrīkiyya* (2009, *The American Granddaughter* (2012)), these novels portray women as witnesses and survivors of different calamities, be they war, detention or economic hardship. The task of bearing witness is specifically incumbent upon women, who as survivors speak up for themselves but also for the missing ones, the *desaparecidos* – those who disappeared, whether inside the dictator's jails, in mass graves or in successive wars.[60] These novels also tackle the issues of feminine identity and the new challenges of life for the exiled Iraqi woman, as in Mamdūḥ's *al-Maḥbūbāt* (The beloved ladies, 2007).

This book asks the following questions. How does the Iraqi novel ascertain these modalities of perishable existence? How does it represent the production of 'bare life' and lift the veil from the Iraqi *homo sacer* under Saddam's totalitarian rule and during the decades of war and occupation that have followed the end of his regime? How is the bare life of the warrior, the war deserter, the suicide bomber and the camp detainee elicited in the space of the Iraqi novel?

I argue that these four figures are united by the fact that they all are doomed to a living death in the context of the lawlessness of war and the state of emergency and exception that it creates. Not only must they exist as if in a living death, but, if they are killed, their deaths are not considered a murder. They are outside human and divine laws, as I show in the analysis of their different experiences. From this point of view, they may be said to embody the concept of *homo sacer*. Using this concept, I analyse and discuss the status and the forms-of-life of the warrior, the war deserter, the suicide bomber, and the camp detainee in their relation to 'necropolitics' as depicted in recent Iraqi novels.

By examining how recent Iraqi fiction about war under Saddam's dictatorship or in the context of the occupation and the war on terror portrays the experiences of these realities and the lives of these different war actors in their 'bare life' and in their 'sacredness' as men doomed to death, my book brings to light the overarching continuum in the devaluation of life and the production of *homines sacri* in Iraq. Giorgio Agamben's concept of the *homo sacer* serves as paradigm to elucidate the shared, unprotected condition of these war actors, who, despite their differences, find themselves outside of society and law, existing as the living dead. By showing how instances of *homo sacer* under the dictatorship have been complemented by new instances in the lawlessness of war and occupation, I expand the concept of the sacred man to potentially large portions of the Iraqi population.

The accounts emerging from the novels and analysed in this book offer a strategic critique of the dominant discourses, whether the old Iraqi regime's discourse or the American discourse of the occupation, by positing a set of different perspectives from which to view Iraq – the perspectives of those who have been coerced, silenced, marginalised, abandoned and tortured. These accounts represent what Foucault calls 'subjugated knowledge', offering perspectives from practical experience, which rank low on the hierarchy.[61] In this case, I privilege the perspectives of coerced soldiers, deserters, prisoners, suicide bombers and camp detainees as opposed to the perspectives of high-ranking officers, managers, commanders and political officials. With this approach, my analysis fills an important gap in our understanding of recent Iraqi history.

Novels Covered and Depth of Coverage

My book investigates a selected corpus of novels. Some of them look back at the years of Saddam's dictatorship and the Iran–Iraq War from a new Iraqi perspective: ᶜAli Badr's *The Professors of Illusion*, Naṣīf Falak's *Khiḍr Qad and the Drab Olive Years* and Muḥammad Ḥasan's *The Descent of the Angels*.

Other novels explore the 1991 Gulf War, such as Abd al-Karīm al-ᶜUbaydī's *Loss in Ḥafr al-Bāṭin* and Hadiyya Hussein's *Beyond Love*.

And, finally, other novels denounce the American occupation of Iraq and question the newfound 'freedom' of the Iraqi people, including Jāsim al-Raṣīf's *Ruʾūs al-ḥurriya al-mukayyasa* (The freedom of the bagged heads, 2007), Najm Wālī's *Baghdad Marlboro*, Shākir Nūrī's *The Green Zone* and *The Madmen of Camp Bucca* and Inaᶜām Kachāchī's *The American Granddaughter*.

I chose the novels that I examine in this book for many reasons: they were all written and published after the fall of the Baᶜath regime and during the American occupation of Iraq. They help us examine how Iraqi authors are revisiting old wars and assessing the recent war, the occupation and their immediate effects on the Iraqi people. My selection is by no means exhaustive, nor would it necessarily be a good thing for it to be. Although the book is diverse and representative and aims to cover three different wars in different historical periods, it remains focused on and guided by a central theme and a central approach: the examination of the continued devaluation of human life throughout the past three decades in Iraqi history.

The novels I consider are also representative of the diversity of Iraqi authors today. Some of them are by authors who took part in the wars (Badr, Falak and ᶜAbd al- Karīm al-ᶜUbaydī) or by authors who were war deserters (Falak and Ḥasan). Other novels are by writers living in exile (Badr, Nūri, Kachāchī, Ḥusayn, al-Rasīf and Ḥasan) or by authors who are still living in Iraq (Falak, ᶜAbd al- Karīm al-ᶜUbaydī).

Most of the novels I treat are by male authors, although a few works by female writers are also included. This is not a deliberate imbalance, but rather one dictated by the fact that most fictional accounts of war experience (this book's subject) are written by male authors, some of whom based their writing on their personal experience of war. A fuller discussion of Iraqi women novelists and their works merits a book on its own.

Published mostly in the first decade of the twenty-first century and after the fall of Saddam's regime, the novels I examine are in Arabic, and most are not yet available in English translation (the exceptions are *Beyond Love* and *The American Granddaughter*). Thus, my book will introduce most of the novels to the English-speaking reader. By exploring extreme cases of life's precariousness under the dictatorship and within the context of the failure of the American-promised democracy, my book opens up this fiction to an Anglophone audience and transports the reader inside Iraq and the lives of its people. In addition to the key texts that I discuss in depth, I make brief reference to other authors and texts to broaden my argument and to highlight the prolific creative activity of Iraqi authors.

An Overview of the Chapters

The four chapters in this book follow a simple chronological order and at the same time try to underscore the logic of a continuum in the devaluation of human life and the production of bare life from the times of the Baᶜath regime up to the American occupation and thereafter. Treating the years under the dictatorship and war experiences during the Iran–Iraq War, the first chapter analyses the instances of bare life in the figure of the poet-soldier and the alienated artist deserter. This chapter examines Badr's *The Professors of Illusion* and Falak's *Khiḍr Qad and the Drab Olive Years*, with additional insights from *The Descent of the Angels*. These novels look back at the atrocities committed during Saddam's dictatorship and the Iran–Iraq War from the perspectives of the marginal and the alienated artists coerced to serve in the war, their subsequent desertions and captivities, and their lives in extremis. This chapter is focused on desertion and the conditions of bare life in which unwilling poet-soldiers, artists and bohemians are reduced to an existence in hiding under a totalitarian regime at war or to captivity in Iranian prisons. I argue that the protagonists' desertion, although a bid for agency, in fact reduces them to the position of *homines sacri*. Vulnerable and targeted, in hiding or in captivity, the deserters live under the spectral presence of death, and there remains nothing for them in the profane world but to be killed or to escape and live a life of exile.

The second chapter is on the 1991 Gulf War, which marked the inauguration of a new kind of war in Iraq: the postmodern war. In this chapter, I explore how the postmodern war is represented in the Iraqi novel and analyse the tangible realities for the soldier on the ground and the 'human moments' in a ghost war where the technological gap between the two armies reduced the Iraqi soldiers in the desert of Ḥafr al-Bāṭin to fatal redundancy. I rely on the novels *Loss in Ḥafr al-Bāṭin, Beyond Love* and *Khiḍr Qad* to account for the popular uprising. I argue that the Iraqi soldiers were rendered useless and irrelevant; they became the *homines sacri* of the Gulf War when they were massacred within the confines of the 'Killing Box', a new horrific military strategy.

Chapters 3 and 4 are closely connected as they both examine space and the geography of occupation in the context of the war on terror.

In Chapter 3, I show how, under the exceptional circumstances of the American occupation and in the context of the war on terror and sectarian violence, the occupied Iraqi subject becomes a suicide bomber targeting both the occupier and other fellow Iraqis in sectarian killings. This chapter relies mostly on the novels *The Green Zone* and *Baghdad Marlboro,* but also to a lesser degree *The American Granddaughter.* It focuses in particular on the geography of the occupation and its paradoxes, juxtaposing two antagonistic images: the image of the American and the image of the Iraqi translator who becomes a suicide bomber. This chapter elucidates the occupier/occupied dialectic in the context of the war on terror and explores the circumstances leading to the metamorphosis of the Iraqi into a suicide bomber.

The last chapter draws essentially on the novel *The Madmen of Camp Bucca,* portraying a real camp where suspected terrorists were detained. It examines the links between the global war on terror and the war in Iraq, the vengeful relations connecting them, the torture of the camp detainee and the only way to resist that treatment and to stay alive. This chapter draws on Agamben's theoretical work on the camp and its paradigmatic figure, the *Muselmann,* a sacred man who ceases to be human altogether. My analysis concentrates on two paradigmatic spaces: the city, represented by the Green Zone, and the detention camp, represented by one detention camp in particular, Camp Bucca, as depicted in *The Madmen of Camp Bucca.* In addition to this dichotomy, we find the lawless space where the disenfranchised local communities live in fear of the militias and the sectarian killings. These distinct spaces stand in apparent opposition to one another, but at bottom existence in all realms, as I show in my analysis, is reduced to 'bare life'. As the walled, entrenched space of law and culture, Baghdad's Green Zone opposes the lawless Red Zone and Bucca Camp in the Iraqi desert, where the 'evil of the terrorists' can be contained and where lawlessness and barbarism reign among both the detainees and their captors. I show that all these spaces, despite their differences, converge because they are the sites of moral and legal transgressions, with on the one side terror as the exception to order and on the other side torture as the transgression of law leading to its suspension.

I examine how the lives of the occupants of all these spaces are exposed, targeted, and reduced to 'bare life'.

Notes

1. Jamāl Ḥusayn Ali, *Amwāt Baghdad* (Beirut: Dār al-Farābī, 2008).
2. Burhān Shāwī, *Mashrahat Baghdād* (Beirut: al-Dār al-^{c}arabiyya li al-^{c}ulūm nāshirūn, 2012).
3. Aḥmad al-Sa^{c}dāwī, *Frānkinshtāyn fī Baghdad* (Beirut: Manshūrāt al-Jamal, 2013).
4. Shākir Nūrī, *Majānīn būkā* (Beirut: Sharikat al-maṭbū^{c}āt li al-tawzī^{c}wa al-nashr, 2012).
5. Shākir Nūrī, *al-Minṭaqa al-Khaḍrāʾ* (Dubai: Thaqāfa li al-nashr wa al-tawzī^{c}, 2009).
6. Ḍiyāʾal-Khālidī, *Qatala* (Beirut: al-Tanwīr, li al-ṭibā^{c}a wa al-nashar wa al-tawzī^{c}, 2012).
7. ^{c}Abd al-Karīm al-^{c}Ubaydī, *Ḍayā^{c} fī Ḥafr al-Bāṭin* (Baghdad: Manshūrāt masārāt, 2009).
8. Giorgio Agamben, *Homo Sacer: Sovereign Power and Bare Life*, trans. Daniel Heller-Roazen (Stanford, CA: Stanford University Press, 1998).
9. Ibid., pp. 7–8. Examples of *bios* include *bios theoreticos* (the contemplative life of a philosopher), *bios politicos* (political life) and *bios apolaustikos* (the life of pleasure).
10. Michel Foucault, *History of Sexuality*, trans. Robert Hurley (New York: Random House, 1978), p. 143.
11. Agamben, *Homo Sacer*, p. 8.
12. Nasser Hussain and Melissa Ptacek, 'Thresholds: Sovereignty and the Sacred, *Homo Sacer: Sovereign Power and Bare Life* by Giorgio Agamben; Daniel Heller-Roazen' (book review), *Law and Society Review*, 34, 2 (2000), pp. 495–515.
13. Derek Gregory, 'The Black Flag: Guantanamo Bay and the Space of Exception', *Geografiska Annaler, Series B, Human Geography*, 88, 4 (2006), pp. 405–27.
14. Peter Fitzpatrick, 'Bare Sovereignty: *Homo Sacer* and the Insistence of the Law', *Theory & Event*, 5, 2, 2001, p. 1.
15. Agamben, *Homo Sacer*, p. 82.
16. Hussain and Ptacek, 'Thresholds'.
17. Giorgio Agamben, *Language and Death: The Place of Negativity*, trans. Karen E. Pinkus with Michael Hardt (Minneapolis: University of Minnesota Press, 2006), p. 105.
18. Agamben, *Homo Sacer*, p. 83.

19. Harold Bennett, 'Sacer esto', *Transactions of the American Philological Association*, 61, 1930, p. 5.
20. Ibid., p. 18.
21. W. Warde Fowler, 'The Original Meaning of the Word *Sacer*', *Journal of Roman Studies*, 1, 1911, p. 58.
22. Agamben, *Homo Sacer*, p. 82.
23. Ibid., p. 83.
24. Ibid., p. 85.
25. See Salām Ibrāhīm, 'al-Riwāya al-ᶜIrāqiyya: Raṣd al-kharāb' (The Iraqi novel: an account of destruction), *Tabayyun*, 2, December 2012, pp. 175–98.
26. Ibid., p. 1.
27. Fabio Caiani and Catherine Cobham, *The Iraqi Novel: Key Writers, Key Texts* (Edinburgh: Edinburgh University Press, 2013), p. 19.
28. Roger Allen, *The Arabic Novel: An Historical and Critical Introduction* (Syracuse, NY: Syracuse University Press, 1995), p. 48.
29. Caiani and Cobham, *The Iraqi Novel*, p. 14.
30. Ibid., p. 73
31. Ibid., p. 76.
32. Allen, *The Arabic Novel*, p. 82.
33. Caiani and Cobham, *The Iraqi Novel*, p. 116.
34. Ibrāhīm, 'al-Riwāya al-ᶜIrāqiyya', p. 3. All translations of Arabic material are mine unless otherwise noted.
35. Ibid., p. 4.
36. Caiani and Cobham, *The Iraqi Novel*, p. xiii.
37. Ibrāhīm, 'al-Riwāya al-ᶜIrāqiyya', p. 4.
38. Among the writings of Khuḍayyir Mīrī is *Ayyām al-junūn wa al'asal*, a novel published in 2000.
39. Ibrāhīm, 'al-Riwāya al-ᶜIrāqiyya', p. 5.
40. Ibid.
41. Ḥamza al-Ḥasan, 'Ḥāmil fānūs al-nahār: jīil riwāʾī jadīd' (The bearer of the daylight: A new generation of novelists), unpublished manuscript, copy in the author's files.
42. Caiani and Cobham, *The Iraqi Novel*, p. 243.
43. ᶜAli Badr, 'Iraq: A Long Phantasmagorical Dream for Those Who Are Not Part of the New Capitalism or Retired Communism', in *We Are Iraqis: Aesthetics and Politics in a Time of War*, ed. Nadje al-Ali and Deborah al-Najjar (Syracuse, NY: Syracuse University Press, 2013), p. 105.

44. Even Arab writers were urged to participate in the literary project of Qādisiyyat Saddam to immortalise Iraq's victory in the war. They were invited to meet with Iraqi writers and to learn from their experiences and exchange notes with them. See Salām ᶜAbbūd, *Thaqāfat al-ᶜunf fī al- ᶜIrāq* (The culture of violence in Iraq) (Cologne: Manshūrāt al-Jamal/Al-Kamel Verlag, 2002), p. 189.
45. Caiani and Cobham, *The Iraqi Novel*, pp. 164–5.
46. Ibid., p. 165.
47. See ᶜAbbūd, *Thaqāfat al-ᶜunf fī al-ᶜIrāq*, and Ibrāhīm, 'al-Riwāya al-ᶜIrāqiyya', p. 6.
48. This is a paraphrase of a quotation from al-Takarlī given in Caiani and Cobham, *The Iraqi Novel*, p. 165.
49. Ibid., p. 164.
50. Hākim ᶜAli, 'Mahdī ᶜĪsā al-Ṣaqr fī al-intiẓār', *ᶜIrāqiyyūn* (*al-Madā* supplement), 8, 20 January 2011, pp. 8–9, quoted in ibid., p. 169.
51. Ibrāhīm, 'al-Riwāya al-ᶜIrāqiyya', p. 8.
52. Ibid.
53. Among the texts published by the exiled authors, in addition to the ones I mention in this introduction, are the novels by Shākir al-Anābrī *al-Kalimāt al-sāḥira* (Magic words, 1993) and *Layālī al-kākā* (The nights of the kākā, 2002); Jinān Jāsim Hillāwī, *Amākin Ḥārra* (Hot spots, 2006); Fāḍil al-ᶜAzzāwī, *ʾĀkhir al-malāʾika* (1992, *The Last of the Angels* (1992)) and *al-Aslāf* (Ancestors, 2001); ᶜAli Badr, *Bābā Sartre* (2006, *Papa Sartre* (2013)) and *Ḥāris al-tibgh* (2008, *The Tobacco Keeper* (2011); Hadiyya Hussein, *Bint al-Khān* (The daughter of al-khān, 2001); Muḥsin al-Ramlī, *Ḥadā'iq al-ra'īs* (The gardens of the president, 2012), and *al-Fatīt al- mubaᶜthar* (2000, *Scattered Crumbs* (2003)); Najm Wālī, *al-Ḥarb fī ḥayy al-ṭarab* (War in the neighbourhood of rapture, 1993); and ᶜĀliya Mamdūḥ, *Ḥabbāt al-naftalīn* (Mothballs, 2000).
54. Sinān Antūn, *I 'jām: An Iraqi Rhapsody* (San Francisco: City Lights Books, 2007).
55. Sinān Antūn, *The Corpse Washer* (New Haven, CT: Yale University Press, 2013).
56. More than five million Iraqis live in exile today, spread throughout the different continents. Novels dealing with the issues of exile and identity include *Taḥta samāʾ Copenhagen* (Under the sky of Copenhagen, 2010) by Ḥawrā' al-Nadāwī; *al- Maḥbūbāt* (The beloved ladies, 2007) by ᶜĀliya Mamdūḥ; *Mawṭin al-asrār* (The locus of secrets, 1999) by Shākir al-Anbārī; and *Aqmār ᶜirāqiyya sawdāʾ fī al-swīd* (Black Iraqi satellites in Sweden, 2003) by ᶜAli ᶜAbd al-ᶜĀl.
57. Al-Ḥasan, 'Ḥāmil fānūs al-nahār'.

58. For more details, see miriam cooke, 'Flames of Fire in Qādisiya', in *Women and the War Story* (Berkeley: University of California Press, 1996), pp. 220–66.
59. Inaᶜām Kachāchī, introduction in *Paroles d'Irakiennes: Le drame Irakien écrit par des femmes* (Paris: Le serpent à plumes, 2003).
60. Ikram Masmoudi, 'Portraits of Iraqi Women: Between Testimony and Fiction', *International Journal of Contemporary Iraqi Studies*, 4, 1–2, 2010, pp. 59–77.
61. Michel Foucault, *Power/Knowledge: Selected Interviews and Other Writings, 1972–1977* (New York: Pantheon Books, 1980), p. 81.

1

The Iran–Iraq War and the Bare Life of the War Deserter

At a time when one might expect Iraqi authors to write about the devastating effects of the 2003 American war on Iraq and the chaos and violence that engulfed the country thereafter, it is surprising to see that they dedicate much of their creativity and imagination to excavating the past and re-examining old wars, portraying previously undiscussed phenomena such as desertion – particularly during the Iran–Iraq War (1980–8) – opposition to war, and the relationship between war and art. It is as though these authors, now without the ideological burden of censorship and fear, have new reason to look back at the Iran–Iraq War, which had already been covered in regime-approved fiction, poetry and other forms of art during its eight lengthy years. Today, three decades after the end of that war, a new generation of Iraqi authors has decided to return to the past to examine the historical records of previous wars so as to better understand what shaped their history and the complexities and paradoxes of their present.

During the Iran–Iraq War, there were many instances of individual desertion at lower levels of the military hierarchy despite the severe punishment in place for it. Many young Iraqis fled the war, only to end up in Iranian detention centres. As we will see in Chapter 2, the mass desertion during the 1991 Gulf War was unique in that it affected both higher- and lower-ranking military personnel. Many of the deserters surrendered or were captured, becoming prisoners of war in American or Saudi detention camps. During the 2003 war, there were cases of mass desertion among high-ranking officials, followed by desertion among other soldiers and conscripts. Anthony Cordesman credits these high-level desertions for precipitating the sudden fall of Saddam Hussein's regime.[1]

Desertion is usually negatively defined as the abandonment of a duty or post without permission and with no intention of return. In Iraq, it is a crime punishable by death. As such, it stigmatises the soldier who makes this choice and dooms him to death and oblivion, banishing him from war records. Stigmatised and erased from official history, the deserter becomes an 'other' confined to silence, unworthy of study or attention. In fact, the phenomenon of war desertion in modern Iraqi culture and history has received little official documentation, if any. Almost no history explores the circumstances and motivations behind it, as if the deserter's life and history are not worthy of documentation. It is in the fiction written three decades after the end of the war that its deserters are beginning to find narrative representation. Fiction's different relationship with politically aberrant phenomena such as desertion offers the possibility of an alternative history, one with space for deserters and their stories. Part of the power of fiction lies in its willingness to unearth voices otherwise disqualified from documentation, due to their marginality, the stigma placed on them, and their capacity to disrupt the claims, interests and coherence of dominant discourses.

In this chapter, I examine recent and avant-garde Iraqi novels published after 2003 that look back on the Iran–Iraq War from the perspectives of soldiers, deserters, fugitive poets and other alienated artists who were coerced into serving in the war and sought to escape it. Some were put to death for deserting, some became prisoners of war in Iranian camps and others managed to flee and survive but remained both hunted by the law and haunted by the spectre of death. I examine three novels in particular: *Asātidhat al-wahm* (The professors of illusion, 2011) by ᶜAli Badr, *Khiḍr Qad wa al-ᶜaṣr al-zaytūnī* (Khiḍr Qad and the drab olive years, 2006) by Naṣīf Falak and *Hubūṭ al-malāʾika* (The descent of the angels, 2013) by Muḥammad Ḥasan. I have chosen to focus on these novels for several reasons. They offer fictional accounts of desertion based on their authors' own wartime experiences, giving us an insider's view of the anti-war spirit that animates these soldiers opposed to the Baᶜath Party and the war. These novels contain biographical and autobiographical elements: two of them (*Khiḍr Qad* and *Descent of the Angels*) are first novels by their authors. The voices we hear in these accounts are either of a narrator survivor of the war or of the deserters who were put to death and later voiced through a narrator who bears witness to their experiences. The narrator of *The Professors of Illusion* sets out to give an account of the lives of his two deceased friends. Both friends were poets and soldiers, but one sacrificed his life on the battlefield, and the other was put to death for desertion. The narrator compares these friends while celebrating their ideas as poets opposed to the war. In *Khiḍr Qad*, the narrator inherits and publishes the manuscript of his friend Khiḍr, who also opposed the war and deserted. Death finds Khiḍr many years after his escape from the Iran–Iraq War, during the popular uprising that followed the 1991 Gulf War. In *The Descent of the Angels*, the narrator is a deserter still on the run after escaping war and execution. While searching for asylum somewhere in Europe, he tells us his story and that of his fellow deserters and their clandestine life in Iraq.

Each novel provides a specific account of the precarious life of a war deserter. I argue that these deserters cease to be fully living because they fall into the vulnerable space between life and death, an unstable position that endangers their very existence. They can be said to embody the concept of *homo sacer* discussed in Giorgio Agamben's work, as noted in the introduction and discussed more fully here. By exploring the deserters' conditions and recovering a narrative of their unfulfilled dreams and lives, these works unearth the buried knowledge of the stifled voices of what Michel Foucault terms 'subjugated knowledge'.[2] It posits the deserters' histories as an irrefutable and integral part of the landscape and history of the Iran–Iraq War.

The Iran–Iraq War and Literature: A Short Background

The Iran–Iraq War began in September 1980, when Iraqi forces invaded Iran following a long history of border disputes and fears of Shiᶜa insurgency among Iraq's Shiᶜa majority. Those fears were augmented by the success of the Iranian Revolution in 1979. Saddam Hussein decided to attack at a moment when the new Iranian regime seemed vulnerable and weak. He had different reasons for entering what he expected to be a short, minor war. First, it was hoped that the war would achieve modest territorial acquisitions, including several parcels of land that the Shah had promised to hand over in the 1975 Algiers Accords between Iran and Iraq, as well as Khuzestan, an oil-rich province in south-west Iran with a largely Arab population. Second, Saddam accepted a large sum of money from Kuwait and Saudi Arabia to initiate the war because both of these countries feared the consequences of the 1979 Iranian Revolution. Third, there was the calculation on Iraq's side that a successful outcome to the war would mean a favourable end to the dispute over the Shaṭṭ al-ᶜArab waterway. Fourth, there was also the fear that the Islamic Revolution would inspire southern Iraq's Shiᶜa population and, through them, would spread into the country.[3] And fifth, from a broader regional perspective, it was hoped that a military victory would be an opportunity for Iraq to gain a more prominent role in the Middle East, with Egypt's stature in the Arab world falling in the wake of its peace agreement with Israel. Fritz Fisher sees this conflict as a 'war of illusion' because each side made calculations based on assumptions and misconceptions about the other side.[4] Many Iraqi officials assumed that the Islamic Republic was weakened by the revolution, while Ayatollah Ruḥollah Khomeini thought the majority Shiᶜa population of southern Iraq would rally around the revolution and thus turn the tide of the war.

For many observers, 'the war seemed to be between secular Arab nationalism and Iranian universalist religious ideology',[5] but Iranian motives were also nationalist in nature and were expressed in terms of national identity. As the war dragged on, the conflict turned into 'a war of identity,' as Sandra Mackey puts it: Saddam described it as a war to reclaim 'the civilization of Mesopotamia' against 'the machinations of the forces of darkness'.[6]

The war was often compared to the First World War in its tactics and battles over trench lines. It was a 'broken-back'[7] war with alternating periods of stalemate and intensity. Each side suffered horrific casualties: one million dead, more than two million wounded, and millions more made refugees.[8] During the war years, the world seemed content to let each side grind the other down. The White House sided with Saddam's secular and anti-Communist regime against the clericist and isolated regime in Tehran. Because of the meddling of outside forces, the war dragged on for eight years where 'neither side could win and neither side was willing to surrender'.[9] Finally, a United Nations-brokered cease-fire was signed in August 1988, leaving Iraq virtually bankrupt and heavily indebted to Kuwait and Saudi Arabia.[10]

Historians argue that the Iran–Iraq War played an important role in shaping the history of Iraq as well as the Iraqi people and the region. Its outcome triggered many events that led to Iraq's becoming more militarised and more aggressive, leading to the invasion of Kuwait and thus yet another war in 1991. Despite the fact that the Iran–Iraq War was one of the longest wars of the twentieth century, it was almost immediately overshadowed by the 1991 Gulf War, and it continued to be forgotten during the lengthy years of economic siege on Iraq and especially after the 2003 American invasion. Today, however, not only historians but also novelists and intellectuals are re-examining this war and its records to reassess its impact on Iraq's recent history. They now have the advantage of the passage of time to allow for reflection on the war and its consequences. And with Saddam's regime being gone, Iraqi fiction writers are capable of contemplating the war without fear of censure or reprisal.

One vital component of the war was the large-scale mobilisation of the population in favour of the war and its projected victory. This concern for the future was accompanied by an interest in reshaping the past, with Saddam emphasising his direct relationship to King Nebuchadnezzar and the Babylonian historical past. It was within this framework of conceiving a victorious future continuous with the glorious past that the Baᶜath manipulated and mobilised the population in support of the war.[11] Thus, the expected victory was first projected domestically through the co-optation of artistic and cultural output. From the beginning of the war, artists, poets, writers and architects were dragged into the mobilisation effort. Many were drafted as war reporters and soldiers not only to fight but also to glorify and immortalise the war in their artistic and literary work.[12]

From start to finish of the war, the regime established literary competitions, poetry festivals and contests with large prizes for what was then known as the 'Qādisiyyat Saddam', all in an effort to entice writers and poets into the propaganda effort. Many poets and novelists who participated received material favours, privileges and literary prizes for the work they entered into the literary competitions; miriam cooke documents this phenomenon in the chapter 'Flames of Fire in Qādisiya' of her book *Women and the War Story*:

> As I browsed through these volumes, I kept noticing this name Qadisiyat Saddam, meaning Saddam's Qadisiya in connection with literary activities surrounding the war. It was attached to a book series, to a literary competition, even to an entire museum. Qadisiya refers to the 637 C.E. battle that marked the first victory of the Arab Muslim forces over their Sassanian Iranian enemy . . . Artists and writers had to be mobilized to sculpt, paint,

> write and sing the glories of the war that even if they were not quite glorious, might in time become so thanks to pens, brushes, chisels, and lutes.[13]

The result of this campaign was an extraordinary amount of literature produced by novelists, short-story writers, poets and intellectuals, all of which served the regime's wishes by justifying the war and glorifying the Baᶜath enterprise in their writing. According to some critics, during the war years literary production exceeded the amount of Iraqi fiction produced up to that point. In the chapter *Riwāyat al-ḥarb wa al-adab al-ᶜarabī al-ḥadīth* (The war novel and modern Arabic literature), written in 1984 during the war, the Iraqi Palestinian novelist and critic Jabrā Ibrāhīm Jabrā expressed surprise at the number of books and novels about war published during the first years of the Iraq–Iran War.

> Two or three years into this conflict, it turned out that war literature in Iraq, whether the novel or the short-story genre has made an important and substantial contribution to modern Arabic literature . . . It is rather extraordinary for more than eighty novels to be written in two or three years in any Arab country. And all these novels were written about the war experience.[14]

Although acknowledging the high literary quality of certain war novels and their contribution to modern Arabic literature as a whole, Jabrā highlighted the existence of two kinds of war texts during this period, underscoring the immediacy peculiar to this literature:

> Many have it that most of what Iraqi novelists and short-story writers have produced [in these war years] falls under the banner of propaganda literature. Some publications fall under this category, but there are also others with an absolute value enjoying vitality beyond their time. And both types in times of war are possible, legitimate and important . . . War novels, whether in Arabic or in other literatures, are usually written after the end of war. The novelty for us, in Iraq, is that novels and short stories about war are written *during* the war, in such a way that they look as though they come directly and immediately from the battlefield and the arena of killing; and this makes them closer to journalistic-style reports coming from the lines of fire.[15]

ᶜAbd al-Sattār Nāṣir, a fiction writer and a critic, emphasised the immediacy of this war literature and maintained that it must 'record now and not tomorrow the extraordinary heroisms of the Iraqis. If the Iraqi pen did not speak today about the martyrs, the sacrifices and the legendary battles, when will it speak and participate in the defense of the land and children of Iraq?' [16]

Authors commissioned to be official pens for the war include ᶜAbd al-Sattār Nāṣir, Wārid Badr al-Sālim and ᶜAli Khayyūn among many others. And among the poets, ᶜAbd al-Razzāqᶜ Abd al- Wāḥid, ᶜAdnān al-Ṣāyigh and many others were sponsored.[17] The themes depicted in the fiction written by these authors include bravery and heroism, humanitarianism, patriotism, sacrifice and jingoism among women.

Critics such as Khuḍayyir ᶜAbd al-Amīr believe that the Iran–Iraq War brought Iraqi literature to maturity:

> It inflamed the writer's imagination and provided them with rich material . . . [W]ar literature in Iraq became a phenomenon that attracted the attention of Arab readers and critics . . . The more the battles raged and the victories multiplied, the surer and maturer became the fiction, to the extent that . . . it could stand alongside international war fiction.[18]

Other literary critics such as ᶜAbdallah Ibrāhīm and Jabrā Ibrāhīm Jabrā underscore the emergence of the 'warrior', a literary figure who masters the art of war and whose political and cultural awareness makes him a strong and a committed character, a positive hero who directly opposes the negative hero who dominated the Arabic literature of the 1960s, usually depicted as an alienated, pessimistic and unstable figure.[19]

In his 1987 book *al-Shiᶜr fī zaman al-ḥarb* (Poetry in times of war), Aḥmad Maṭlūb documents more than forty-nine Iraqi poets who celebrated Iraq's leadership and the heroism of its warriors and wrote collections about Qādisiyyat Saddam.[20] These collections were published under the auspices of the Iraqi Ministry of Culture and Information. Poems in these collections had titles such as 'The War' and 'Songs of the War'. In one of his poems, the poet ᶜAbd al-Razzāq ᶜAbd al-Wāḥid addresses Saddam Hussein, saying:

> You stood among the people like a radiant lance / you were Iraq, challenging and proud // The currents of Tigris and Euphrates in your eyes / were churning, the anger in them a cosmic space // You stood like a lance had anyone dared to touch / the skies would have split and cracked // All Iraqis'

> eyes / watched humbly your shining eyes // And when you spoke it was as if our martyrs / all spoke with your voice for us to hear // They told us with your solemn voice that / it is Iraq alone, all other talk is false // [. . .] Oh you, Iraq's pride and glory / oh you best of all brothers, leaders, and all.[21]

In his 2002 book *Thaqāfat al ʿunf fī al-ʿIrāq* (The culture of violence in Iraq), Salām ᶜAbbūd condemns the Baᶜathification of culture and history during the war years as well as the atmosphere of censorship it engendered. For him, writers' and poets' participation in the war effort was a form of enslavement. ᶜAbbūd describes the different stages in the production of propaganda culture and literature:

> The sovereign power launches its war, and the writers weave it into literary texts, while out of [this process] critics construct cultural values and the state distributes prizes. As for the sons of the nation, they are left with the absolute freedom to enjoy two things: the calamity of war and the calamity of the culture that gives expression to it.[22]

The artistic mediocrity of some of the novels and short stories produced in this period, in comparison with the potential power of their testimonies, was, by Salām ᶜAbbūd's account, a result of censorship and the existence of the death squads:

> It was [a choice] to write either about what was permitted or about the shadows of the death squads and the party's torture of entire families. The war writers chose the picture where death squads and torture were invisible. The reality that was depicted in war literature was a probable one in some respects and was not opposed to the regime. It wasn't close to the sociological and psychological horror of individuals and groups who were led to their death while gangs stood behind them and torture groups spread among their families. When he was writing, the author didn't see this dark side of the image. He was standing on the other side of the river, observing only one side of the landscape of destruction. This is why we said that this literature, whether by Baᶜathists or non-Baᶜathists, was a literature of the regime. It was part of the culture of the institution and not of the people.[23]

Poetry, Desertion and Bare Life: *The Professors of Illusion*

Mr. President,
I send you a letter that you might read
If you have time
. . .
Mr. President,
    I do not want to go to war
    I don't live To kill the
    poor. Don't be upset
I have to tell you that
I made my decision to be a war deserter.

(Boris Vian)[24]

ᶜAli Badr's recent novel *The Professors of Illusion*, published in 2011, is about the existence of underground groups of poet-soldiers during the 1980s who were drafted into the war but who chose not to be part of the mainstream war efforts. Through a fictional investigation of the literary, cultural and political landscape in Baghdad during the 1980s, the novel sheds light on the Iran–Iraq War, exploring how some Iraqi intellectuals and poets dealt with the devastating realities of wartime. A vocal critic of the war and the dictatorship of Saddam Hussein, a poet and a veteran who fought in two wars (the Iran–Iraq War and the Gulf War), ᶜAli Badr left Iraq in the early 1990s soon after the Gulf War. In *The Professors of Illusion*, he draws from his own lived experience, exposing the hidden tensions that dominated the psyches of Iraqi intellectuals during the war years and illustrating their resilience in the face of coercion and violence.

The novel's narrator is the only survivor among a group of poets who served in the war. He bears witness to the plight of his fellow poet-soldiers, who are torn between obligatory service and their dreams of reaching out beyond the limits of language and culture. Central to the poets' feelings of alienation is their deep frustration with their country's increasingly grim social and political realities, palpable in the details of their daily lives. Poetic pursuits soon become their only refuge from the world of politics, ideology and war. Poetry saves them from war and its delusions but deepens their alienation and schizophrenia. The novel's unnamed narrator focuses on two figures in the group of poet-soldiers: his close friends ʿĪsā and Munīr. He explains their attitudes toward the war, their visions of poetry, and their aesthetics of noncommitment. He draws psychological portraits of ʿĪsā and Munīr, whom he meets at the front in 1986, where they all participate in the battle of al-Fāw on the southern border with Iran.

Both Munīr and ʿĪsā die in the war: Munīr as a soldier and ʿĪsā by execution for deserting. After ʿĪsā deserts and renounces his political life and rights, he becomes a fugitive, taking refuge in Baghdad's Christian neighborhood al-Battāwīn and living on the margins of society. He thus falls into a no-man's land, where he remains between death and life. With his desertion and rejection of politics and ideology, he takes refuge in metaphysical meditations, experimenting with language, poetry and art. The bare life of the deserter, the killing of whom is permissible and whose life is without value, finds meaning beyond the materiality of life in the metaphysical truth of poetry. Through his meditations and experimentations with poetry, ʿĪsā's poetic life functions in *The Professors of Illusion* as an alternative to his political life.

In exhuming the stories of his fellow soldiers' desertion and death, the narrator is in fact motivated by the urge to answer questions posed by Munīr's sister Laylā, a literature student. Researching Russian poets who died in prison or in detention camps under Stalin's rule and the poets who died in the Second World War, Laylā needs to include cases of Iraqi war poets who participated and died in the Iran–Iraq War. She also wants to explore the cases of those who were tortured under Saddam's rule. Her project is based on the assumption that similar political and social circumstances in different places can create similar personalities. The similar circumstances faced by Russian poets who died unknown under Stalin and by the Iraqi poets who died in the Iran–Iraq War give Laylā the idea to draw parallels between the Russian and the Iraqi poets. This research project prompts her to contact the narrator, who was a close friend of and had served in the war with her brother Munīr. Because the narrator is the only survivor in the group, he is necessarily Laylā's only source for details of her brother's life during the war and his ideas as a poet. Laylā sends her request to the narrator in the year 2003; it comes at a time when he is already preoccupied by the newest war that has just begun. Before trying to answer her, he wonders,

> Another war has just broken out, and I am busy with it. How can I set aside a current war for the sake of an old one? Or perhaps it is true for our case that war never disappeared from our life and never became a past. It is not wars but a continuous single war.[25]

Confronted with the difficult task of witnessing, the narrator is overwhelmed by a guilty conscience and paralysis. How can he make a story from the death of his dear friends? But as the only survivor of the group, he has a duty to speak and bear witness to their lives and ideas, specifically those of the deserters. He also feels compelled to challenge what he calls 'literary terrorism' in reference to the erasure of these poets-soldiers from literary history, wherein the act of not acknowledging their existence re-enacts their execution.

While retracing the history of ᶜĪsā and Munīr, the narrator situates their stories in the broader context of a lost generation of imaginary secret groups based on groups that he knew in Baghdad during the 1980s. He describes several of these underground groups and networks, including the Bahiyya Group, a strange literary and surrealist group named after Bahiyya, a famous prostitute in Baghdad during the 1950s, and the Poets of Five O'Clock. Both groups were communities of marginal poets, playwrights and actors who were secretly opposed to Saddam Hussein's regime and the war against Iran. According to the narrator, nobody knows the exact number of adherents to these groups and or their full stories because all members were eventually captured and killed. What is certain is their daring in opposing the war and even turning their backs on it, if only to return to a clandestine life in their home cities:

> The Bahiyya Group was like a political organisation, but underground. They produced in the open, but their meetings were held clandestinely. They had no political or ideological affiliation. They were like the members of music bands producing collectively. Their poems and novels were collective productions. To finance their activities they used to steal. The group named itself 'Bahiyya' and signed their poems and novels under this name. They ended up opposing the war on the basis of the assumption that war was against art, and they celebrated the war deserters . . . The [Bahiyya and Poets of Five O'Clock] had a tragic end, and perhaps I am the only one

who survived death in the year 1987, the year when most of my poet friends were killed. (pp. 29–30)

According to the narrator-survivor's testimony, the deserters' executions were carried out in public squares using the cruellest methods, demonstrating the ancient and absolute 'right of the sword' (the sovereign right over death and life, as Foucault puts it)[26] in order to teach a lesson to those who were tempted to attack the sovereign's will and law. For the narrator, the scene of those executions was reminiscent of medieval practices and stood in stark contradiction to the project of modernisation and westernisation that Baghdad embraced at that time:

> As soon as the authorities captured a deserter, he was immediately put to death, and sometimes the execution was carried out inside the city, in public. Indeed, this was a repeated scene in a city that was on the one hand heading towards modernisation and westernisation and on the other hand reminiscent of old empires in presenting scenes of public killing, where the deserter was displayed against a wood panel and shot in front of the people. (p. 72)

The narrator, who miraculously survives the hunts and executions, confesses that it was not fear of death that kept him from deserting but the destructive anxiety of living in hiding and the fear of being captured, tortured and killed. According to his testimony, the deserters who remained in the cities were condemned to a nocturnal existence. They frequented those coffeehouses and taverns known to be havens for deserters, where they would meet and mingle in relative safety:

> During daytime, they would rarely go out, but at night they would spend their time in bars and clubs with thieves, prostitutes, and other fellow fugitives. It was a whole world made up of those fugitive intellectuals, a world that existed parallel to the daylight world of the authorities. It was strange that the poet deserters always met on Abū Nuwwās Street, in the taverns that opened only at night. Most of the deserters infiltrated these bars, which were also attended by off-duty soldiers who would spend their breaks there. (p. 73)

Each of the narrator's close friends – Munīr and ᶜĪsā – belonged to one or the other of these secret groups of poets who were opposed to the war. They were all part of an oppressed generation of intellectuals and poets who found in Western poetry and biographies of famous poets an inspiration to help them resist the oppression and the lack of freedom in their country. In the ideas of peaceful protest movements, political activism and war desertion, they found ways to break free of the chains of tyranny and destruction. But the discrepancies between their dreams and the real world caused them to be alienated from Iraqi society in general and to live on the margin of life: 'They were really alienated from their society. The books and the dreams they contained cut them off from their environment; they were uprooted' (pp. 102–3).

Munīr, ᶜĪsā and the narrator share a fascination for poetry and world literature. They are especially drawn to and influenced by Russian poetry, thanks to Munīr, who was born to an Iraqi father and a Russian mother. Munīr's Russian mother and his own claims of fluency make him the group's designated Russian–Arabic translator. Fond of poetry, biographies of famous poets and anything that distracts them from the unpleasant realities of Baghdad, ᶜAli Badr's poet- soldiers cultivate their poetic universe by reading and translating from Russian poets. At the same time, however, they cannot help but witness the decline and disintegration of living conditions in Iraq under Saddam. Reading and translating poetry and poet biographies in other languages bring the group closer to Russian and European poets but deepen their disconnection from their own environment and its closed horizons. 'We were more like children who enter a basement and like life there so much that they refuse to leave that place until death', the narrator comments (p. 60). The image of children hiding and playing in a cellar is not an innocent one. It calls to mind a more significant and powerful motif drawn from the Islamic tradition and modern Arabic literature: the fable of the People of the Cave or the 'Seven Sleepers',[27] who were persecuted for their faith and were saved only by falling asleep for hundreds of years, cut off from their real environment. The appropriation of this enigmatic fable by the three poets gives their plight a quasi-mythological dimension. Like the Seven Sleepers, on the days of their short leaves from the war, the poets wall themselves up in Munīr's mother's house, translating, reading and writing poems. They try to find salvation in poetry, as if faith, truth and an escape from the cruelty of their time are to be found only in these meetings and that anything outside them is false. In his appropriation of and identification with the People of the Cave, ᶜĪsā goes so far as to fashion his own version of the tale, jokingly telling the story of their sleep in his own poetic terms. For him, the People of the Cave didn't really fall asleep: 'They just didn't want to leave the cave because somebody was translating Russian poems for them, and they lost track of the time!' (p. 61). The young poet-soldiers would not mind living in a cave as long as doing so frees and protects them from outside persecution and oppression and allows them to read and write poetry.

The young Iraqi poets cherish an imagined, idealised community of Russian poets united in their artistic inspirations and living in existential circumstances under a totalitarian regime. This fascination and identification with Russian poetry were common during the 1970s and 1980s in certain Iraqi intellectual circles. The totalitarian ideologies in Russia and Iraq and the terror that both regimes inflict on artists and poets have moved these young underground artists to identify with their Russian counterparts. Unable to look for political asylum in a Russia that terrorises its own poets and intellectuals, the young Iraqi poets in Baghdad find refuge in a 'substitutive textual homeland', as Muḥsin al-Mūsawī puts it,[28] by simply celebrating and writing about these Russian poets.

Fascinated by anything and everything Russian, the poets ensure that their meetings are suffused with a Russian scent: the house where they meet, the furniture around them, the books they read, the air they breathe, the poems of Mayakovsky (1893–1930) and Anna Akhmatova (1889–1966). Badr's inclusion of Anna Akhmatova – an icon of Russian literature and history whose son Lev Gumilyov (1912–92) and husband, the poet Gumilyov (1886–1921), were persecuted and sentenced respectively to imprisonment and death – is not coincidental. Akhmatova was not only a prestigious poet but also an opponent of Stalinist repression, the Great Purges and terrors. She suffered censorship, persecution and surveillance; the Communist Party considered her poems anachronistic and anti-revolutionary, and she was expelled from the Union of Soviet Writers. In the 1930s, Akhmatova's work had to be circulated in secret.[29] Under Stalin, many Soviet poets were attacked, and some, such as Osip Mandelstam (1891–1938) were deported to labour camps for their activities against the state.

> What was happening to us? We were fleeing from devastated Baghdad and the unpleasant times to Russia, to the beautiful days. We had to forget the calamities of the past. Īsā claimed that the dimmed atmosphere of the room was more in tune with the poem. The beautiful elegant print of the books and their leather covers, the letters and numbers of their series excited us . . . We were looking for great poetry that made us shiver, and we found it here . . . It's just that we found these fine ink-printed lines that Munīr started reading for us, rendering them in a language that we understood so that we understood the meaning of our life. (pp. 59–60)

But what ʿĪsā and the narrator believe to be great Russian poetry, translated and read to them by Munīr, is not Russian at all. Munīr only pretends to translate from the Russian as he reads aloud in Arabic poems that are his own compositions. He is almost illiterate in Russian, a fact the narrator discovers only after his friend's death:

> When I met [Munīr] he claimed that he knew Russian and translated it. I found out after his death that he had very little knowledge of Russian, if any, and that the poetry he was pretending to translate for us was in fact of his own improvisation. Everybody at that time was under the influence of his poetry, assuming that it was some of the most prominent Russian poetry of the 1930s and 1940s, when it was his own. (p. 36)

Even though the narrator confesses that Munīr is a great poet who might have influenced all who read his poetry, he chooses to focus more on ʿĪsā because of his originality as a poet, his heightened sense of alienation and perhaps also because of his tragic end by execution. It is ʿĪsā who is first called 'the professor of illusion', or the most delusional among the group of poets.

But, according to the narrator, he is possibly also the most truthful:

> ʿĪsā, whom Munīr called the professor of illusion, was the most truthful among us because he was the only one who lived the life he wanted despite all obstacles . . . In particular, he was the most alienated among all of my friends. He felt deep alienation and disgust for a society that couldn't offer him experiences similar to those given to the poets he admired by their own societies. (pp. 85, 103)

So who was ^{c}Īsā, the soldier, the poet and professor of illusion? How did he become so alienated?

The Poet-Soldier

> ^{c}Īsā never paid attention to life or to the news of the war. He was withdrawn, as though he were living in another world, a different world than the one in which we were locked. He looked at the world through the prism of metaphors and metonymies. For him, the world was not real, but a metaphor for another, and life a metaphor for unreachable beauty. As for war, it was a metonymy for cruelty and violence, for our world was a world of excessive cruelty, which expressed itself in conflicts. This is what ^{c}Īsā thought. (p. 117)

This brief portrait of ^{c}Īsā at the war front, where the narrator initially encounters him, depicts him more as a romantic outsider or a surrealist poet than as a soldier. The two men are in a unit that is called in as reinforcements against an Iranian attack during a ferocious battle on the northern border in 1987. In the midst of bloodshed and blown-up bodies, ^{c}Īsā, imperturbable and unconcerned, first surprises the narrator with his sense of calm and his withdrawal:

> Despite all the chaos around us, the bloodshed on the rocks, the ferocious fighting and the terror on everyone's face, ^{c}Īsā, with his outsize khaki uniform and his thick medical glasses, was still reading from *Artificial Paradises* by Baudelaire, a French poet who died almost a century ago in Paris. (p. 113)

^{c}Īsā's awkward and weak body, his defiant attitude and the way he carries himself, silently withdrawn into his own world apart from the front, are his way of challenging the imposed discipline of the military world and the brutality of war.

> At the front, ^{c}Īsā chose to sit on a rock . . . He was reading *Artificial Paradises*. It wasn't easy to get him out of his world, except for military orders, which he hurried to execute, only to return to his book . . . On the front, he was reading more than talking, unlike the days of the break where he used to talk all the time.

> . . . His military clothes were too big for him, and his medical glasses kind of thick. He was reading and not paying attention to what was around him. (p. 114)

During short leaves from the front, ᶜĪsā and his poet friends spend their time in Baghdad's famous literary cafés, such as the Brazilian Café and the Ḥasan ᶜAjamī Café, discussing poetry. There, according to the narrator, ᶜĪsā is even more eccentric – with his cultivated nineteenth- century look, the strange clothes he buys from secondhand shops, his booming voice and the books he always carries with him, in particular Colin Wilson's (1931–2013) *The Outsider*, published in 1956, which had cast a spell over an entire generation in 1980s Baghdad.

> Among the authors that fascinated ᶜĪsā was the popular English author Colin Wilson. It is not an exaggeration to say that this writer was far more popular in Baghdad than in London. His translated books, especially his book *The Outsider*, take the entire responsibility for the loss of the minds of many. I doubt any of my friends failed to read it. (p. 119)

Alienated from the real world, ᶜĪsā's idealism leads him to feel that he is living in the wrong time and place.

> [ᶜĪsā] could not see anything but the war, that's why he wanted to exchange this world for another. He didn't see anything other than soldiers' helmets and the pink intestines of the wounded. Even Baghdad's moon was dead and cold and had lost its shine. (p. 134)

ᶜĪsā is appalled by the militarisation of life, the nightmarish reality of the war and the destruction and the decay it engenders. For him, Baghdad 'is drowning in blood' (p. 134) – it is a world where 'sectarian banners and vengeance knives are the main merchandise' (p. 134). He feels thrown into the war, although he has no ambition to be inscribed into history as a fighter and a killer of innocent people. At the front, he has no enemies. His only enemy is a totalitarian regime that creates its own enemies and sees them everywhere. All that ᶜĪsā needs is a way to escape the coercion of this regime and extract himself from the war and a bloody history. 'I understood him,' says the narrator about ᶜĪsā:

> He wanted to rise above history because they wanted him to be inscribed in the middle of history. But what kind of history? They wanted to make him a fighter against the enemies (Iran, Europe, and America). They wanted to make him a killer of all kinds of enemies. He had to be a hero, a nationalistic hero . . . And they would bring out the killer that was hiding inside him, the bloodthirsty nationalistic hero, although he was only an evil poet and a corrupt liar who had no desire for vengeance. (p. 139)

At a time when it was rare for Iraqi intellectuals not to be politicised and affiliated with the Ba^{c}ath Party or with one of the opposition movements, whether Communist or Islamic, ^{c}Īsā rejects all kinds of action, has no interest in politics, and disdains ideology and the fashionable ideas of engagement and commitment for causes.

> What interested him were those trivial little things in so far as they didn't have any claim of action on history because he sneered at all kinds of actions on history . . . ^{c}Īsā was living outside history. He didn't care about any ideology or any movements. He was completely free of feelings of hatred toward the authorities who were terrorising him day and night. He was an individual par excellence, and his individuality prevented him from politics. (p. 193)

The ever-present nightmare in his country makes the poet abandon many constraining, empty concepts and irrelevant ideas that restrict his longing for freedom. ^{c}Īsā's rebellion leads him into a dream about a new world, a nomadic world with no roots or borders. The author does not include any poetic excerpts from ^{c}Īsā's poetry in the novel; instead, he has the narrator refer to the main ideas of some of ^{c}Īsā's poems. In one of the poems, ^{c}Īsā portrays himself as a cosmopolitan poet without ties, country, homeland or history. Like an anarchist, he rejects any idea that may limit his imagination or restrain his inspiration. He rebels against the dominant ideas of a culture he perceives as stagnant and ossified. He is distraught by the morbidity of the dying world of ashes where he is imprisoned, a 'world made of skulls and of birds without wings', as he puts it (p. 126). Like a 'passing cloud', he wants to be free without predeterminations. He strips himself of all kinds of historical, cultural, and geographical determinations.

> He lives in a nightmare; he wants to flee – he wants to be a universal poet, a poet without a homeland, without a history, without a nation, and without a people; a poet with no folklore, no determined language. He wants to be from a passing cloud, with a fluid, nonrigid identity, from an undetermined world, a created, patched world, a world made of different homelands, different cultures, and different worlds, new and old worlds. (p. 126)

Once ᶜĪsā deserts, with meagre financial means, cut off from the outside world and immersed in his world of poetry, he lives a bohemian life – stealing food and books he cannot afford, selling vegetables to earn money and living in the popular al-Battāwīn neighbourhood. In brief, ᶜĪsā is the ideal incarnation of the figure of the outsider as described by Colin Wilson, whose works he carries with him wherever he goes. Steeped in the work of nineteenth-century poets such as Baudelaire and Mallarmé and of surrealists such as André Breton, and having read Colin Wilson's books, ᶜĪsā has a surprising conception of poetry given the time and place where he is living.

'My only comfort in this life is that I am a poet' (p. 137), proclaims ᶜĪsā, who christens himself after the French poet Baudelaire, 'if he [could] be a poet like any poet in Europe or in America' (p. 124). ᶜĪsā, the self-proclaimed Baudelaire, thus links himself in some ways to the character of Sharīf, another self-proclaimed Baudelaire, in Ghāᵓib Tuᶜma Farmān's novel *Khamsat Aṣwāt*. In Farmān's novel, the Sharīf character is said to be based on the bohemian poet Ḥusayn Mardān.[30] Both Sharīf and Mardān have humble backgrounds, and, even though they dreamed of Paris, Baghdad for them is a 'wondrous place full of marvels'.[31] But for ᶜĪsā, the Iraqi Baudelaire in Badr's novel, the quagmire of the war is not inspiring, and the 'festival of third world trivialities and terrors' (p. 125) is an obstacle in the face of his poetic ambitions.

> Poetry was the only magical and mythical tool that could save him from the country where he lived, from the sky left by the wars empty of stars and where only catastrophes and more destruction loom at the horizon . . . Poetry was the only way to straighten the huge divine mistake in which he found himself. For ᶜĪsā, in poetry everything gained its right place. (pp. 136–7)

The Nausea of Existence: ᶜĪsā and Purity

ᶜĪsā perceives everything in his existence as marked by a profound lack of beauty, from his own physical appearance to the larger contours of the life that surrounds him; everything is ugly, dirty, and lowly, as the narrator comments: 'Here, it was the country of real poverty. There were no towers, no gothic churches, no French bars, no picturesque atmospheres like what we found in the poetry of Baudelaire and Rimbaud' (p. 242). In addition, ᶜĪsā is ashamed of his humble and poor family origin and nauseated by the ferocious figure of the man who is suffocating the people. It is only in poetry that he can find freedom, transcend the physical ugliness of his world, and replace it with a metaphysical beauty found in the imaginary, language and poetry. Poetry becomes ᶜĪsā's raison d'être. It is in language and contemplation and not through action that he intends to rectify the divine mistakes of his existence. Soon, however, the process of reading the biographies of famous European poets dazzles ᶜĪsā and makes him lose his compass. His weariness with his existence and his exasperation with the war and its decay make him fall under the spell of the European poets whom he is reading. Poetry and the biographies of poets, once a liberating escape for him, turn into a dangerous trap of alienation in which he is gradually ensnared. His rejection of his own image functions as a metaphor for the concomitant rejection of his life, his person and the troubled times of war:

> Thinking about poetry purified his image, beautified it and made it harmonious. He imagined himself in the image of the handsome European poets whose images and biographies he read, and so his own image faded totally, and suddenly a totally different one appeared . . . He wanted his appearance to be like the printed portraits of European poets on the covers of their books. He wanted to look in the mirror and instead of his own image see the portrait of Lord Byron in black and white. (pp. 170, 173)

Once ᶜĪsā has deserted and thus rejected his *bios politikos*, he cultivates his *bios poetikos* as an alternative qualified life so that he can transcend his *zoe*, his targeted natural life. Needing to create his own biography and remodel his image, he has to fashion a new identity for himself, an identity tailored according to criteria that, he hopes, will elevate him to the level of the poets of nineteenth-century Europe. His weariness with the war and the politics of coercion and his exasperation with the general decay of Iraqi society lead him to search for a conception of poetry that transcends the heaviness of life and purifies him so that he can rise beyond the forces of darkness that pull him down, crushing his humanity. In his conception of poetry, he wants to go beyond meaning, to bypass straightforward content that refers to ideas, doctrines and beliefs.

For ᶜĪsā, the language of poetry should be an abstract language, like the language of mathematics and algorithm, rigorous and rich in condensed symbols, using concise images and metaphors with well-calculated words, raising his verses above the wordiness and heaviness of experience.

In order to transcend the limitations and the constraints of the physical conditions of his existence, the mediocrity of his localism, and the decay of his country, ᶜĪsā forges for himself an imagined biography in line with his aspirations, one that can free him from his limited world and propel him to the exceptional and cosmopolitan:

> He had to fix the problem. He had to rectify his bio in accordance with the life of poets. It had to be an exceptional bio, the bio of a great poet, born in new times . . . In his poems, was he not the incarnation of the god of language who would defeat the men who were fighting for ideas? Then his bio had to be an excellent one. (p. 137)

Inspired by myth and magical realism, ᶜĪsā purges the fleshiness and materiality of his existence to achieve a poetic status that is also prophetic. In rewriting his biographical data, he starts by negating his family affiliation and suppressing his father's name in a gesture of rebellion and rejection of tradition: he rewrites his birth certificate using just his first name – thus like Oedipus symbolically killing his biological father. Like Jesus Christ, whose name he shares,[32] he breaks free from the power of tradition, negates his materiality, and claims the spirituality of a prophetic status:

> Oedipus . . . He said laughingly. He was born out of the poetic moment of creation, out of the painstaking of ideas and great wisdom, and not from the petty sexual pleasure of Irwīd, his father and the desire of Ṣabriyya, his

> mother. He was born out of the eternal truth, the creative flame, and not from the fleshy marble of his parents' bodies. (p. 152)

Self-originated like God, the poet rejects the idea of being physically conceived and engendered by his parents, thus freeing himself from his alienation, imitation of European poets and the constraints of his own physical condition. At the end of the novel, he is believed to have risen from his tomb and ascended into the sky toward his God. Like Christ, ᶜĪsā joins the world of myth. The trope of Christ, the miracle worker, is used to reinforce the very possibility of ᶜĪsā's poetic promise.

His idealism and his metaphysical contemplations about poetry lead ᶜĪsā to meditate upon a spiritual system of art and love that transcend the fleshiness of things and the materiality of life. His disgust at being the result of the union of his father's sperm and his mother's egg, his nausea at the thought and reality of sperm, sweat and all body excrements, and his reluctance to have sexual intercourse with Nāzik, a woman who likes him, are but a few instances of his rejection of the materiality of life and his yearning to achieve being and purity through poetry, music, forms and geometry.

> He raised a very important issue about how to reach a spiritual system related to the poetic theory and to sublimation, a system that enabled one to rise beyond the body and its secretions and to achieve purity like the transparent purity of poetry . . . He cultivated formalism and abstraction in poetry; he wanted poetry to be like the abstraction of music, mathematics and geometry. He wanted it to distance itself from the trivialities of everyday language. (p. 207)

This obvious concern for formalism and abstraction in poetry recalls the trend of depoliticisation of art forms and poetry in particular that was at the centre of the cultural and literary debates during the 1970s and 1980s in the wake of Jean-Paul Sartre's distinction between prose as committed literature and poetry as an art form in which words are used not as a means of communication but as things and materials with which the poet creates his or her own poetic reality. Sartre's 'poets are men who refuse to utilize language'.[33] However, Iraqi political officials condemned this trend and deemed it treasonous. In the Iraqi context of a war waged by a totalitarian regime, there was no room for the creed of art for art's sake.

> What [ᶜĪsā] wanted was a message that goes beyond meaning and beyond contents, something far from the straightforward because meaning always grows in the midst of gloom and ugliness. ᶜĪsā wanted to distance himself from the impurity of living in the midst of meanings and contents. Words for him always referred to ideology, and doctrines, while he, like poetry, aspired to abstraction, geometry, emptiness, transparency and music. He wanted obscure symbols, signs that referred to the absolute and the eternal. (p. 206)

Poetic Vision

The poets in *The Professors of Illusion* share a total disengagement from the world in which they live, a general disdain for politics, and an abhorrence of ideology. ᶜAli Badr's poets have withdrawn into their subjective world. Self-absorbed and self-educated intellectuals, they have little interest in the real issues of their country (other than the war as it affects themselves) and no respect for its politicians.

Are these poet-soldiers idealist lunatics, individualistic dreamers and lazy outsiders who turn their backs on their homeland at a critical moment of its history and ignore their historical responsibility as poets? Should we perceive them as narcissistic formalists who have fallen under the influence of the West in their poetic imitations and creations? Is it possible for them to denounce a war they do not believe in? Is it conceivable for them to express their doubts about the war? In their poetry, can they condemn those who have pushed the nation into a senseless war? These questions might seem too naive in the context of a totalitarian regime like that of Saddam Hussein.[34] The poets on the margins of the society cannot take such a risk in an atmosphere where each member is like an actor on 'a theatre stage, a stage burning in flames' (p. 126) and where everyone is required to carry out his assigned role, as ᶜĪsā puts it. Yet these poets are not even interested in the idea of using poetry to convey their opposition to the war or to describe their experiences as weary soldiers, but, even if they were, it is simply too risky for them to be openly opposed to the regime or the war. In truth, for these non-propagandists, anger is useless, and optimism is impossible. Disillusioned about the war and its motives and too intensely aware of the social and political ills, the non-mainstream poet-soldiers in ᶜAli Badr's novel are not likely to compose poetry in support of the war or in defence of the homeland. *The Professors of Illusion* dramatises the dilemma of this group of Iraqi poets and their aesthetic choices in the middle of their participation in the war. Underlying their debates is the question of poetry's function and whether it should concern itself with eternal issues or temporal ones, such as politics. It is useful here to underscore with Muḥsin al-Mūsawī how modern Arabic poetry from the mid-1940s to the 1970s was permeated by the 'politics of urgency'. As he puts it,

> The challenge of the modern in the Arab world since the mid-1940's and perhaps until the 1970's was prompted and colored by the politics of urgency, especially insofar as the Palestinian question is concerned. It was imbued with Cold War politics and their aftermath. Against imperial and multinational interests in the geopolitics and natural resources of the region, the political assumed greater urgency than the social. The poet who was intellectually committed to such issues was bound to develop a register of potency to measure up to an agenda of some sort.[35]

The novel abounds with references to surrealist and symbolist European poets such as Breton, Rilke, Baudelaire and Akhmatova and to modernist Iraqi poets such as Badr Shākir al-Sayyāb, Ḥasab al-Shaykh Jaᶜfar and Saᶜdi Yūsuf. The discussions of poetry are centred on the importance of the individual experience. Through the novel's focus on the main character ᶜĪsā, who has the most tragic fate among the marginal poets, ᶜAli Badr resuscitates the cultural polemic of poetry's role in society. The poets try to redefine poetry within the context of war, violence and coercion. Their idea that poetry should represent metaphysical truth and should not meddle with war, politics and circumstances can be interpreted as their main counteraction to the oppression of war. In this condition, they retreat into *a noncommitted conception of art and aesthetic of poetry*. However, poetry for them is not merely an escape from the absurdity of the war. Their ideals and aesthetics are an alternative to violence and coercion, an antithesis to the war and its calamity. Between co-optation and silence, they seek art. In his aspiration for renewal and innovation, ᶜĪsā wonders if he can just simply be like European or American poets, with the freedom to write poetry about urban life; but the decay of Baghdad and the poverty of the al-Battāwīn neighbuorhood are not inspiring. ᶜĪsā dreams of Baudelaire, Breton and Eliot; he reads their poetry in their original languages and is fascinated by their biographies and their portraits on the covers of their books.

On the one hand, we see Badr satirising ᶜĪsā's fascination with and blind imitation of the symbolist and surrealist poets, highlighting his illusions and his alienation. On the other hand, Badr blames the war for the devastation it wreaks not only upon the country and the people but also upon language, the arts and the artist aspiring to freedom, beauty and independence.

The poet-soldiers' unconventional literary and poetic attitude toward the war places them outside the canonical and official circles of poets and writers commissioned to justify the war. In their jingoistic productions, the mainstream poets describe their heroic war experiences while boosting the morale of the troops and the public, celebrating patriotic sentiments and martyrdom, and urging the people to sustain their support for the war. At the same time, Badr's poets share a bohemian idea about art and poetry in general. They do not conceive of poetry as a tool to change the world, and they do not use their words to service causes such as war or ideas such as 'the nation' and 'the homeland'. They value art in and of itself and do not see their artistic production as a condemnation of the dictatorship or the war. They believe in the creed 'art for art's sake': 'Art means art and has nothing to do with anything else' (p. 255), states ᶜĪsā in reply to a friend's suggestion that they write a collective novel to condemn the war and the society at large. But most of their efforts and attempts to instil a new life in their poetic experimentations fail and remain tentative theorisations of an escape. Victims of the war, a brutal dictatorship, imitation, and their own illusions, the poets in the novel remain in constant search of ideas, but their premature deaths cut short their efforts, as the narrator confesses:

> Poetry was not for us a tentative attempt to reach perfection . . . we were living in real terror; we tried to jump beyond language, but we failed, yes, we all failed, we stumbled and we fell, and we nosedived into the cadaver. (pp. 84–5)

The novel provides many indications that Badr is alluding to the literary and poetic debates that took place in the second half of the twentieth century and the modernist trends that shaped the emergence of modern Arabic poetry. In this case, it is very likely that he modelled his characters after the poets of the 1960s poetry group Shiʿr (Poetry), who modernised Arabic poetry despite their short-lived experience as a group. First, there is the characters' debate about poetry's role in society, their attempts at defining a theory of poetry and their aspiration to renewal, innovation and cosmopolitanism. Second, we find that their perception of history and of their decaying present as a burden, coupled with their longing for a new world, connect them to major themes developed by modernists poets such as Adūnīs (b. 1930), who was one of the pioneers of modern Arabic poetry. Shiʿr was founded by the Syrian Lebanese poet Yūsuf al-Khāl (1917–87), and its views were expressed in his short-lived review by the same name, which he started in Beirut at the end of the 1950s and kept going until 1964. Shiʿr was a rallying point for modernising Arab poets. Al-Khāl pioneered a trend in Arabic poetry and pressed for an opening to influence from the West after his return from the United States. Some of the members of this group acknowledged later their fascination with modern Western poets such as Baudelaire, Mallarmé and Breton and how this fascination enabled them to rediscover Arab modernity in Arabic poetry, as Adūnīs confesses in *An Introduction to Arab Poetics*.[36] For this avant-garde group, 'man is the first and last subject of poetry', and poetry ought to be free from political commitment and causes and based on the expression of real-life experience and the expression of a vision (*ruʾyā*). Adūnīs even condemned *engagement littéraire*. Shiʿr gathered around Yūsuf al-Khāl and included such promising names of the time as the Syrian poet Adūnīs, the Iraqi Badr Shākir al-Sayyāb (1926–64) and Khalīl Hāwī (1919–82), among others, who revolutionised Arabic poetry in both form and content.[37] A look at the editorial of the first issue of the review *Shiʿr*, where a quote from the American poet Archibald MacLeish (1892–1982), whom al-Khāl met along with other poets during his stay in the United States, not only reveals the Western influence on the Shiʿr poets but also resonates with some of the ideas of the poets in Badr's novel:

> Those who practice the art of poetry in a time like ours do not have to write political poetry or poetry that solves the problems of the period, they have

> to practice their art for its own purposes, knowing that by their art life is touched on in the past and will be seized too in the future.[38]

It is this debate on whether to practise poetry for its own sake or to use it for other purposes that preoccupied the poets of Badr's novel in a context marked by war. *Shi*^{c}*r* and its advocacy for the liberation of the individual Arab through art and art forms was seen by some as being against the condition of a time marked by more pressing issues such as occupation and imperialism. In her study 'La vie littéraire autour de la revue Libanaise *Shi'r* (1957–1970)', Dounia Badini underscores how through his revolutionary message Yūsuf al-Khāl 'aspired to culturally and ontologically liberate the individual Arab', at the same time, she argues that the Shi^{c}r movement 'inscribed itself against the current of a political context marked by the exacerbation of nationalism in the face of the West perceived as synonym not only of progress but of occupation, colonisation and imperialism'.[39]

Bare Life: The Death of Men and the Death of Language

In *The Professors of Illusion*, the poet-soldiers live with the threat and smell of death surrounding them. Whether at the front or running from a death sentence because of desertion, they live in symbiosis with death, but without totally belonging to the world of the dead. At war, they are assured of their death, but they do not know when it will strike, so they are kept in a waiting zone between life and death. According to the narrator, the idea of symbiosis with death is well represented in Munīr's poems, as if writing about death is a way of escaping or exorcising it. His poems are contemplative and infused with sadness. The obsessive image of worms attacking the flesh of Munīr captures the narrator's attention in particular:

> Once, Munīr confessed to me that his favourite game was to imagine himself dead and worms feasting on him. He used to feel a huge quantity of worms eating his flesh and nesting in his eye sockets. After his death I always had this nightmare, seeing his flesh ripped from him, the worms feasting on his bones, making his cadaver like a sponge while he is breathing slowly, moaning and crying like an old man, the image of a dead man suddenly caught but still full of an extraordinary life. (p. 279)

As the only survivor among his friends, the narrator confesses that the idea of the certainty of death was inseparable from their presence at the front:

> In reality, we all were obsessed by the idea of death, not only Munīr. Yes, for sure the idea of death had taken hold of us; otherwise, what would the war mean? War is to pick up your breath in the shadow of an assured death; you just don't know when it will strike. However, you feel you are nevertheless dead. *It was this idea of being dead and alive at the same time that was killing us in a cold and bureaucratic way.* Death here took the form of a death penalty; it was a kind of an administrative death. You obeyed the administrative order, and you submitted to meeting your fate without any objection. (p. 278, emphasis added)

With their biological lives literally at stake, the poet-soldiers are also traumatised by this lingering state between life and death. It is this constant oscillation between the two that impels them to try to transcend their bare condition with poetry, to push the threat of death away from them by instilling a new kind of life into language. For language, too, suffers a symbolic death during the war through its use and misuse in the media, in propaganda and in sponsored war poetry and war novels. The poets' attempt to save the spirit of language in poetic experimentations is an attempt to save their own bare lives. The narrator confesses that he too was one of those who tried to instil a new spirit into language through narrative experimentations:

> I used to write long prose passages where I was experimenting with a new kind of language, new words that I was looking up in dictionaries and old books. I was also looking up the derivation system of the words in Semitic languages . . .
>
> Perhaps [these activities were part of] the obsession to escape death, which we felt so close to us. It was our obsession to distance ourselves from what was common and widespread, in particular in language, because the common language at that time was the language of the media. It was a hyperlanguage, a discourse that was completely out of touch with reality. This was how we ended up looking for a new language, new and virgin words, new usages that were not corrupted by the language of the media and the language of the war. (p. 181)

The poets see Iraq as the incarnation of Eliot's *Waste Land*, where the idea of death and waste is reiterated and not limited to the human condition but extended to language, art and creation. The language is emptied of its spirit and needs to be regenerated; it needs to challenge war and death. These poets feel that it is their responsibility to save language from death and by doing so they will also be saving their own lives:

> In fact, this was our dilemma during the 1980s: we were wondering about what was left in the language after it was used in the war, in the press and in the media in these disgusting ways because nothing was left for poets to explore other than a deep silence. This is how we were thinking at that time. We felt that some ideas were being dissipated and wasted and only silence was manifest. (pp. 282–3)

Like a prophet, ᶜĪsā stands alone in his poetic journey and in his conception of the poet's role amid war and dictatorship, while the regime poets – the poets peddling propaganda – were ready to kill and die for ideas. ᶜĪsā's idealism and his poetic choices put him on the path to desertion, and his metaphysical meditations pave the way to his status as *homo sacer*. His desertion reinforces his outsider status, as he becomes a target, chased by the authorities and vulnerable to his fate as *homo sacer*. ᶜĪsā's initial plans for desertion include getting smuggled from Iraq to Turkey and from there to Europe or probably Russia. But he has to abandon the naive idea of taking refuge in a country 'that tortured its own poets' (p. 64). Instead of going to Russia, he finds a kind of spiritual refuge in poetry. After his desertion, he abandons his old place in Ḥaydar Khāna in Baghdad to hide with the pariahs of al-Battāwīn, a poor Christian neighbourhood in Baghdad. He lives there under a false identity thanks to the help of his friends in the clandestine Bahiyya Group. Al-Battāwīn includes all those who are excluded from society at large. The poor and the marginal groups of Baghdad find refuge here: prostitutes, criminals and drug dealers live alongside new immigrants from the countryside as well as people from the Christian minority who formed the first inhabitants of this quarter, and now, during the war years, deserters and political dissidents have joined them. ᶜĪsā is included in this community of the excluded, the potential *homines sacri*. Exiled in al-Battāwīn, he continues to rely on poetry as a defence mechanism. He withdraws into his readings and at night wanders about or drinks in Abū Nuwwās Street taverns. It is this double dimension of being at once of the profane world where he can only be killed and the transcendent world of metaphysics and poetry that defines him as poet-deserter and *homo sacer*. Peter Fitzpatrick elucidates this intermediate condition:

> As sacred *homo sacer* occupies a meditative domain in-between the profane and the transcendent beyond. *Homo sacer* is still of the profane. He fugitively occupies an all too solid world in which he can be killed without sacrifice. Yet *homo sacer* is also of the transcendent beyond . . . The life of this sacred man is 'bare' then, only because it has been consigned to an empyrean, leaving nothing for it in the profane world but to be killed.[40]

The narrator portrays this domain in the novel:

> In those days in 1987 I used to see [ᶜĪsā] at night walking along the Tigris. He was a fugitive after his desertion, and a death sentence was awaiting him. Munīr and I wondered how much longer he could go on like this and when he would escape his death sentence. (p. 265)

After his friends from the Bahiyya Group are captured, ᶜĪsā takes refuge in yet another ghetto. At the end of 1987, an amnesty is issued for all war deserters, but, when ᶜĪsā surrenders, he is accused of belonging to a banned organisation 'threatening the national security of the state' (p. 271) and is put to death. Saddened and shocked by the death of 'this funny magician', the narrator wonders, 'In what country are we living? What threat? And what security could have been threatened by a person like ᶜĪsā?' (p. 277).

'Bare' before the law, ᶜĪsā the deserter experiences the law in its most abstract and formal death-dealing capacity. However, Badr applies a mythical end to his protagonist in his sacredness by producing a mystery regarding a possible final escape. Like Christ, ᶜĪsā finds death but joins the realm of myth when his grave is by chance discovered empty of his cadaver. This final narrative twist redeems ᶜĪsā as a poet, a martyr and a prophet. As if to counteract the inhumane killing of the poet-deserter, his final salvation functions here as a sublimation of his fate and an elevation of the *homo sacer* deserter into the realm of the divine.[41] Murdered as a *homo sacer* whose killing is permissible and goes unpunished, ᶜĪsā becomes a sacrificial symbol. The narrator explains that rumours of dead war martyrs believed to have returned and to have shown themselves to the living as ghosts or phantom forms are common during the war years:

> Thousands of stories like that circulated in Baghdad. The dead would manifest themselves to the living, while the living would appear like defeated gods . . . [E]ven in the case of the martyr buried by his own family, they would end up believing that the cadaver they buried wasn't their son; and then all of a sudden a woman or a man would come to claim that he or she had run into the deceased alive in some city, and the family would buy the story! . . . What can people do in the face of the incurable disease of war if not indulge in hallucinations and illusions? (p. 275)

Like Christ, ᶜĪsā is believed to have risen into the skies:

> Didn't you hear there is a soldier who broke his tomb and left it . . . and people are saying that his name is ᶜĪsā, after Christ . . . He rose to the sky, said one of his friends from the theatre . . . It was his resurrection, and it was in the month of March. What a coincidence his death was like that of Jesus and his resurrection was also in March. (p. 276)

The mystery of the disappearance of ᶜĪsā's body from his tomb is not solved until 1992, after the narrator stumbles on an announcement relating how the authorities found out that it was Salīma, ᶜĪsā's sister, who removed the cadaver from the tomb with the help of her relatives and buried it in her garden: 'The Iraqi authorities captured Salīma Irwīd, who was accused of keeping the cadaver of her brother, the criminal ᶜĪsā Irwīd, after he was put to death in 1987' (p. 277).

The *homo sacer* deserter finds in fiction an ultimate redemption of his suffering and killing, wherein he is elevated from the realm of the human to the realm of the divine through the use of the Christ trope of sacrificial death and resurrection.

Desertion in *Khiḍr Qad and the Drab Olive Years*

Unlike in *The Professors of Illusion*, where the narrator is the only survivor of a marginal group of poet-soldiers who die in the war or are executed because of desertion, in Naṣīf Falak's novel (*Khiḍr Qad and the Drab Olive Years*) it is the voice of the deserter that we hear, without the mediation of a narrator. The protagonist Khiḍr records his adventures and the circumstances of his escape in a manuscript, which he entrusts to his friend Karīm, who publishes the chronicle after Khiḍr's death. In his manuscript, Khiḍr, a dramatist, is not tormented by the problematic of the relationship between art and war or taken by the philosophical question of the role of drama. Instead, using a combination of tragedy and dark comedy, he focuses his narration on the practical aspects of his experience of the years of the 'drab olive' rule, the circumstances of his miraculous desertion from the Iran–Iraq War, and his death in the Shiᶜī uprising after the Gulf War. He represents all those *homines sacri* among the Iraqi people who stood up for their humanity and dignity against the dehumanizsing practices of the Baᶜath and the horrors of war.

Largely autobiographical, *Khiḍr Qad and the Drab Olive Years* is the first novel by Iraqi poet, playwright, actor and novelist Naṣīf Falak. It was first published by the Baghdadi newspaper *al-Ṣabāḥ* in 2006 and sold on newsstands. Falak fled Iraq in the early 1980s, and after years of flight he was arrested and sentenced to life imprisonment by the Saddam regime. The novel refers to the adventures of the protagonist Khiḍr Qad and his experiences during the decades of the Baᶜath rule in Iraq, the Iran–Iraq War, and the Gulf War (1991). The title of this novel combines the main male character's name (Khiḍr Qad) and the metonymy 'Drab olive' (the colour of the official Baᶜath uniform), symbolising the militarisation of life under the Baᶜath and the successive wars it brought upon the Iraqi people. 'Drab Olive' refers not only to the Baᶜath era but also to its iconic figure, Saddam Hussein. Thus, the title juxtaposes and opposes the two main figures of this fiction: Khiḍr Qad the war deserter – potential sacred man – and the figure of a sovereign whose name is a conflation of the words *Baᶜath* and *Saddam*: Bahḍām. The strange-sounding name is like a monster's name.

The curious name 'Khiḍr Qad' raises many questions, combining as it does the name of a prophet, al-Khiḍr, and the linguistic particle *qad*. In Islam, al-Khiḍr[42] is a revered figure, a mysterious prophet and a spiritual guide who is described as having wisdom and secret knowledge. The bewildering particle *qad* in formal Arabic generally conveys doubt, vague possibility, uncertainty (similar to the English words *perhaps* and *maybe*). This word suggests, as discussed more fully later, the main character's uncertain and mythical fate as well as his constant oscillation between reality and fantasy, life and death, imprisonment and freedom, hope and despair, being and extinction. This original and unusual nickname, 'Qad', sticks to Khiḍr after he is found one day in a public square crying and sobbing before a reproduction of the Freedom Memorial in Baghdad. Khiḍr is lamenting the artist Jawād Salīm, who created the memorial, and at the same time lamenting his country: 'Oh my father. Oh my brother. Jawād Salīm, oh my brother. Freedom Memorial, oh my father!' [43] Hearing this wailing, Comrade Muḥān, a Baʿath official from Khiḍr's neighbourhood, rebukes Khiḍr, telling him in colloquial language to stop his ridiculous excess, or he will be taken to a mental health hospital. To all the comrade's threats, Khiḍr has only a one-word perplexing answer: 'Qad' (Maybe). Since that incident, this bewildering particle has stuck to Khiḍr, replacing his real name and evoking the uncertainty and openness of his destiny.

The novel is satirically picaresque, depicting with realistic and humorous detail the wit, fantasies and adventures of a hero who is alienated from reality and resembles Don Quixote in his utopianism, battling the giants of the 1980s. Khiḍr was born in one of the poorest and most marginal neighbourhoods of Baghdad, Madīnat al-Thawra (Thawra City), renamed 'Sadr City' after the 2003 war. It is home to three million Shiʿīs. The novel retraces Khiḍr's repeated escapes from Madīnat al-Thawra and his defences against a situation marked by the lack of freedom and the constant abuse of the people who live there. First, he escapes the grip of reality by becoming an alienated artist and a dreamer living on the margin of society. Then he miraculously escapes from the war, the authorities and the security services. His desertion forces him to live on the fringe; he is *homo sacer* occupying an ambiguous space, a threshold between the world of the living and the world of the dead. Finally, he flees the country and finds refuge in Iran, where he is held captive in a camp for many years. He makes his final return to Iraq to join in the uprising that occurs in the aftermath of the 1991 Gulf War. All along, the narrative moves geographically with the main character, following him in his freedom flight from one place to another – from Baghdad to Kurdistān, from Kurdistān to Iran, then back to Iraq during the popular uprising. It is there that Khiḍr eventually ends up buried alive in a mass grave, reunited with Sallāma, his lover.

Khiḍr Qad not only tells the poignant story of the deserter's perishable life as *homo sacer*, his virtual death, and his freedom f(l)ight but also depicts a profoundly realistic and grim tableau of life during the drab olive years of the Baᶜath society, marked by the rule of exception and abandonment of the sacred men and by the subjection of their biological lives to the control of the sovereign.

The State of Nature and the State of Exception, or Living under the Baᶜath

The novel *Khiḍr Qad and the Drab Olive Years* is set in a dehumanised world ruled by a constant state of fear and savagery. Khiḍr's description of life under the Baᶜath and of the power relations characterising the society during the war years recalls the Hobbesian state of nature and the conditions of violence where 'man is a wolf to men' (*homo homini lupus*) and where everyone exists in 'bare life' and each is *homo sacer* to everyone else.[44] The fight for survival is the engine that justifies the bestial conditions of savagery and terror in this endless 'war of every man against every man'.[45] Under the Baᶜath, the overlap between the state of exception and the state of nature is total. As Agamben has shown in his critical analysis, 'The state of nature and the state of exception are nothing but two sides of a single topological process in which what was presupposed as external (the state of nature) now reappears . . . in the inside (as state of exception)'.[46] In the 'juridically empty' space of the state of exception, anything that the sovereign deems de facto as necessary can happen. Reflecting on the state of struggle of 'all against all' and the hunt of man by other men, Khiḍr wonders how he can extract himself from this eternal struggle:

> I imagined that I under my skin I carry my ancestors' species . . . My grandfather couldn't for one instant ignore the danger all around him. He spent his days from sunrise to sunset caught in the vicious circle of killing, fighting the claws that open up from all sides . . . Am I outside the scope of this fight? And how can I extricate myself from the doom and perpetual loss? Millions of men, billions, where are they all now? They were wasted in one fight and one destiny. How can I escape and distance myself from this fight and its fatality? How can I save my existence from this nihility? (p. 61)

Khiḍr views himself as belonging to a separate species, one opposed to the arrogant and brutal species of men like the monster Bahḍām, his loyalists and the lords of the war. Khiḍr fears that

> perhaps I'm the last one of my kind. If I die, my species will disappear, and there will be disequilibrium. The existence of Bahḍām and his party will also cause a huge disequilibrium in nature. He is a natural disaster with no remedy. It is either he survives and preserves his species, or I survive and save my species. It's a fight for survival. (p. 60)

In the state of exception during the Baᶜath dictatorship, law can be suspended, the distinction between life and law is blurred and liberties are questioned. It is permissible to target, torture, and eliminate not only political adversaries but also whole categories of the population that resist being integrated into the political system. The latent threat of violence lurks everywhere. Under the Baᶜath regime, one is assumed guilty just for being Kurd, Shiᶜī or Communist because this identity represents a threat to the enforced monolithic doctrine. This existence marks the potential of being condemned to a ghost life in a zone of unlimited suffering and fear, expecting arbitrary incomprehensible harm. It is a life in symbiosis with death. As Omid, the narrator's Kurdish friend, comments, the unpolitical (the fact of being born Kurd and Shiᶜī) is treated the same way as the political (the fact of having embraced Communism by one's own choice):

> I am entangled in three problems; each one is more dangerous than the other. First, I was born Kurdish, and that was out of my hands. Second, I came to the world as a Shiᶜī, and this is also beyond my control. Third, I entangled myself wilfully and by my own choice when I joined the Communist Party. They have the right to punish me only on this last account because it was my own deed. (p. 56)

Paradoxically, under the totalitarian regime, the physical abuse and torture of biological life are not only the monopoly of the state but also self-inflicted. Lurid depictions of patterns of self-inflicted physical violence abound in Khiḍr's chronicles. Khiḍr's friends, for example, train themselves daily using a strange exercise: they sit naked on the necks of Pepsi-Cola bottles, which are sarcastically called 'Baᶜath Cola'. They do this training in preparation for the day they get arrested, interrogated and tortured. This exercise of self-inflicted physical pain is conceived as an activity that may lift their fear and psychological pain. As Elaine Scarry argues, 'Physical pain is able to obliterate psychological pain because it obliterates all psychological content, painful, pleasurable and neutral.' [47] This feared scenario is eventually what happens to Khiḍr's friend Omid, who in himself amasses all possible crimes against the state by being at once Kurdish, Shi^{c}ī and Communist. But the exercise with the Pepsi Cola bottles is to no avail for Omid. And to no avail are the terror and the persecution that the Iraqi male seems to be subjected to from a young age in the family, at school and up to adulthood. Once incarcerated, Omid is subjected to all kinds of torture, and as a result during a 'persecution party' he mentions Khiḍr's name, and the two end up in the same cell, where, despite all the torture and pain, they both are convulsed with hysterical laughter:

> Omid, says Khiḍr, I'm perplexed by this crazy laughter that has seized us while we're sitting here in the abyss of hell. It's like laughter during a difficult lesson at school when the teacher is so strict and shows no understanding. We try to suppress and silence the laughter, but it only increases in intensity, and we can't stop it. I'm afraid we'll explode in laughter like madmen. We're laughing more here than we ever did outside. (pp. 24–5)

What remains of Omid after being subjected to unlimited torture in the Ba^{c}ath prisons is the bare life of a man who can be counted among neither the living nor the dead, an unbearable condition that makes Omid yearn to be 'a lost dog in lost valleys, not even deserving to have a stone thrown at him'. Worse, he wishes to be 'a stone among millions of stones, self-sufficient and independent, where nothing gets into it and nothing goes out of it' (p. 32).

Anselm Haverkamp rightfully points out that, 'for Agamben, "bare life" is "what remains" (*quel che resta*) of the state of exception. "Bare life" is what remains of the unlimited application, not of the law, but of its own suspension inscribed within it'.[48] Omid's friends, who have literally lost their lives and become the living dead, comfort Omid not by voicing the usual expression 'Long life to you' but rather by wishing him only the state of mere survival of what remains of him and just to be able to hang in there. Falak's grim portrait of Iraq during the years of the dictatorship and the war is made palpable through the use of raw, crude language closer to spoken than formal Arabic. Even the odours of that society are distinct and repugnant. They are 'the smell of the Ba^{c}ath and poverty, the smell of dirty art in the backstage of politics, and the smell of human fat in detention and interrogation rooms, and the smell of lies and hypocrisy' (p. 14). The irritated and distorted faces of the Baᶜath Party loyalists are 'the faces of shit smellers', with Bahḍām 'the greatest shit smeller' of them all (p. 135). The distortion is frozen forever on their faces. 'The shit-smelling feature was spread out in the geography of the Baᶜathist comrade's face in Iraq' (p. 42), thinks Khiḍr, and this is how he views the Baᶜathists in Iraq. During the Baᶜath years, some insignia were distinctive among the mob, such as beards or moustaches. To grow a beard in the Baᶜath-controlled society during the war was to be suspected of belonging to an Islamist party and thus to be suspected of treason. A moustache was the distinctive sign of Baᶜathism – loyalty and virility. Those without hair on their faces were considered pro-Western effeminates and were subject to laughter and mockery.

Falak demystifies and ridicules some elements of the founding mythology of the totalitarian regime that justified the Baᶜath and was used in the propaganda for the war against Iran. In particular, he points to the use and abuse of the Palestinian question as a means of subordinating the individual and manipulating the mob's emotions. According to this mystique, the road to free Palestine passes by Iran (or by Kuwait, as we will see in Chapter 2) and is paved with the idea and the reality of the Arab nation. This myth has hypnotised a whole generation, Khiḍr says. To debunk the myth and deconstruct its hypnotising narrative, Khiḍr appropriates it, ironically making himself the prodigy hero the Baᶜath saw in Saddam Hussein, but in this case only to mock its propaganda and its lies:

> They kidnapped me when I was about to liberate Palestine, all of Palestine from the river to the sea. I got hold of the people of Tel Aviv and the rest of the Israeli cities. I put them to deep sleep and put the Palestinians to sleep too. I hypnotised them with a potion . . . Everything was under my control, even the atomic weapons, but the security people kidnapped me in front of the library. (pp. 28, 29)

The novel refers to the Iran–Iraq War as the 'Dog War', alluding to a campaign where those who did not join were denounced, captured and sold like dogs to the authorities in exchange for a piece of land, a car or ten thousand dinars. The 'Dog War' is also a reference to the dogs who feasted on the cadavers of fallen soldiers from both sides. 'Dogs alone are victorious in this war, and it is indeed a dog war' (p. 40), explains the narrator. The Dog War is also responsible for drawing into the country a multitude of foreign workers – Egyptians, Pakistanis and Bangladeshi – to make up for the men at the front and the fallen soldiers. The novel also calls the Iran–Iraq War the 'Forgotten War' because of its eight lengthy years and its absurdity. In making the decision to join or not join the front, you are faced with a choice between death and death: either you keep dodging your fate in the battles at the front, or you expose yourself to the death penalty by not joining, which requires your family to pay the cost of the bullet that kills you, exclaims the narrator. In either case, the individual man is reduced to the status of a potential sacred man. The author reports and describes with bitterness and dark humour the ruses that young men use to evade draft and conscription. Students, for example, keep failing the same classes again and again in the hope that they will not be called up or that the war will end. The backstage activity of the war is also characterised by the widespread use of what the author calls the 'Amputation Workshops', where young men purposefully inflict violence and pain on their own bodies in order to avoid the draft. The most popular thing is to sacrifice index fingers and thumbs of the right hand. Some break a hand or a leg, and, worst of all, some go as far as sacrificing an eye.

The horror and the production of *homines sacri* are best revealed and exposed in the metaphoric expression 'Arḍ al-Sawād', the Land of Blackness, to refer to Iraq.[49] This expression was first coined and used by early Arabs to refer to Iraq as a land of fertility and greenery thanks to its rivers. But the expression takes on an altogether different meaning in the novel when it is used to refer to a land where fields of buried black human hair can testify to arbitrary mass killings, massacres and the execution of sacred men. This macabre scene is suddenly revealed to Khiḍr when he makes his way on foot from Iran back to Iraq in 1991 by crossing through the marshes. The scene is both a horrendous reminder of the genocide of the Kurds in 1988 and an ominous presage of the mass killing that will take place during the Gulf War and its aftermath with the Shiᶜa uprising. As Khiḍr walks into an endless black field that looks at first as if grass had been burned on it or as if it is being prepared for cultivation but then turns out to be the most unexpected thing, he is overwhelmed by the nightmarish scene with its familiar yet strange appearance. He sees on one side clouds and fog clogging the horizon and on the other a sea of terrifying black human hair buried in the marshes and swaying with the breeze. This black grass entangles itself around Khiḍr's fingers. 'This is not grass, this is hair . . . I stand in the middle of blackness, human black hair is surrounding me from all sides' (p. 152).Trying to pull the hair from the ground, he is shocked to see that it is attached to a human head, still bleeding, a head that reminds him of Omid, his Kurdish friend:

> The locks of hair entrapped my hand, tightening their grip around my fingers . . . When I decided to pull out the hair from its roots to free my hand . . . I was taken aback to see that it was a slaughtered human head still dripping in fresh blood . . . I got up to leave the field of black hair and realised there was a multitude of slaughtered heads. This sight gave a totally new dimension to the designation of Iraq as the Land of Blackness. (pp. 151–2)

This abomination exposes all the killing that has gone unpunished and functions here as a metaphor for all the *homines sacri*, foreshadowing yet more killing in the Gulf War and in the subsequent uprising, of which Khiḍr too will fall a victim.

Alienation and Desertion

> A crazy man, whose feet don't touch the ground, a war deserter expelled from his loved ones.
>
> Naṣīf Falak, *Khiḍr Qad*

Perhaps the common feature that links Badr's novel and Falak's is their focus on artists and alienated characters. Like ʿĪsā, who lives in his world of illusions, Khiḍr is completely disconnected and lives on the fringe of the real world. On the one hand, he is all too aware of the evil of the Baʿath, and on the other he harbours dreams and illusions that cut him off from reality and in vain embolden him to brave and challenge reality even though he is not equipped for the fight. Karīm Kashkūl, the character in the novel who inherits Khiḍr's papers and converts them into a novel, writes a short foreword in which he mourns Khiḍr and reflects on his friend's deep disconnection from reality. He says:

> Do you see this escapee from his own time and space? He is tying the lace of his shoes in the public square and looking back like a legendary film hero

> before, at the last minute, he saves the world. He looks around and looks to the sky, imagining hundreds of cameras behind him, out of breath, taking pictures of him minute after minute. (p. 5)

In his narrative, Khiḍr explains that he has been able to live through chapters in his life and his story by comforting himself and believing that what was happening was only mere fiction, a movie or a screenplay. As a way of coping with the fantastical aspect of the horror that is taking place and to comfort himself by reminding him of its ephemeral nature, he keeps repeating, 'Everything is just acting'. He believes that everything is unfolding according to the authority of an omniscient invisible film director who is creating all the events and scenes. That is why after every difficult or confused situation he reassures himself that

> every morning I celebrate life along with the birds and kids, innocent, clear of the previous day's dirt. What is happening is mere acting, nothing else. As soon as my role ends, I will return to myself anew and start another movie, another dream or another illusion that has the taste of life. In one word, my problem is that reality has washed its hands of me. It has failed to bring me to believe in it and to obey its conditions because there is always a safety zone of artistic and dreamy ambiguity standing between me and what takes place in such a way that I can neither fully believe nor categorically deny. (p. 9)

A graduate in theatre from the Art Academy in Baghdad, he sees himself as an excellent actor who lives outside reality. One day, in a reckless move, he dares to show up at Baghdad Radio and Television station to offer his acting skills. 'I am an excellent actor,' he tells the director; 'please don't deprive the public of me' (p. 7). He is immediately pushed out of the building in a humiliating way, followed by insults. In another display of his audacity and recklessness, he shocks his friends and the public with a play he wrote with veiled references to the evil and stubborn dictatorship. While the youth of his neighbourhood, whether Kurds, Communists or Shiᶜa, one by one become members of the community of the missing (the *desaparecidos*), Khiḍr remains afloat – as if he were wearing a talisman to protect him, he thinks, poking fun at himself. For Khiḍr, the frontier between reality and fiction is constantly blurred. Once when he is arrested and interrogated, he challenges and confuses the security official with a philosophical reference from a play about Abū al-Ṭayyib al-Mutanabbī, the famous ninth-century Iraqi poet, saying that, no matter what the nature of one's move is, it all amounts to one thing – one step – and that nothing makes any difference to him.

Even after his file is transferred to the security services and he remains under observation, Khiḍr is still divided: 'Half of me is shadowed by dreams and the other half is spotlighted under the glare of reality. I sleep on the bed of illusion covered with the sheet of truth' (p. 10). Is it his theatre training, his book reading, his fondness for art and cinema or his love for Sallāma (whose scent defeats all the odours of reality) that alienates this character and makes him feel that he is living outside the realm of reality?

> I am inhabited by the jinni of the arts. How many times has this tempting and cursed jinni alienated me from reality? I have completely lost touch with it. How many times has it got me into big trouble? But is it also possible that this jinni has saved me from inevitable death without my knowing? Is it he who's saved me from many catastrophes, without my even being aware of it? Will this jinni turn into a guardian angel that will save me at the last moment? (p. 86)

Khiḍr ceases to perceive reality as such not only because he is inhabited by the jinni of Sallāma and the 'jinni of the arts' but also because reality itself – its cruelty, violence and catastrophes – has gone beyond belief in its fantastic and mysterious qualities.

It is not just the character who escapes his time and space, but reality itself seems to overflow its temporality. For Khiḍr, the only way to cope with reality is to make an attempt to defy and surpass it. Khiḍr is like Don Quixote in his utopianism, tilting at windmills and battling the giants of his time. His misfortune is in trying to put a fantasised end to the evil of the Baᶜath and to deliver the Iraqi people from it, his quest echoing that of his ancestor Gilgamesh. Alienated and unrealistic, Khiḍr entrusts himself with the utopian mission to bring down Bahḍām and his regime. As in folktales, he says that a prophecy was made about and transmitted to him, the hero. At his birth, the midwife who delivered him saw three moles on his left arm and predicted that he was the promised child who will put an end to Bahḍām. It is this secret knowledge that empowers him and further alienates him. He has been selected by fate to play this important role:

> 'Here I am', says Khiḍr, 'the promised child, the child who will save Iraq, the region of the Middle East, and the world from the evil of Bahḍām and his party. How and with what means? I do not know.' (pp. 80–1)

Khiḍr, who has lost touch with reality, chooses not to join the war. 'Who gave me the right to squander my life while all my friends behave in a disciplined way? Since the beginning of the Dog War, they all have joined without delay. They have no choice: either they are executed, with their families forced to pay for the price of the bullet, or else they dodge death at the front' (p. 34). As in the case of the poet-soldiers of *The Professors of Illusion*, death in the Dog War is assured whether one joins or refuses to join or deserts once he has joined. The non-joiner, the deserter, is a doomed man who becomes taboo and sacred in the way he is set apart and cursed. Khiḍr becomes a burden on his family and a threat to their existence, endangering their lives and their livelihood. His father warns him about the security forces who pursue draft dodgers, chasing them from one roof and street to another. His older brother, a first sergeant in the army, fears for himself in shielding a coward and promises 'to settle [Khiḍr's joining of] the war without death penalty, imprisonment, or any punishment' (p. 35).

Succumbing to his families entreaties, Khiḍr eventually joins the war and 'wears the ugliest uniform in the history of mankind, from the mulberry leaf up to the uniform of astronauts, a despicable uniform the colour of dog shit' (p. 35). At the front, he avenges himself by reading novels – just like ᶜĪsā, who reads poetry at the front. 'I read *The Brothers Karamazov*, *Moby-Dick* and *Caligula*' (p. 35).

When one day Khiḍr comes close to death in a battle, he is mistakenly transferred to the morgue. Ironically, it is thanks to his flatulence, which signals that he is still alive, that he is plucked from the surrounding heap of cadavers and saved, after which he decides to desert. Over the course of the next three years, Khiḍr, insane in his recklessness and out of touch, spends a night here and a night there with friends and family members, making them feel as if they are in an emergency state for sheltering a deserter. His uncle rebukes him and urges him to spare his family and friends from the constant horror. 'Join, like any other soldier. Everyone will die on his own day!' (p. 43).

The deserter's exclusion and banishment and his final expulsion from the community as a threat to the life of his family and friends are crystallised in his uncle's rebuke. He is a dead man, and as such he should be set aside from the living so that he does not endanger them.

He becomes the perfect incarnation of what was known in ancient Germanic law as *friedlos*, 'without peace'. In the chapter 'The Ban and the Wolf' of his book *Homo Sacer*, Agamben draws on Germanic law in identifying the concept of *friedlos*, which he refers to as a 'brother' concept of *homo sacer*:

> Ancient Germanic law was founded on the concept of peace (*Fried*) and the corresponding exclusion from the community of the wrongdoer who therefore became *friedlos*, without peace, and whom anyone was permitted to kill without committing homicide.[50]

Rejected and excluded, Khiḍr becomes a man without peace, on the run in Baghdad, sometimes not knowing where to sleep, awaiting sunrise and dodging the eyes of the Baᶜath security forces. He reaches a point of no return when he makes the irrevocable decision not to return to the army and the front even if it costs him his life:

> I won't return to the army even if they kill me in front of our house and my father pays for the bullet. I won't return to the front like any coward who sells his blood in exchange for a car or a piece of land. I won't be the martyr of my own treason to myself in the Dog War . . . The last thing I said was, 'You won't see me after today', and I left without a farewell. (p. 44)

Excluded and considered taboo by his community, with a forged identity and still inside Iraq, the deserter secures three full years away from the war – hiding at al-Mustanṣiriyya University, the Academy of Fine Arts in Baghdad and wherever he could safely spend the night, fearing the most dreadful demand: 'Your ID, brother!' The only time he is asked for his identity is when he steps into a coffee shop known as 'the café of deserters'. But here again luck is on his side. Finally, having had enough of the bitterness of three years of 'inside desertion' within the confines of the city of Baghdad, he decides to leave Iraq. His 'outside desertion' starts with a ruse: he joins a military weather forecast unit in order to leave the army forever from the northern Kurdistān area.

> I decided to flee from Iraq. I had had enough of the bitterness of my flight inside the country. For three years, I have been vomiting my death out of bitterness . . . I have been suffocating in Baghdad, at every step I am walking on the mine of the death sentence . . . I sit naked on a Pepsi Cola bottle's neck . . . Three years of whole terror . . . Will I flee alone or through the service of an agent who will ask unknown sums, or will he stab me in the back as I pass? I know my shitty luck when it entangles me in *death without real death*. (pp. 54–5, emphasis added)

Two days before the expiration of a decree granting amnesty to deserters, Khiḍr takes the opportunity and joins a military unit in Mosul, with the firm intention of crossing over the mountains of Kurdistān into Iran. After a month in this unit, he escapes, turning his back on Baghdad and setting off toward Iran, trying to find his way through a forest of entangled trees and branches. His ride in a 'war car', rattling in the language of death, carrying soldiers who look alike with black holes for eyes and terrified expressions, ends abruptly in a deserted area and leads him to change the path of his death – from the death chosen for him to a death he chooses for himself, preferring 'the thrill of an unknown destiny to the gloom of an assured fatality' (p. 58).

The Werewolf and the Topography of Desertion

Living under the state of exception in the cities of the Baᶜath society, Khiḍr wonders how to save his species and how to escape from the fatality of a fight where man is a wolf to men (*homo homini lupus*). His desertion and subsequent flight take him from the condition of 'lupization of man' to the state of the 'humanization of the wolf',[51] from the Baᶜath state of exception to the state of nature, which emerges, according to Khiḍr's descriptions, as paradoxically less dangerous for him, the hero. This might explain why after he frees himself from his fears in the forest, he feels ready and able to hug and embrace wolves and tigers!

> I don't fear a bear or wolf because I'm free like them. Imprisoned in my chest is a call to all the wolves: Come! Let's run together. I too have

> recovered my lost wildness, the wildness of my first nature. My loneliness in this world is now supplanted by this friendly wildness. I'm ready to hug tigers and to spend the night in the company of wolves. Here, it's a party for rallying animals, not men. (p. 96)

Banned and abandoned by the law, a bandit and a *homo sacer*, the deserter can thus be associated with the figure of the werewolf, which Agamben uses to delineate the condition of the man rejected by his community and banned from the city. 'Such a man is defined as a wolf-man and not simply as a wolf. Having a hybrid nature, both human and animal and divided between the forest and the city', the werewolf, according to Agamben, is 'a hybrid of human and animal' who occupies a space where he is not a man and not an animal; rather, he is caught metaphorically in

> a zone of indistinction between the human and the animal . . . The life of the bandit is the life of the *Loup garou*, the werewolf, who is precisely neither man nor beast and who dwells paradoxically within both while belonging to neither.[52]

Desertion as Liberating Event

After Khiḍr joins the military weather unit, he is offered a job as a reporter, but he declines it because he has made an irreversible decision to flee. Through the description of Khiḍr's flight, the novel portrays the adventures and fears of a flight through the mountains of Kurdistān that many Iraqi deserters historically took. On a moonless, cloudy night, he crosses the forest, groping his way in the darkness through the valleys and the branches in a marathon against the moonlight. As soon as he sets out, he experiences the most frightful shock he has always feared and yet never experienced, even when he was a deserter at large in Baghdad. After his first steps, he is suddenly grabbed from behind and frozen by terror into a statue. In this moment *friedlos*, without peace, he is a dead, dumb statue. As the silence persists, the spectre of death has never been so close to the deserter, immobilised in this position, who fears not so much death in itself but torture, humiliation and vengeance.

> What's this silence, why aren't I hearing insults and curses? How come they don't hit me with the butts of their guns? Strange that nobody's spitting on

> me! In any case, I have an excuse: I've lost my way as this is the first time I've taken a leave. . . . [T]he rope of silence is stretching around my neck and around the neck of the valley. Is it possible that he who grabbed me is so sadistic? . . . I decide to break this intolerable silence; the death sentence is more bearable. I turn quietly while my heart sinks and see a tree with a branch exhibiting five hooks grabbing me like a hand at the level of my waist. (p. 75)

The similarities between the two novels discussed in this chapter are quite striking; in both, desertion is conceived as a spiritual quest and liberating event that not only delivers the deserter from a forced duty but divorces him from oppressive and diminishing cultural constructs and biological constraints. The deserter yearns for a rebirth, a new immaculate existence that reconnects him with the force of the spirit. In language echoing that of ᶜĪsā, the poet-deserter, Khiḍr expresses his desire to free himself from biological, social, cultural and political determinations and communicates his hatred of politics and false ideologies. He renounces the politics that has called his life into question. For Khiḍr, crossing into Kurdistān out of the geographical space that is under Baᶜath control is a celebration of freedom, individuality and selfhood. His flight frees and purifies him from 'worn-out concepts' such as the Arab Nation and Iraqi nationality and renders him a nation unto himself, a free man who does not want any followers because, as he says, 'a free man doesn't follow another free man' (p. 85). In his flight through the mountains of Kurdistān, Khiḍr reunites with nature in an immaculate rebirth, free from 'the filthy vocabulary of Baᶜath society' as well as 'the burden of responsibility', the burden of nations, and 'the illusion of identities' as he puts it.

> I'm free now, with no nationality, religion, geography, or time. For the first time I'm returning to the womb of my great mother, to the womb of nature without biological parents or brothers . . . I'm going back to my spiritual homeland after a long exile that has lasted from my birth until Mount Qindīl. (p. 96)

As Khiḍr makes his way through the forest, it is as if its natural environment turns into a humanizing force that helps him recover his humanity and legitimates and covers his action with the blessing of the universe. This mystical force is represented in a strange, creative sentence that Khiḍr repeats like a refrain in 'the symphony' of his flight: 'I was with, not by, myself'[53], perhaps referring to the patron saint al-Khiḍr, his spiritual guide and guardian angel. Unable to give a name or identity to the universal force or spiritual energy that is supporting and accompanying him in his flight, Khiḍr, in an unusual sentence with twisted syntax, condenses disparate elements:

> I was repeating to myself a strange sentence that I made the main refrain in the symphony of my flight: *I was with, not by, myself,* as though I knew who was with me. Or perhaps I wasn't sure how to name this company. Was it God, my mother, the totem of fear, the instinct of preservation, the spirit of nature or all these entities at once that I condensed in my twisted sentence? (p. 83, emphasis added)

This statement – 'I was with, not by, myself' – captures the original feeling of freedom that the protagonist's desertion is supposed to provoke. Unfamiliar and strange in its syntax, the statement establishes that in fact Khiḍr is not alone in his desertion but has company, without specifying the nature of the entity that keeps him company, in an open-ended declaration that encompasses life-asserting forces.

During this journey and on top of Mount Qindīl, the deserter overcomes his fears. He enters into communion with the spirit of the universe and feels in harmony with all those who have walked away from the oppression of their societies:

> I am a nation by myself and everyone who unites with freedom is a nation. Perhaps the prophet Abraham experienced this freedom when he meditated the falsehood of his family and society, so he dropped it and freed himself from it when he left and made his way through the desert. (p. 85)

It is on Mount Qindīl that Khiḍr finally sheds the remnants of his old and shattered self. He tosses away his military beret and declares that 'a head was saved from the grinding machine of the war, a head recovered its humanity'. But 'if only', he exclaims, 'the beret could fly and end as spit on the face of the war' (p. 84).

Taking refuge on top of Mount Qindīl, Khiḍr – like ᶜĪsā, who compares himself to Christ – compares himself to Moses on Mount Sinai. In a language no less poetic than that of ᶜĪsā, the poet, Khiḍr personifies nature, experiencing his consciousness of freedom like a revelation: 'Goodbye, my brother Qindīl. You are free and by yourself, and I am free and by myself. On your summit I discovered that *I am a nation*' (p. 85, emphasis added).

Khiḍr's journey through 'the forest of bones', where the tree branches are entangled and look like the bones of the dead, and through the mountains of Kurdistān recalls Gilgamesh's journey into the cedar forest in his search for freedom from death and mortality. Like Gilgamesh, who, after he loses his friend Enkidu, sets out looking for eternal youth and freedom from death, Khiḍr, after the loss of many of his friends to torture in Bahḍām's prisons, flees from the fate of death in war and under the totalitarian regime. His journey is an attempt to recover his agency and humanity. It also evokes other legendary journeys, such as the journey of the prophet al-Khiḍr with Moses and with Alexander the Great, wherein al-Khiḍr was believed to impart wisdom to his companions and to teach deep gnostic meanings.[54] It is at this moment in Khiḍr's flight that his name reveals all its potential and its symbolism. Khiḍr in the novel is not conceived as just a man against the war, an alienated artist who tries to save himself, but as amysterious, spiritual and heroic figure who identifies with the prophets and immortal men of wisdom and knowledge.

Beautiful as his flight may be, it is not free of dangers. Descending from the summit of the mountain, Khiḍr must traverse a frozen river, a dangerous path with only a hair's width of ice separating him from imminent death in the violent current beneath the ice. This dangerous path through mountains and valleys might bring death, but that death would be liberating:

> If I die on the mountain . . . if I die during my slippery descent on my belly, it would be a free beautiful death, unlike death in the war or the death sentence. To die during this flight is to capture the essence of freedom, a nonhumiliating, total death, a death of an endless rebirth. (p. 97)

Unfortunately, this is not the death the deserter will get. The refuge in Iran turns out to be a prison, 'a smaller Iraq', as he says, and a nightmare where he loses the freedom and essence of existence he captured during his flight through the mountains of Kurdistān. After a few years there, dying a slow death, he is tempted by the crazy idea of returning to Iraq after Saddām issues an amnesty to all the deserters inside and outside Iraq. But, if he surrenders, he fears that they will 'open up an investigation going as far back as his ancestors and Utanabishtam [Gilgamesh's ancestor], up to his children and grandchildren until the last person of his offspring' (p. 135). Nevertheless, Khiḍr clandestinely returns to Iraq by foot, crossing through the fields of the marshes with a guide until he reaches the city of al-ᶜAmāra. But with his 'shitty luck', he arrives only a few hours before the start of the Gulf War, also known as 'Desert Storm for the Americans, the Mother of all Battles for Saddam, and the mother of all shame for the soldiers' (p. 143).

The journey back to Iraq is motivated by Khiḍr's decision to put an end to the monster Bahḍām:

> Alone, I advance unarmed, with my greatest secret running in my blood . . . I will stand alone in the face of the Coalition and overthrow Bahḍām and his party in accordance with the prophecy of the old lady who delivered me and saw the three moles on my arm: 'this child will kill a king and shake the world'. (p. 143)

Khiḍr's utopianism not only leads him to believe in the midwife's prediction for him but also spurs him to cross marshes and prepare for his prophesied role. 'The role is made for you, and no one else, but you will do it . . . Now it's your turn to change the destiny of your country and that of the world. Don't hesitate; the world is waiting for you' (p. 144). Without identity papers, Khiḍr is like a newborn, sneaking into Baᶜath territory.

Intent on going to Baghdad to kill the monster Bahḍām, Khiḍr, naked, without a weapon, is shocked when his utopianism is violently crushed under the brutality of the regime. In the final apocalyptic scene, he ends up killed and thrown into a mass grave in the city of al-ᶜAmāra. It is a scene where the climax of the morbidity in this movie of Khiḍr's life is reached and where the film's director fails to save the hero from a gratuitous, arbitrary death, closing Khidhr's eyes on the final ominous image of crows crossing the sky and screaming, 'Qad . . . Qad . . . Qad . . .'

This cry echoes the nickname that had stuck to Khiḍr and opened his fate to precariousness and uncertainty – a requiem for the tragic *homo sacer*, who finds his fate as less than a human and less than an animal.

The Descent of the Angels

Other novels about desertion and the anxiety it causes to the soldiers have similarities to the two novels discussed in this chapter. Many of the deserters in these other novels are alienated artists who end up living a clandestine life. But there are also some differences. In *The Professors of Illusion* and *Khiḍr Qad*, the deserters do not survive. In contrast, *The Descent of the Angels* by Muḥammad Ḥasan features deserters who survive and do not end up mythologised as ᶜĪsā and Khiḍr do in their quests for freedom.

In *The Descent of the Angels*, Khalīl, the narrator, is also an artist, a tailor, and, because of his desertion from the army during the Iran–Iraq War, a fugitive. He bids farewell to his friends, a group of Iraqi exiles living in Germany, and sets out to Belgium, where he hopes to find asylum after he is denied residency in Hamburg.

At this point, the novel flashes back to Khalīl's life in Iraq during the war, his friendship with a group of Iraqi youths both before and during the war at the front, their flight from the war and their subsequent lives on the edge of death, whether in Baghdad or outside Iraq. Few of them make it to safety; most end up either in the hands of the police or in the prisons of neighbouring countries. Those who are really unlucky, such as Raᶜd – a close friend of the narrator – suffer death because of their desertion and deception of the authorities.

First, there is Mālik, nicknamed 'al-Ḥazīn', 'the Sad One' or 'Mālik the Sad'. His nickname almost supplants his real name because of the pain and suffering he goes through. His story is a succession of flights. After serving four months in the southern front of the war, he deserts but then is captured and put in prison. When he manages to escape from his prison, his only chance is to put his fate into the hands of smugglers from Iran through the mountains of Kurdistān. As he makes his way to Iran, his fate entangles him once more with the war, where the Peshmerga forces[55] ask him to take part in the attacks against Iraqi army units. Finally, he ends up in an Iranian camp, where he suffers hunger, mistreatment and diseases such as diarrhoea and hysteria, both of which are common and widespread among the detainees. Luck is on Mālik's side when he finally manages to escape the Iranian detention camp. With the help of some Iranians of Iraqi origin, he comes to possess a new fake ID with which he is able to travel to Turkey and from there to Pakistan. In Pakistan, where he is awaiting relocation by the United Nations Refugee Office, he is followed by the Iraqi secret services and spotted in a protest against the gassing of the Kurds. He is arrested and taken back to Iraq, where he is imprisoned in one of the basements used by Saddam's secret police. Subjected to harrowing 'parties of humiliation and torture',[56] as he puts it, he is castrated as a punishment for his desertion and treason. He is then transferred to Abū Ghraib prison to join those prisoners awaiting the death penalty. Every morning he fears that his name will be called among the names of those whose turn it is to be killed. Every day, at dawn when the prison guard opens the gate, Mālik involuntarily loses control of bladder and bowel motion out of fear, further diminishing his humanity and dignity. This is a common reaction among the detainees:

> He was seized by severe attack of diarrhoea every time he heard the sound of the key turning in the door, and there were those who lost their control and peed on themselves while waiting for the announcement of those who were to be shot dead or hanged. (p. 182)

Mālik, however, is miraculously saved from the death penalty day after day until he is numbered among those who receive amnesty on the occasion of the president's birthday. He again entrusts his fate to smugglers, from Iraq to Istanbul, to Greece and from there to Germany, where he is finally granted asylum.

The narrator, Khalīl, improvises his desertion after a short leave, simply deciding not to return to the war:

> The days of the leave passed quickly, then another three days, and then seven days, ten, twenty. After that I spontaneously freed myself from the army and told myself in an improvised tone: 'I won't fire another bullet in this cursed war. Damn! I hate this despicable war.' Then I started living outside the law, and I kind of liked this feeling. (p. 101)

As a deserter in the midst of a huge crowd, Khalīl is one day a witness to a horrible scene where three deserters are put to death at a soccer field at al-Karrāda. The three deserters, their heads covered with plastic bags, are tied to pillars fixed in the ground. In a cruel and inhumane scene, the officers first aim at their victims' bellies and chests, provoking their cries of pain and suffering. The horror ends with final shots that end their lives.

In his first year of being a deserter, Khalīl enjoys walking freely but cautiously along the streets of Baghdad. He watches the war news on television and earns his living from his paintings and drawings. He is able to live in relative peace of mind, thanks to false medical leaves that his friend Raʿd provides for him or to fake IDs. The capture and tragic end of Raʿd, however, are a turning point for the narrator. Raʿd has planned to leave Iraq for Lebanon with a fake British passport. In trying to escape the country, he disguises himself as a Lebanese priest. The authorities discover his false claims and arrest him at Baghdad airport.

The last encounter between Raʿd and Khalīl at the Abū Ghraib prison where Raʿd is awaiting his execution is very painful and filled with sadness and sorrow for the two friends, who together defied the regime and its war. Helplessly standing by Raʿd's side in the final moments of his life, Khalil the artist naively wishes they could be turned into fictitious creatures of pen and paper so as to avoid pain and suffering. His wish is a profound human cry of powerlessness and hopelessness in the face of unjust death: 'In this atmosphere filled with weakness and submission I wished for the skies to turn us into paper creatures or into cartoons that can easily be destroyed and not to be of blood and flesh' (p. 214). Raʿd's comments come to Khalīl heavy and full of meaning, like a cautionary tale, reminding Khalīl, who is still on the loose and whose fate remains open to all possibilities, including capture and death: 'Death is tough, but he who deserts the war has to know well in advance that sooner or later he has to pay the bill'. Raʿd's execution understandably terrifies Khalīl. He hurries back to the army after years of desertion. He joins after an amnesty decree is issued for all war deserters.

When Khalīl returns to the army, the war is winding down. However, he has to continue serving in order to make up for the years he was in flight. Caught by another war (the Gulf War) and long years of economic siege, he finally manages to participate in a cultural trip to an Iraqi art festival in Paris. This trip gives him the opportunity to cut his ties with Iraq once and for all. Yet, as indicated at the beginning of the novel in his move from Germany to Belgium, he is still on the road, looking for a place to settle somewhere in Europe.

Conclusion

Banished from the official records of the war and its literature, deserters from the Iran–Iraq War finally find redemption in fiction. By investigating and retrieving the hidden memory of the deserter and uncovering his experience and his voice as an important figure of the cultural and political landscape of 1980s Iraq, the novels discussed in this chapter offer an alternative history for them.

ᶜAli Badr's novel about the existence of underground groups of poet-soldiers who were coerced into the war and who chose not to be part of the mainstream represents a challenge to assumptions that all Iraqi poets of that period were co-opted by and succumbed to the Qādisiyyat Saddam. By presenting the views of marginal groups of poets and artists who were coerced into joining the war and were sentenced to death when they subsequently deserted, and by stressing their anxiety and their deep alienation from their milieu, the novels discussed in this chapter stand in stark contrast to the official literary records of this important period in Iraqi literary history. In revisiting this war three decades later and after the fall of Saddam, Iraqi authors break through the fear and the silence surrounding this issue. The narrator of *The Professors of Illusion* expresses this relationship between written history and power when he says, 'I was thinking about this other world that grows out suddenly, this unrecognised world which springs up out of the blue to undermine and destabilise the written history.' He continues:

> What is the secret power of the written that wants to erase everything else? . . . I understand that history is a tool in the service of power when it needs to remove the bodies of these youths who were there, those poet soldiers who stood in a vacuum vis-à- vis that history that we contemplated. What is this strength attached to publication that wants to ignore their bodies, which did exist? . . . Who can convince me that they did not exist when in truth I knew them not only in life but also in the field of writing? It is true they did not publish, and their pictures did not feature in newspapers as they have dreamt. Their names did not sparkle on the covers of their books, but they marked with their young bodies a whole period . . . What is this history that wants to cancel them and say that they simply did not exist, even though they had a deep impact during a difficult confused time and

> inaugurated a decisive experience? . . . They died . . . Yes, they died, and they did not publish, and nobody heard of them. But they are there in the beyond, in the dreamt city. (pp. 92–3)

Through the accounts of desertion during the Iran–Iraq War given in these different novels Khiḍr, ᶜĪsā, Khalīl, Raᶜd and Mālik all incarnate the 'other' soldier – the one who refuses to kill and die in the name of ideology. These deserters represent a contemporary embodiment of the sacred man, the man who is set apart because of his action and who is captured in the sovereign sphere, where it is permitted to kill without committing a homicide. Their desertions can be read as liberating events to contest the politics of war and terror and to reclaim some form of agency, but they also reduce these actors to 'bare life', leading them to their final dehumanisation. Most of them are alienated artists who reject their political existence for another qualified life. ᶜĪsā finds in poetry a way to transcend his natural life and his exposed condition, and in his freedom flight Khiḍr sheds his political self to reconnect with an immaculate self. The death of these deserters revives in its raw form the old sovereign right over life and death and connects them to the archaic figure of ancient Roman law: the *homo sacer*. In particular, Khiḍr and ᶜĪsā find in fiction salvation and redemption as prophetic figures who join the myth.

Notes

1. Anthony Cordesman, *The Iraq War: Strategy, Tactics, and Military Lessons* (Westport, CT: Praeger, 2003).
2. Michel Foucault, *Power/Knowledge: Selected Interviews and Other Writings, 1972–1977* (New York: Pantheon Books, 1980).
3. Rob Johnson, *The Iran–Iraq War* (New York: Palgrave Macmillan, 2010), p. 43.
4. Fritz Fischer, *War of Illusions* (London: Chatto and Windus, 1975), cited in ibid., p. 7.
5. Johnson, *The Iran–Iraq War*, p. 7.
6. Quoted in Derek Gregory, *The Colonial Present: Afghanistan, Palestine, Iraq* (Malden, MA: Blackwell, 2004), p. 153.
7. See Johnson, *The Iran–Iraq War*, p. 6.
8. Gregory, *The Colonial Present*, p. 153.
9. Mackey, quoted in ibid., p. 153.

10. It was when Kuwait and Saudi Arabia demanded their money back after the end of the war in 1988 that Saddam Hussein decided to invade Kuwait.
11. miriam cooke, *Women and the War Story* (Berkeley: University of California Press, 1996), pp. 230–1.
12. See Salām ᶜAbbūd, *Thaqāfat al ᶜunf fī al-ᶜIrāq* (The culture of violence in Iraq) (Cologne: al-Jamal, 2002).
13. cooke, *Women and the War Story*, pp. 223–32.
14. Jabrā Ibrāhīm Jabrā, *al-Fann wa al-ḥulm wa al-fiᶜl* (Art, dream and action) (Baghdad: Dār al- shᵓuūn al-thaqāfiyya al-ᶜāmma, 1986), 52.
15. Ibid., pp. 52–3, emphasis added.
16. Quoted in cooke, *Women and the War Story*, p. 238.
17. ᶜAbbūd, *Thaqāfat al ᶜunf fī al-ᶜIrāq*, p. 198.
18. See cooke, *Women and the War Story*, p. 237.
19. ᶜAbdallah Ibrāhīm, *al-Bināᵓ al-fannī li-riwāyat al-ḥarb fī al-ᶜĪrāq* (The artistic structure of the war novel in Iraq) (Baghdad: Dār al-ṣhᵓuūn al-thaqāfiyya al-ᶜāmma, 1988), pp. 114–15.
20. Aḥmad Maṭlūb, *al-Shi'r fī zaman al-ḥarb* (Poetry in times of war) (Baghdad: Dār al-Shᵓuūn al-thaqāfiyya al-ᶜāmma 1987).
21. (This poetic excerpt is quoted in Leslie Tramontini '"Speaking Truth to Power?" Intellectuals in Iraqi Baathist Cultural Production', *Middle East-Topics & Arguments*, 1, 2013, p. 56.) And according to my colleague Roger Allen who 'attended the Marbid Festival in 1988 which was almost entirely devoted to a celebration of the war's end, among the poets who recited ringing odes to Saddam Hussein were Nizār Qabbānī, Muḥammad al-Faytūrī and Suᶜād al-Sabāh' (private conversation with Professor Roger Allen).
22. ᶜAbbūd, *Thaqāfat al ᶜunf fī al-ᶜIrāq*, p. 198.
23. Ibid., pp. 246–7.
24. Boris Vian, *The Deserter*, quoted in *The Professors of Illusion* (see next note), p. 213.
25. Ali Badr, *Asātidhat al-wahm* (The professors of illusion) (Beirut: al-Mu' assasa al-'arabiyya li-dirāsāt wa al-nashr, 2011), p. 89. Page references are given parenthetically in the text after this point; my translations throughout.
26. Michel Foucault, *Society Must Be Defended: Lectures at the College de France, 1975–76*, ed. Mauro Bertani and Alessandro Fontana, trans. David Macey (New York: Picador, 2003), p. 240.
27. The story of the People of the Cave is featured in the Qur'ān (*Ahl al-Kahf* 18:9–26). *People of the Cave* is also the title of one of the plays that the Egyptian playwright Tawfīq al-Ḥakīm published in 1933.

28. Muḥsin al-Mūsawī, *Arabic Poetry: Trajectories of Modernity and Tradition* (New York: Routledge, 2006), p. 15).
29. The writings of Akhmatova and Mayakovsky, among other Russian poets, were available in Arabic in Baghdad during the 1980s, translated by the Iraqi poet Ḥasab al-Shaykh Ja^{c}far, who studied and lived in Moscow for many years.
30. See Fabio Caiani and Catherine Cobham, *The Iraqi Novel: Key Writers, Key Texts* (Edinburgh: Edinburgh University Press, 2013), p. 123.
31. Ibid., p. 124.
32. '^{c}Īsā' is the Arabic name for Christ.
33. Jean-Paul Sartre, *What Is Literature? And Other Essays*, introduction by Steven Ungar (Cambridge, MA: Harvard University Press, 1988), p. 29.
34. It is not an exaggeration to say that the mere idea of the existence of these poets in Baghdad during the 1980s is difficult for many to believe. If not for the testimony of ^{c}Ali Badr, with whom I had a conversation and who attested that these poet-deserters were his fellow soldiers at the front, I would be unable to support my claim that these groups did indeed exist. Badr's and Falak's novels as well as Muḥammad Ḥasan's are otherwise the only source I have found regarding these groups. Some of the Iraqi writers with whom I have discussed these groups of poets just laughed at the mere idea.
35. Al-Mūsawī, *Arabic Poetry*, p. 55.
36. Adūnīs, *An Introduction to Arab Poetics*, trans. Catherine Cobham (Cairo: American University in Cairo Press, 1992), pp. 80–1.
37. Roger Allen, *An Introduction to Arabic Literature* (Cambridge: Cambridge University Press, 2000), pp. 130–1.
38. *Shi^{c}r* 1, 4, quoted in Ed De Moor, 'The Rise and Fall of the Review *Shi^{c}r*', *Quaderni di studi arabi*, 18, 2000, p. 93.
39. See Dounia A. Badini, 'La vie littéraire autour de la revue Libanaise *Shi^{c}r* (1957–1970)', *Middle East Literatures*, 13, 1, April 2010, p. 89.
40. Peter Fitzpatrick, 'Bare Sovereignty: *Homo Sacer* and the Insistence of the Law', *Theory & Event*, 5, 2, 2001, p. 52.
41. The image of the resurrection of Christ as sacrificial death and as a trope for suffering is a common one used in Iraqi poetry; see David Pinaut, 'Images of Christ in Arabic Literature', *Die Welt des Islams*, New Series, 27, 1–3, 1987, 103–25.
42. Even though he is not mentioned by name in the Qur'ān, al-Khiḍr is a mystical figure and a spiritual *persona* identified with the figure in the Qur'ān 18:64 'One of our servants, unto whom we (God) had given mercy from Us, and had taught

him knowledge proceeding from Us.' According to the story in the Qur'ān, Moses set out to seek wisdom and knowledge. He encounters al-Khiḍr, who initiates him into divine, esoteric knowledge. See *The New Encyclopedia of Islam*, pp. 257–8.

43. Naṣīf Falak, *Khiḍr Qad wa al-ᶜaṣr al-zaytūnī* (Khiḍr Qad and the drab olive years) (Baghdad: Manshūrāt al-Jamal, 2006), p. 67. Page references are given parenthetically in the text after this point; my translation throughout.
44. According to Agamben, the Hobbesian state of nature 'is not necessarily to be conceived as a real epoch, but rather could be understood as a principle internal to the State revealed in the moment in which the State is considered "as if it were dissolved"' (*Homo Sacer: Sovereign Power and Bare Life*, trans. Daniel Heller-Roazen (Stanford, CA: Stanford University Press, 1998), p. 36).
45. Thomas Hobbes, *Leviathan*, ed. Richard Tuck (Cambridge, Cambridge University Press, 1991), quoted in Foucault, *Society Must Be Defended*, p. 89, see also note 1. p. 112: 'During the time men live without a common Power to keep them all in awe, they are in that condition which is called Warre; and such a warre, as is of every man against every man' (quoted on p. 88).
46. Agamben, *Homo Sacer*, p. 37.
47. Elaine Scarry, *The Body in Pain: The Making and Unmaking of the World* (New York: Oxford University Press, 1985), p. 34.
48. Anselm Haverkamp, 'Anagrammatics of Violence: The Benjaminian Ground of *Homo Sacer*', in Andrew Norris (ed.), *Politics, Metaphysics, and Death: Essays on Giorgio Agamben's* Homo Sacer (Durham, NC: Duke University Press, 2005), p. 140.
49. *Arḍ al-Sawād* is also the title of ᶜAbd al-Raḥmān Munīf's trilogy, 1999, Beirut: al-Muʾassasa al-ᶜarabiyya li al-dirāsāt wa al-nashr.
50. Agamben, *Homo Sacer*, p. 104.
51. Ibid., p. 106.
52. Ibid., p. 105.
53. The original Arabic sentence is: 'kuntu maᶜa laysa waḥdī'.
54. The story of the prophet al-Khiḍr is narrated in the Qur'ān in sūra 18.
55. The Peshmerga are the armed Kurdish forces who fight for an independent Kurdistān.
56. Muḥammad Ḥasan, *Hubūṭ al-malāʾika* (The descent of the angels) (Beirut: al-Tanwīr li al-ṭibāᶜa wa al-nashr wa al-tawzīᶜ, 2013), p. 179. Page references are given parenthetically in the text from this point on; my translation throughout.

2

Postmodern War, the Gulf War and the Iraqi Soldier

In the first chapter, we saw how desertion from the Iran–Iraq War could lead to the deserter's banishment from his country, from life and from history. In this chapter, I explore the soldier's experience as depicted in novels about the 1991 Gulf War and how the soldier is a perfect example of the *homo sacer*, whose killing is permissible and goes unsanctioned during the war. This chapter focuses on the tangible realities of a 'ghost war' on the ground; it is structured around three major moments in the Gulf War as glimpsed through the novels *Ḍayāᶜ fī Ḥafr al- Bāṭin* (Loss in Ḥafr al-Bāṭin, 2009) by ᶜAbd al- Karīm al-ᶜUbaydī, *Mā baᶜd al-ḥubb* (2003, *Beyond Love* (2012)) by Hadiyya Hussein, *Khiḍr Qad wa alᶜaṣr al-zaytūnī* (Khiḍr Qad and the drab olive years, 2006) by Naṣīf Falak and *Baghdad mālbūrū* (Baghdad Marlboro, 2012) by Najm Wālī. These narratives expose both the myth of the 'Mother of all Battles' (ʾUmm al- Maᶜārik) and the myth of a clean, precise and bloodless war.

Loss shows us the Gulf War from the ground through the eyes of an Iraqi soldier, the protagonist and narrator, thus resituating the geographical horizon of this conflict from the virtual space of the monitor screen where the war was displayed and inflated into a worldwide war back into the forgotten real space – the desert of Ḥafr al-Bāṭin. Owing to the postmodern nature of this brief but deadly conflict, the novel shows how Iraqi soldiers who were stationed in the front at Ḥafr al-Bāṭin were rendered irrelevant and obsolete creatures on the field, meeting their invisible enemy only after the end of the operations, when they were lost in the desert and became prisoners of war. Using language fraught with irony and sarcasm and prose infused with dirty, obscene images, the anti-war hero debunks both the Iraqi regime's false rhetoric and the Americans' sanitised version. He exposes the coercion, corruption and vices inside the Iraqi army. In his utter solitude, he is able only to observe and describe the deadly result of an invisible but assumed one-sided action that makes the surrender and desertion of high-ranking Iraqi officers and soldiers one of the most palpable realities of the conflict and an obscene spectacle.

To this first moment in the conflict we can juxtapose the last episode in the ground offensive of this war, as depicted in Hadiyya Hussein's *Beyond Love*. Through the poetic testimony of one of the returning Iraqi soldiers, this novel gives us a vivid description of a war executed as a sovereign 'police operation' and manhunt. This manhunt is most visible during the bloody return of soldiers from Kuwait to Basra and in the targeting of the retreating troops along the trail – the 'Highway of Death', as it was called.

The other two novels, *Baghdad Marlboro* and *Khiḍr Qad*, show the third major moment in this war with the burial of Iraqis while they are still alive, whether in the desert at the end of the war or during the crushing of the Shiᶜa revolt that followed the war. In *Baghdad Marlboro*, an American lieutenant, Daniel Brooks, comes to Iraq after the 2003 war to try to meet the families of the victims he buried alive in the desert in 1991 as a way to express his repentance, and in *Khiḍr Qad* (which I also discussed in Chapter 1) the main character, who had deserted the Iran–Iraq War, returns to his country during the Gulf War and finds death in the Shiᶜa uprising, thrown like garbage into a mass grave along with the many anonymous victims crushed during the revolt.

Through the accounts of these different novels, we gain insight into some of the 'human moments' of the Gulf War, but I argue that these 'human moments' turn out to be not so much human as *subhuman*: Iraqi soldiers are dehumanised as 'sandy objects in fusion with the desert';[1] they are hunted down and massacred or melted down with the metal of their carbonised vehicles on the Highway of Death or thrown alive into mass graves. I argue that war as a contest is absent from the novels; it is instead a police and extermination operation where paralysed soldiers are massacred as *homines sacri*. Because of the asymmetrical aspect of Operation Desert Storm, the Iraqi soldiers did not experience the war existentially. Though stationed in the real space of Ḥafr al-Bāṭin, they found themselves locked into non-action because the war did not offer them the option to affirm their agency. A feeling of inadequacy and futility filled them and degraded them. Their only activity was the circular and vicious wandering in the desert and the feeling of loss they incurred after the desertion and the surrender of their officers and their subsequent situation as prisoners of war. *Beyond Love* depicts the retreating soldier in his biological life, targeted from above and exterminated; in this episode, we witness the emergence of the camp as a structure where law can be suspended and extermination becomes possible. Along these lines, I look at the targeting and extermination of the retreating soldiers in the Killing Box, a US military bombing technique used in the war, as a *virtual camp*, which is paralleled in its atrocity by the mass graves into which thousands of Iraqi rebels were thrown, some of them alive, during the uprising immediately following the war. All of those who were killed, whether in the virtual camp or in the mass graves constitute the *homines sacri*, sacred men, of this war.

Before discussing the novels' portrayal of the soldier's experience of the war, I retrace the characteristics of the Gulf War as a postmodern, virtual and media war that caused the disappearance of the existential dimension of the war.

The Persian Gulf War: Mythologised and Forgotten

Unlike the Iran–Iraq War, which, as we saw in Chapter 1, generated a substantial body of literature, including novels, short stories and poetry, much of which was propaganda, the 1991 Persian Gulf War and Iraq's defeat are marked by an intriguing cultural and literary silence. Saddam Hussein obviously had no time to commission writers or poets to celebrate Iraq's invasion of Kuwait or to denounce the Coalition war in response to this invasion. Iraqi authors understandably could not celebrate the regime's bitter defeat in the Mother of All Battles. Those among them who were homebound could not condemn the regime's brutality and recklessness. At the same time, they did not denounce and condemn the Coalition war, which surpassed the Second World War in its firepower. In *Baghdad Marlboro*, a novel published in 2012, Najm Wālī's narrator confesses the blackout of information about what really happened in the southern front of the country during the 1991 Gulf War:

> We didn't know anything about the news of the war on the southern front except for what we heard on the official radios and some other foreign radio

> stations . . . We had to travel outside the country, or to wait until 9 April 2003, to see what we were not allowed to see or to discover what was forbidden, but even after we saw the images and pictures of the battles that took place there [the southern front], they couldn't give us an idea about what really happened.[2]

Today, more than ten years after the fall of Saddam's regime, Iraqi writers now focus on the occupation of Iraq that began in 2003 and the sectarian war. It seems as though the 1991 Persian Gulf War was consigned to oblivion; not much attention is given to the re-examination of this war's historical and cultural records, despite its structural and strategic importance in the history of modern Iraq.

A few authors did not forget the Gulf War, however. In 1993, Kanan Makkiya, an Iraqi academic living in exile, published his polemical book *Cruelty and Silence: War, Tyranny, Uprising, and the Arab World*.[3] A diatribe and a condemnation of Arab intellectuals at large for not speaking out against the crimes of Arab rulers, in particular Saddam, and for their lack of self-criticism, this book is also a vast catalogue of different experiences and testimonies by Iraqi Arabs and Kurds as well as Kuwaitis who suffered during the invasion of Kuwait, the Coalition war, the Shiᶜa uprising and the massacre of the Kurds. Among the early novels on the 1991 Gulf War, miriam cooke mentions in her essay 'Flames of Fire in Qadisiya' the 1994 novel *Maṭar aswad . . . maṭar aḥmar* (Black rain . . . red rain) by the female Iraqi author Ibtisām ᶜAbdallah.[4] Dunyā Mīkhāᵓīl's *Yawmiyyāt mawja khārij al-baḥr* (The journal of a wave outside the sea), published in 1995, is a series of prose poems describing the poet's reactions to the events of the war. Both works were published by the Iraqi Ministry of Culture and Information relatively shortly after the war.[5] Nuha al-Radi's *Baghdad Diaries* (2003),[6] a chronicle of life in Baghdad during the days of the Gulf War, is an excellent document portraying the daily endurance of Iraqis during Operation Desert Storm. In 2007, on the occasion of the fourth anniversary of the occupation of Iraq, Raᶜd al-Ḥamdānī, a former general of the Iraqi Republican Guard, published *Qabla an yughādiranā al-tārīkh* (Before history leaves us),[7] a military history that retraces Iraq's involvement in war from 1973 until the 2003 invasion. Other references to some of the episodes of this war are made in novels portraying the duress of life under the embargo and the years of sanctions (Hussein's *Beyond Love*); the war's virtual and media aspect as reflected on Western television networks (Batūl Khudayrī's novel *A Sky so Close*);[8] the war's aftermath, especially the post-defeat Shiᶜa rebellion and the horrific burial alive of close to one thousand soldiers on the Hafr al-Bāṭin front (Falak's *Khiḍr Qad* and Wālī's *Baghdad Marlboro*). Besides these few titles, literature that is dedicated in full to the fictional exploration of what happened during this war and that takes us to the theatre of operations from an Iraqi perspective is scarce indeed.

Of the four novels to be discussed in this chapter – *Beyond Love, Loss, Baghdad Marlboro* and *Khiḍr Qad* – all but *Beyond Love*, which has been translated into English, are unknown to English-speaking audiences. It seems as if a literary and cultural silence envelops the 1991 war and clouds its memory, despite its strategic importance in the chain of wars in the past three decades of Iraqi history. The intellectual history of this forgotten war is yet to be written. The lack of materials undermines the effort to understand and analyse the Iraqi perspective on the events in their historical political, cultural and literary contexts.

In contrast, in the West the Gulf War in its multiple facets as a media war, a virtual war and a postmodern war has generated an abundant amount of mostly non-fiction literature, ranging from the immediate media coverage at the time of the operation to critical academic controversies, novels and documentaries. This is not surprising as this war saw a new dawn in the history of warfare.

The munitions dropped on Iraq and Kuwait produced a destructive power equivalent to five Hiroshimas, making it the most firepower-intensive conflict since the Second World War.[9] The Gulf War was almost mythologised in the literature and the minds of those who witnessed it (or at least the censored version of it) live on television all over the world. It gained the comparison to a world war because of its representation. Despite its local aspect, the French theorist Paul Virilio does not hesitate to describe it as a world war:

> The Gulf war was a reduced world war . . . It appeared to be a local war in the sense that its battlefield was very small compared with the Second

> World War. However, considering its representation it was a worldwide war, . . . live with all the special effects.[10]

The literature about the Gulf War has generated a profusion of names and labels for the war. Norman Schwarzkopf, the commander of Operation Desert Storm, talks about a 'technology war'.[11] Some call it a 'new war', an 'electronic war' and a 'clean, high-tech war' that sold us a 'Spectacle War'.[12] Yet others prefer to call it a 'postmodern war'. The importance and relevance of information to postmodernity and to the Gulf War make Chris Gray opt for the last label, identifying the Gulf War as one of the finest case studies of postmodern war.[13] Computers and informational networks dominated the war, and a new type of 'warrior computer operator' emerged, operating from an installation thousands of miles away from the targeted space. Paul Virilio writes about a

> first total electronic war or a pure war . . . that allows confrontation with the enemy almost without touching as if by nothing less than a miracle, with the electromagnetic environment above the Iraqi territory effectively substituting for the normal milieu, the sphere of armed men.[14]

The mythical aspect of this war is perhaps best captured, as Briemberg would like to put it, in the formula 'It was, and it was not', the traditional words Arab storytellers use to begin a story – 'Kān wa mā kān', which is perhaps a variation of the formula 'kān yā mā kān' used here to ponder the contradictory and perplexing qualities of the new war:

> It was and It was not . . . a war. The massive weapons of armies were used but where were the battles? . . . It was and it was not . . . in the Gulf. It was and it was not . . . a television spectacle. In North America it was the wide western screen, malignant with its infotainment . . . In Iraq and Kuwait the consequences were burned flesh and spilled blood.[15]

In addition to its mythical aspect, the Gulf War was surrounded by a huge controversy among theorists and postmodernist thinkers regarding its new rhetoric, its 'hyper-real' character and its video game imagery and mass-media simulation. Beyond the war's media character, Western theorists and academics were also very engaged in the debates and arguments that divided them pertaining to the 'real' versus phoney aspects of the war in a postmodern-exacerbated context where the relevance of distinctions such as 'truth' and 'falsehood' is undermined, to say the least. Among the most controversial attitudes was that of French thinker Jean Baudrillard, who published three provocative essays before, during and after the Gulf War.[16] His main thesis was that the Gulf War is not a war if we are to understand by war 'an antagonistic and destructive confrontation between two adversaries'.[17] In the first essay, written before the war (in the context of French refusal to sanction it), he claimed that the Gulf War would not take place, given that there was no longer any difference between the war rhetoric, the media simulation of it during the build-up and the event in itself. Indeed, a loss of boundaries between these three categories made it irrelevant, according to Baudrillard, to talk about the outbreak of a war as we used to define it. In the context of the media simulation of this war, the French thinker went so far as to doubt the outbreak of the war because it had not been declared in the first place, and therefore, according to him, the simulacrum of the war could go unchecked.

To use Baudrillard's words, the 'reality gulf' that emerged between the war and its postmodern substitute in the form of the ubiquitous, pervasive media-simulated images made it difficult, if not obsolete, to think in terms of an existing 'truth at the end of inquiry'.[18] Baudrillard's epistemological scepticism led him to reject not just appearances but also the idea of any truth behind them, whether through investigative and critical journalism or any other form of inquiry, because all possible actors – from the viewer to the combatant, the strategist and the politician – were caught up in the pernicious game of the all-too-powerful media-simulation machine:

> If we have no practical knowledge of this war – and such knowledge is out of the question – then let us at least have the skeptical intelligence to reject the probability of all information, of all images whatever their source.[19]

Christopher Norris found Baudrillard's thesis cynical, 'absurd' and 'ill-equipped to mount any kind of effective critical resistance'.[20] But in fact what Baudrillard questioned and lamented was the lack of any means of access to what happened during this conflict other than what was offered by the official, government-approved media images and the virtual war. The other side of the picture was to be found in what the media did not and could not show.

Because of the technology and the media aspect of the war, the distinction between categories such as 'actor' and 'spectator' became totally blurred. At the same time, each side of the war was totally locked into its own time and space. On one side, the human actors or spectators were caught in the media machine under the supervision and dominance of computer monitors, networks and amazing pictures in real time, and on the other side they were locked into a time and space that was more traditional and dominated not by network communications and computers but by the scarcity of control and the lack of intelligence, communication and networks. The latter were grounded into the slow time and naked space of the desert without technological mediation; miriam cooke says that, because of media coverage,

> in February 1991 American citizens were there with the American military in the Persian Gulf. They entered the briefing room. They joined the journey of the bomb from its launch to the moment when the electronic eye warned that it was about to hit its target.[21]

The viewers of Western networks were unified into an imagined community of war watchers, and in addition to their quality as spectators they acquired a new dimension as actors in this war thanks to the media, in which the spectator's eye was 'endowed with the symbolic function of a weapon'.[22] Virilio adds to this symbolic function an almost divine quality:

> We were living in a theatre of operations, spectators of a theatrical production (mise-en-scène). We have been living in a complete fiction . . . and turned into 'divine beings.' Curiously, telecommunications put properties of the divine into play in civil society: the ubiquity (to be all present together at the same time), instantaneity, immediacy, omnivoyance, omnipresence. Each of us is metamorphosed into a divine being, at once here and there at the same time. Whence our arrogance: I could say what I think about what is going to happen to a guy in six months or fifteen hours in the Arabian desert, although I know so little about him. It is totally absurd.[23]

Whereas some spectators were turned into 'divine beings' with a god's-eye view regaled by the most spectacular images of damaged infrastructures and lit skies over Baghdad, without the shadow of any human being on the image, other war actors or spectators were turned into something less than human as they experienced and witnessed their own debacle, and even into something less than spectators, becoming like 'strange wooden marionettes' in the desert, as one of the Iraqi soldiers puts it in *Loss*.[24] They were the creatures who looked like the 'ghostly sheep', which the media images could have shown had they not been censored and blocked, as one reporter who managed to see some forbidden gun-camera shots filmed from Apache helicopter raids described:

> [The Iraqi soldiers were like] ghostly sheep flushed from a pen – bewildered and terrified, jarred from sleep and fleeing their bunkers under a hellish fire. One by one they were cut down by attackers they could not see . . . blown to bits by bursts of 30 mm exploding cannon shells.[25]

Taken from above, these censored images testifying to the existence of the hidden dimension of the war-echoed images, perspectives and experiences coming from the ground and later found in novels and memoirs such as *Loss*. The narrator and protagonist of this novel gives us some of the instrumental 'practical knowledge', the absence of which Baudrillard lamented and something that we have been lacking in works about this war.

The 'Human Moments' in the Gulf War

> The bulk of Iraqi forces on the front lines was composed of young, relatively untrained conscripts, with a sprinkling of veterans from the Iran–Iraq War. The veterans were mostly older men fed up with years of pointless fighting. Further in the rear stood the flower of Iraq's army: the Republican Guard.
>
> Alberto Bin et al., *Desert Storm*

In his book *The Future of War*, Christopher Coker shows how, as a complex human activity, war has changed dramatically in its existential and instrumental dimensions. This change was caused by three major events in humankind's history: the Industrial Revolution, the information revolution and the biotechnological revolution. For Coker, war is made up of three interrelated dimensions: instrumental, existential and metaphysical. War is 'a rational instrument employed by states in a controlled, rational manner for purposes that are either economic or political'. The existential dimension contains those who practise it: the warriors; and as a metaphysical concept war 'invests death with meaning translating it into sacrifice'.[26] In his book *Waging War without Warriors?* Coker shows that, from the *Bhagavad Gita* and the Samurai tradition to *The Iliad*, war offers an existential experience that is life-affirming in so far as it allows for a sense of self and agency, offering the warrior an experience to discover and assert himself and to affirm his humanity.[27] It helps the warrior to actualise himself and become something higher, giving life meaning.

As Coker argues, 'In his willingness to put his life on the line for a warlord, feudal master or king, or a people, the warrior defines himself as a man . . . he rises above his animality'.[28] But with the technological age and the development of nuclear weapons, the existential dimension of war became obsolete, and with the American way of warfare the warrior became redundant in the age of computerised bombs, drones and smart weapons. Coker pointedly questions the 'death of the warrior' tradition. He notes that the new emphasis on technology has made war almost entirely instrumental, devoid of the existential experience and as such at odds with Western humanism in that it is leading to a *posthuman* world in which the warrior is devalued. The change incurred with modern and then postmodern technologies has caused war to be a disenchanting and alienating activity.

Although the Gulf War allowed for the emergence of a new kind of warrior, the virtual warrior or the computer warrior battling at a distance and enthralled with the high-tech instrumental aspect of this new war, it also unveiled the alienated soldier, locked into non-action, self-defeated and imprisoned by this same ultramodern technology. The Iraqi soldier was doomed to redundancy and to occupy the position of spectator. He entered the war against his will, as a hostage or prisoner, and if he didn't die in it, he exited it as a humiliated prisoner, relayed from the hands of the Iraqi generals to those of the Americans and then the Saudis, feeling useless during the time he was stationed in the desert. For the Iraqi soldier, both the instrumental and the existential dimensions of war were non-existent. The cancellation of this doubly important dimension created a void in which the Iraqi soldiers felt their total inadequacy and therefore their irrelevancy in the landscape of this war. As the novels discussed in this chapter show, after the order was given to hide the artillery, the terrified soldiers took refuge in their bunkers and shelters. Like rats in the desert, they hid in their holes. The news of the surrender and the desertion of their superiors confirmed the magnitude of their loss, their abandonment and their vulnerability in the desert.

Deployed Men and the Moral Conditions of a Deployment

Loss is a narrative of war told by a soldier who was there and witnessed the events. It was written in 2005–6 and published in 2009, after the fall of Saddam's regime and almost twenty years after the war. One of the reasons for this long wait is certainly the regime's censorship. A direct tale narrated in the first person, this novel chronicles, in the distinct and individual voice of a soldier, what happened in the desert of Ḥafr al-Bāṭin during the forty-three days of the war. It is the personal witness of an ordinary man who was there and a story about what the war was like for the Iraqi soldiers in the desert – what they did, how they felt and what war did to them. It is through these particulars that we gain the 'practical knowledge' otherwise absent from media accounts of the war. In his book *The Soldier's Tale*, Samuel Hynes stresses the importance of the 'particulars' in the personal narrative of war:

> Because the soldier's tale is told by the fighting men themselves, it is a tale of particulars: one man or a few men, in a trench or on a beach, in a plane or a ship, acting, feeling, suffering. And because it is particular it is the human tale of war.[29]

These particulars 'bring the war down to the human realm', as Aharon Appelfeld notes in his remarks about the Holocaust, by 'making the events speak through the individual and his language, to rescue the suffering from the huge numbers, from dreadful anonymity'.[30]

Loss describes the circumstances of the deployment and how it was marked by coercion, corruption and propaganda – major practices that undermine the existential dimension of war from the inside. It uncovers how the soldiers were led by force to the front in Ḥafr al-Bāṭin and how desertion was very present as an idea and already quite widespread as a practice even before the war started. Moreover, the novel is keen in unveiling the rampant corruption at all levels, from politicians to officers, soldiers and civilians.

A reservist from Basra and a veteran of the Iran–Iraq War, the narrator is a lost, penniless and unemployed young man whose youth has been punctuated by two wars: one that has just ended and another to start soon. He is to join the front only a few months after his release from the army after seven years of service in the Iran–Iraq War. Still not fully recovered from previous traumatic experiences and morally devastated, he has no choice but to be led back to the front. The idea of dodging the draft is on his mind, but his family warns him against the terrible consequences of desertion. Submitting to his fate, the narrator unveils the real conditions of the capture and coercion of soldiers and their subsequent forced transfer to the front while exposing the prevailing corruption at different levels of command. The soldiers are first captured, taken hostage, and then driven under the threat of arms to a unit prison, where they spend the night to ensure they cannot desert before they are taken to the front. After a night in the prison, where, according to the narrator, humans beings are heaped on top of each other and entangled with one another, the narrator's friend Mālik the ᶜAmāratlī (literally 'the man from the city of al-ᶜAmāra') exclaims: 'I swear by al-ᶜAbbās,[31] I'm totally exhausted. And they want me to fight. Fighting is not within my reach'.[32]

The narrator uses an abundance of expressions referring to insects and animals in his descriptions of the group of captured soldiers led to the desert. They are like a 'flock of lost ants,' 'slowly moving bugs,' 'crushed cockroaches', and 'crowds on their way to death' (p. 31). This is how the narrator perceives his fellow soldiers after they have spent twenty-four hours in a prison, waiting to be transferred by force to the desert of Ḥafr al-Bāṭin with no word to their families. Some of the soldiers have never even heard of this location and object to the way they are being rushed to the front:

> 'How do we go to Ḥafr al-Bāṭin without our belongings or luggage and without even bidding farewell to our families? Are there any soldiers in the world who are asked to defend their homelands in this savage way?' The officer's reply was unequivocal: 'What families, what are you talking about? Your country is being targeted by the Zionists and the imperialists, and you think about your families?' (p. 31)

But, as Elaine Scarry has argued in her book *The Body in Pain: The Making and Unmaking of the World*, the structure of war requires the undeniable solidity of individual bodies to lend substance to its insubstantial fictions.[33] The coercive methods used to recruit the soldiers are complemented by propaganda. By appropriating these unprepared, untrained and exhausted bodies, the state confers substance and credibility on its narrative and its propaganda. This is also visible in the first political orientation lecture the soldiers receive in the desert. The captain of political orientation briefs them about the Zionist and imperialistic conspiracies, stressing

> the necessity of the return of the branch to its origin and the importance of Kuwait as a step towards the liberation of Palestine . . . The captain recited old, empty statements about the conspiracy of the enemies against our country and the backwardness of some Arab countries . . . then he said that the road map to free Palestine goes through Kuwait first! (p. 42)

The narrator's humour and sarcastic reserve are the best weapons he has to cope with such fallacies. He misses no opportunity to recall with dark humour how the same road map to free Palestine had a different route in previous narratives, hinting at the same propaganda that justified the war against Iran. Not without irony, he points to the demagogy of the Iraqi regime comforting him and his friend with the thought that, as long as it requires only the invasion of neighbouring countries, things are manageable; however, 'the worst is to be feared if that imaginary road [to free Palestine] has to go through faraway lands like the islands of Guinea or Burkina Faso!' (p. 43).

In addition to coercion and propaganda, desertion as an expected reaction to enforced deployment is yet another disconcerting phenomenon that affects the early phase of the war (as well as its end phase, as we will see later). The narrator reports how on the way to the front many conscripts take the opportunity to flee at every checkpoint, while others bargain for their release; he notes how those who are recaptured are savagely punished and humiliated for trying to flee.

Following their arrival in the desert, the soldiers complain about the difficult conditions, the scarcity of provisions, the humidity and the bitter-cold nights in the desert. They share pieces of bread, and lucky indeed are the ones who have water to boil some tea: 'It was as if we were living in the early history of humankind, the living conditions are so difficult here' (p. 47).

In this gloomy landscape, corruption is the last resort for those who cannot flee. Amid these lost, hungry soldiers, the truck driver occupies a key lucrative position because he is the only intermediary between desert and cities. He takes advantage of his position, smuggling all sorts of goods and selling them to the soldiers for a high price. At night, the driver is able to earn good sums of money for smuggling deserters who can afford his fee, using different excuses to get them safely away from the front. 'All the officers with their different ranks saw in him [the driver] their only intermediary between desert and cities. They knew how to manage him and have him take care of their needs; they courted him so as to spare him for the close defeat' (p. 44). Soldiers follow their officers in their submission to the driver and have to pay his steep prices for goods and especially to secure their flight from the desert: 'The driver realised his importance very early on . . . The soldiers knew that he was a professional thief' (pp. 44–5). Some soldiers are lucky enough to serve under officers whom they knew originally from their own neighbourhoods, something that enables them to secure jobs serving as liaisons and couriers between the officers and their families and mistresses, making weekly trips to cities and bringing back food and cigarettes. But when battle is imminent, they are smart enough to turn their backs on their masters and flee from the front. The commander of the unit and his closest circle, along with the cook and his helpers, the first sergeant of the unit and his guards, form a self-serving, opportunistic gang, while the rank-and-file soldiers are the real victims, at times ready to fight each other for a sip of water, a piece of bread or a handful of grain. In addition to the bitter cold and harsh conditions of the desert, the scarcity of food and the lack of equipment and logistical support, the narrator lists illness, epilepsy and strange behaviours among some soldiers, whom the desert and the conditions of living have turned into subhuman creatures. One of them is Mālik the ᶜAmāratlī, the narrator's friend, who behaves erratically owing to his epileptic fits. Some soldiers live on the edge, depressed and sad. In an excess of hysteria, complaints, insults and ironic expressions against the regime and its figures circulate freely on the tongues of the angry, depressed soldiers. The narrator himself, absorbed and estranged from his fellow soldiers, is distracted and astonished by the sight of the rising sun in the desert, spending his days deep into the desert, collecting rare stones of different shapes and sizes. He returns with the stones he has found and happily sets to work classifying them according to their shapes. At night, he holds the radio close to his ear in search of the latest news about the war.

The 'Sons of the New War' and a Very Short Contest

> 'One day we fight the Kurds, and another Iran, then Kuwait and now America . . . How are we supposed to defeat it with the Kalashnikov?'
>
> ᶜAbd al-Karīm al-ᶜUbaydī, *Loss*

> Most of the soldiers were asleep; on that cold night, maybe no one was awake. The world was waiting for a miracle to extinguish the fire to come. But as of now all that is left to them, to us, and to the sky *is just to watch and see. We are all the sons of 3:00 a.m., the sons of the new war.*
>
> ᶜAbd al- Karīm al-ᶜUbaydī, *Loss*

In *The Body in Pain*, Scarry discusses the structure of war, which she sees essentially as a 'contest' 'where the participants must work to out-perform and out-injure each other and where the side that inflicts the greater injury faster will be the winner'.[34] Although she acknowledges the fact that the word *contest* is usually attended by synonyms of peacetime such as *game* and *play*, she insists on the importance of identifying war as a contest:

> War is in the monumental fact of its structure a contest . . . where the participants arrange themselves into two sides and engage in an activity that will eventually make it possible to designate one side the winner and one side the loser (or more precisely makes it possible for the loser to identify itself so that the other side will recognize itself as the winner by default).[35]

According to Scarry, as a contest the structure of war is necessarily marked by a formal duality. But this condition of duality is only temporary and is replaced by the condition of singularity that emerges after one side has been declared the loser at the end of the war:

> In consenting to enter into war, the participants enter into a structure that is a self-cancelling duality. They enter into a formal duality, but one understood by all to be temporary and intolerable, a formal duality that by the very force of its relentless insistence on doubleness, provides the means for eliminating and replacing itself by the condition of singularity.[36]

The contest structure of war is also marked by formal defining moments, wherein the beginning marks the transition from the condition of multiplicity to the binary or dual condition of the contest itself, which eventually must lead to the unilateral situation marking the end of the contest. The insistence on the language of contest is also justified by the fact that it takes into account reciprocity versus non-reciprocity and monodirectional versus bidirectional as major categories in the description of the activity of war.[37]

Scarry sums up the notion of war as contest more clearly when she specifies further the central activity of war in combination with its formal structure:

> Each side begins the war by perceiving physical damage as acceptable and ideological and territorial sacrifices as unacceptable; through the war each side tries to bring about in the other the fundamental perceptual reversal – damage as unacceptable and sacrifices as acceptable . . . Each side works to bring the other side to the latter's perceived level of intolerable injury faster than it is itself brought to its own level of intolerable injury.[38]

Measured against these formal delineations of the structure of war, the descriptions in *Loss* of what took place during Operation Desert Storm do not and cannot show us the event of war because there is no dual condition. The narrator immediately introduces us to the condition of singularity marking the end of either a very short contest or no contest at all.

Of the two hundred pages of *Loss*, the author dedicates only thirty to the panic and horror of the air attack, its disastrous consequences and the debacle at the level of the command and soldiers. The shock of the first air attack that took everybody by surprise, with most of the soldiers asleep at the H-hour, was like a natural catastrophe. The start of the hostility is confirmed only by way of hearing and by the narrator's reports of his fellow soldiers' fear and superstition in face of such a calamity: 'None of us wanted to pronounce the fateful sentence announcing the outbreak of a world-caliber war and become forever stigmatized as the ominous symbol of this calamity' (p. 56). For the narrator, loss is guaranteed, and this perception is already and immediately embodied in the new vocabulary for and the brand names of aircraft he can hear from his radio and of the deadly cargo they are dropping:

> At 3:00 a.m. our loss was a matter of numbers as we got acquainted with tens of strange new words referring to the machinery of war: F-117 Stealth

> bombers saturated the night sky of Baghdad; F-117s obliterated many sites; flocks of A-10 bombers unleashed their missiles on the warehouse provisions along the front lines. Two thousand sorties were scheduled every day; the missiles fired by F-15s destroyed a number of targets in the desert of Ḥafr al-Bāṭin; Tornado fighters attacked the first line of the front. Bombers, Tomahawk missiles, and other attackers created the shock of 3:00 a.m. I put the radio to my ear; bulletins and reports were updated every minute. (p. 58)

The duality normally characterising the structure of war is immediately put to rest by the lists of these brand names and the sight of the Tomahawk missiles, Stealth bombers, Tornados, and F-15s crossing the Iraqi desert, obliterating targets there and heading on toward Baghdad. The soldiers enter a state of passivity and inertia, putting their ears to the radio, while, as the narrator puts it, the commanders and the officers watch 'the game' live on the TV screens in their refuges.

In his provocative 1991 essay *The Gulf War Did Not Take Place*, Baudrillard claimed that 'since this war was won in advance, we will never know what it would have been like had it existed'. And he regretted that 'we will never know what an Iraqi taking part with a chance of fighting would have been like'.[39]

Baudrillard's claims might have seemed at the time pure speculation, but they find substantiation in the narrative of *Loss* as the narrator provides facts from the ground authenticating not the reality of the war but its absence and the stupefaction of the soldiers being bombarded. Amid the panic and horror of the initial shock, the narrator assures us that, although destruction is undoubted and devastation is guaranteed, the confrontation between the adversaries is doubtful because the paralysis of the Iraqi army in the face of the invisible enemy is total, giving the troops an overwhelming feeling of uselessness and the reader of the novel disappointment in the shortage of events.

Virtual and won in advance for the Coalition forces, the Gulf War was lost in advance for the Iraqis, with no point of common ground and no point of contact between the two sides. It is as though we are talking not about the same war, but two totally different wars.

> At first, our anti-aircraft machines took a shot and participated. They released their dense fire but fell silent only a few minutes later. The marksmen hid, and the cannons were also hidden as if the war had already ended. (p. 61)

The narrator reveals how the soldiers were at a loss as their officers begged them to bury the weapons under sandbags and hide and as they became the object of conflicting demands:

> Saddam was asking us to stand up in the face of this bunch of non-believers, while Bush was urging us to surrender or flee in order to save our souls. At the same time, our officers were begging us to hide and not use the arms or bury them with sandbags lest the aeroplanes detect them and destroy us all! (p. 60)

Along with the arms, the war itself goes underground. 'Like an animal,' comments Baudrillard, 'the war goes to ground. It hides in the sand' as it 'hides in the sky'.[40] The order to hide the arms and artillery from the visual field of the Coalition pilots cancels the instrumental dimension of the war for the Iraqis and de facto annuls the engagement and binary relationship characterising the formal structure of war, thus allowing the entrance of the unilateral condition that formally characterises the end of the contest. After the artillery and weapons are hidden, the narrator notes that, in less than twenty-four hours after the beginning of the air campaign, 'Bush's aeroplanes and missiles dance alone in the sky. And around us people watch our slow death live on their television screens. Everybody, oh God, is watching how we burn' (p. 61).

The narrator describes a sense of overwhelming uselessness and obsolescence dominating the general atmosphere and the soldiers' feelings. Torn between different demands, confused and terrified, the narrator feels as if he is getting split in two: one half is dissolving into the sand, and the other is yearning for his wife and family. The non-functionality and heightened feelings of inadequacy are best expressed in the narrator's wish to dissolve into the environment:

> From inside this nightmare we wished we could turn into stones or sand that the wind might blow away, far from that ugly quagmire . . . I returned to the refuge. I was half broken. I leaned against the wall and wanted to cry, but I couldn't even find my tears. The desert has transformed me into a broken piece of wood that loss has brought together with thousands of other wooden creatures lost in the sand and storms. I will die here, in the

> desert. The roof of the refuge that I built will fall apart. This stubborn pillar will destroy my head. I am dead in any case . . .
>
> We have turned into nihilistic creatures with dusty faces, dirty beards and bodies eaten by lice, hunger and thirst amidst that crazy explosion that enveloped us and destroyed us one after another. (pp. 60–1)

In subsequent days, everybody sees the absurdity of the most recent news reports. A sense of uselessness and futility overwhelms the soldiers:

> The nights we spent waiting for the war became a distant memory . . . We laughed at the most recent news reports as they immediately became outdated for us.
>
> Everything was already consumed and had vanished, including the threats, the right and wrong guesses, our existence itself became useless . . . As long as the helicopters of the American army and its air force were over our heads, everything on this planet was obsolete. It is war. (p. 57)

The novel reveals how the empty rhetoric associated with the theme of Arab unity, the nationalistic ideas surrounding the war and the discourse pertaining to the imperialistic and Zionist plans in the Middle East could not withstand the reality of destruction and shock. The soldiers burn and vanish with the fires and are buried along with the unused artillery. The Mother of All Battles is really no battle – only dust storms roaring over the desert. Ideological and territorial sacrifices suddenly become acceptable as the damage increases:

> The discourse of authority lost its meaning. The rhetoric pertaining to the Zionist-imperialist plan and Arab Unity and nationalism vanished in flames. All these pathetic emotions evaporated . . . Illusions dissolved and burned. In the burning desert, even the code name for the war was nonexistent in the burning desert. The 'Mother of All Battles' was just a storm here, Desert Storm that burned us and revealed our loss to the whole world by means of satellite dishes. (p. 63)

The narrator relates how, following the initial shock, many soldiers took the opportunity to flee to Saudi Arabia or al-Zubayr, the closest Iraqi town. These waves of early desertion and surrender to Coalition forces take place even before the end of the 'war'. According to the narrator:

> Many deals were concluded in the open, and many people agreed to be part of groups of night patrols where a military vehicle would take them to the Holy Place. From there they took refuge with the American forces and surrendered. In the evening we would hear news of their desertion and surrender from the radio (p. 65).

The waves of desertion accelerated. Many soldiers disappeared from their units. They would leave all their belongings and accompany any vehicle going to al-Zubayr:

> From the beginning, the fires of the holocaust revealed the weakness of this concentration that was supposed to be strong behind its leadership. The satellites transformed all that weakness into images and movies, and I think they caught that daily scene where the commander of our unit would appear to check on what cannons and anti-aircraft weapons were left. He wanted to make sure that everything was properly hidden under sandbags so that the fighters and helicopters wouldn't see them. As for the political orientation officer, he didn't leave his refuge. Perhaps he couldn't tolerate seeing his illusions burnt in the desert. Or perhaps he was busy thinking of a way to extricate himself. All the illusions quickly vanished. As for us, we were burning. After the weapons and cannons were hidden, our condition deteriorated. I couldn't recognise a single face in the blur of the soldiers' faces. They all were clones of a single dusty face hidden behind a long beard and an untidy, stinky, head full of lice. As for the bodies, they were waning and emaciated, filthy and stinky. (p. 65)

When many soldiers emptied sandbags and wore them to protect themselves from the bitter cold of the desert at night, they started looking like phantom creatures with a ghostly shape. They were metamorphosed into marionettes: 'The sight of our unit became really terrifying: a bunch of swollen, moving bags in the trenches. Nobody could recognise anyone any more' (p. 66).

Bewildered, the narrator cannot help but wonder, not without cynicism and bitterness, how the Coalition pilots interpreted the images they could capture from above and how they made sense of the sight of the 'phantasmagoric creatures' in the desert and the images of empty, scattered refuges after the desertion of many soldiers: 'I still don't know how Schwarzkopf [American general] explained that scene, and I don't know how the generals of the Pentagon understood the messages of the new images coming from Ḥafr al-Bāṭin sent to them through their satellites' (p. 66).

Trying to rationalise the dilemma, the narrator can only advance a couple of assumptions the American pilots may have made. They must have thought either that 'the soldiers down there have gone out of their minds or that the war has already ended!' (p. 67). For the narrator, advancing these ironic assumptions is another way of asking the real questions. It is as if he formulated these questions:

> Were they not able to see with their satellites and sophisticated cameras how we were not worth defeating and not even worth fighting against, totally stupefied, immobilised, and hiding in our holes? And what is the degree of reality of a war where the enemy's weapons are buried? Did they not question the degree of credibility of a war where we, Iraqi soldiers (admittedly the fourth biggest army in the world!), couldn't even take a chance at fighting?'

On the basis of these facts, the narrator believes that the war has already exhausted itself, with no more excitement, no interest, no surprises, nothing. Everybody, Coalition forces as well as Iraqis, should be sent home, if the pilots and generals of the Coalition would only come to understand properly the various signs sent from the ground. That is the real message that is sent to the Coalition pilots. What the narrator cannot understand is why the pilots and their generals stubbornly overlook these signs and continue the one-sided engagement in a relentless and ferocious air campaign. Non-communication and the absence of 'symbolic exchange' is one of the most distinctive aspects of this conflict, despite the fact that, in addition to the unilateral military destruction of the infrastructure, military targets and troops, each side sends other messages. For instance, the Coalition drops leaflets to the Iraqi soldiers urging them to surrender or to desert, and the Coalition jet cameras send images from the ground by satellite into the computers viewed by the pilots. All these messages are just another kind of non-communication devoid of meaningful exchange. Interestingly, at this point, the narrator stops using the word *war* to refer to the air offensive. Instead, he starts using the word *holocaust* to refer to the silent burning and collective death of all the remaining soldiers, clinging to each other in their fear: 'We used to sit in our holes following the flight of flocks of fighters back and forth above our heads. At night fear besieged us, so we stuck to each other in a collective, heavy silence, a silence heavier than that of the graveyard. We all believed that no one would escape this *holocaust*' (p. 67, emphasis added).

> To no avail I was awaiting death. This feeling scared me, especially after our situation deteriorated dramatically as we lacked water and food. After the air raid on our refuge, I was in shock when I saw the sandy red desert turned into a carbonised carpet like charcoal, full of shrapnel and debris of burning tanks and vehicles on fire . . . A rumour circulated among the soldiers that Israel would enter the war. Some said that it was already in from the beginning, while others said that its participation was certain. Rumours grew bigger. 'Wait for the Israeli revenge', said another one. Who was circulating rumours in our unit? The commander and the officer of political orientation were the only ones watching the game from a TV screen inside their refuge. The courier, the commander's cook and some soldiers exaggerated what they heard and saw inside the refuge and disseminated it in a scary way to the soldiers, who made sure to add another layer to scare the rest of us. What we feared most was imminent land attack. Fear from that certain fate reduced the level of readiness of our empty bodies to its lowest degree in the midst of the thunder of aircraft circling above our heads, shelling many targets, and of other planes passing at light speed toward Baghdad and other Iraqi cities . . . Fear became our real existence. We could see its details reflected on the faces of one another and in the rattling of our voices and our anger, while some other vocabularies and rites strangely disappeared. I don't recall that anyone thought of a meal, breakfast or dinner. And nobody talked about water. The explosions became our daily food, and fear circulated in our veins, while our tongues just kept busy with news of destruction and death. (pp. 62–3)

The novel reveals unexpected and unpredictable behaviours and reactions that emerge among the soldiers after they are reduced to 'sitting ducks'[41], numbed spectators of their own paralysis in the face of a virtual war. As if to make up for the loss of engagement and sense of the real, the soldiers fall back to the raw level of concrete, 'primitive', and basic behaviours wherein a sense of action, excitement and suspense reconciles them with the reality and the needs of their bodies, with basic practices of the real world, and with a sense of life. For example, the narrator describes how in their dirty condition at night the soldiers are bitten by lice running everywhere through the hairy parts of their bodies and how, having shed the basic rules of civilised life, they scream and scratch their body parts where the lice bite them. They cannot care less about other strange behaviour:

> Our traditions and rules vanished there, perhaps because we lost our humanity and any notion of modesty. Just a few yards apart from one another, we defecated collectively in the desert, cleaning our butts with sand because we had no water. (p. 71)

The most exciting activity comes when the soldiers from different units attack each other at night in order to steal water, blankets, food and cigarettes. 'We used to steal everything we could carry except guns, which became unimportant to us' (p. 71). Just before setting out with his friend Mālik to try to find a way out of the desert, the narrator wants to have a last look at their unit; he takes time to defecate in front of their refuge, not hesitating to clean his butt with one of the many pieces of paper that the strong wind has scattered from the desks of the political orientation officers – a Baᶜath Party propaganda brochure that reads:

> 'Here in the eastern part of the Arab homeland, we don't fight in defence of Iraq but on behalf of the Arab nation against the plans of the Zionist imperialist camp and all other greedy countries.' The page stuck between my thighs, so I used it to clean my butt and made sure to spread a thick layer of my shit on that page as a way of honouring it and freeing it from the great leader's words. (p. 93)

Other post-traumatic behavioural disorders resulting from the war and defeat include death threats between soldiers, pointing guns at each other in the midst of wanderings in the desert, and animal sexual abuse. The narrator is shocked and disgusted when he surprises his friend Mālik twice sexually abusing the female dog left in the commander's refuge. More obvious and contradictory patterns emerge when the group of soldiers lost in the desert grows bigger, and they are split into those who observe prayers in strict fashion and those who indulge in drinking binges.

The melodramatic aspect of this conflict culminates in the subsequent wanderings and loss of the Iraqi soldiers in the desert. After massive desertions of soldiers and officers, the narrator and his friend can finally leave in peace, provided that they can manage to escape Coalition aircraft flying very low and avoid the deceptive mirage of the dunes. Looking for the road to al-Zubayr, the closest town to Basra, and trying to find a way out of the labyrinth of the desert, they keep circling in the empty space of Ḥafr al-Bāṭin. They are trapped in a featureless, deceptive environment. The senseless loss experienced by the soldiers, whose steps keep taking them back to their point of departure, their refuge, re-enacts two things: the senseless activity of the war itself and its circularity and at the same time the soldiers' own entrapment and condition of paralysis. Caught in the labyrinth of the desert, debilitated and demoralised, the narrator and his friend keep ending up back to their unit, where the only landmarks testifying to their loss and to their desperate quest for a way out of the desert are the boxes of unused artillery and military provisions, looking like corpses left in the sand.

> We were drowning in the moving sand . . . Every morning we felt we were at the outskirts of al-Zubayr, but, with every sunset, we erased that illusion and scored another failure. We ended thinking that, like us, al-Zubayr was turning in the desert and misleading us. (p. 115)

According to the narrator, the Iraqi soldiers wander for about two months in the desert. They head north instead of going south toward Basra. A Saudi helicopter flying low looking for Iraqi soldiers and urging them to surrender does not even want to take them when they show their readiness for captivity. 'Go on foot', says the pilot, but at least he shows them what direction is south (p. 120). They finally come across a landmine field, a landmark for them, but at the same time a test and a dangerous adventure. But it is not just human beings who are lost in the desert: seven camels await the soldiers in the landmine field. In a moment of panic, three of the animals are wounded or finished off by the mines, while all the men cross safely despite the panic stirred by the camels' presence. Trying to get beyond the pain and sadness caused by this scene, some soldiers justify it as a sign of divine intervention, wherein camels, not men, are sacrificed.

'We Are Checkmated'

How can one accept the end of a war that has not really taken place? How can one admit a defeat without having a chance at fighting? The war starts without a formal declaration and when Iraqi soldiers are asleep. The novel also reflects how it ends in the same way – incognito, furtive and evasive. The rumour of the end reaches the narrator long after the officers, the commander and many soldiers have left the desert, abandoning their camels, the commander's dog and the desert rats. The secret and hurried withdrawal of the commander and his guards shocks the narrator and his friend so much that they doubt the truth of the defeat and stubbornly refuse to acknowledge the way everything has suddenly ended for them:

> Did the news of the withdrawal that reached me very late mean that the bloody game had come to an end? . . . Was this the end? But what end? This was just a truce. This was an illusion . . . How could the war end like this, how could the commander desert with his guards and leave us in the desert? Are we no different from his dog and his camels? But why was I stubbornly resisting the defeat? . . . In accepting the defeat, I still feel that I've failed. (p. 81)

As for Mālik, the discovery of the expression *checkmate* during a chess game in one of the evenings of their loss in the desert is like a revelation for him. Ignorant about chess and intrigued by the game and its pieces, he enquires about the pawns and about the use of 'checkmate' to end the game. 'It means the king is dead and the game is over', explains one of the soldiers.[42] Mālik's questions cause a collective hysterical laughter, but, when he understands the analogy, he keeps serving and drinking whisky while repeating, 'Checkmate, checkmate'. When asked why he finds this expression so intriguing, he says:

> 'This expression is perfectly tailored to fit our situation. Do you know what *checkmate* means? Are you aware of the game? No. *We are checkmated.* America said *checkmate*, and the catastrophe came to an end. Now, all of us

are checkmated. You and you and you,' then he turned toward me and said, 'You are the most checkmated one of us!' (p. 118, emphasis added)

Mālik, who up to this point in the novel has been referred to as an insane epileptic and now as a simple-minded conscript, turns out to be more clairvoyant and intuitive than his fellow soldiers. He dismisses the hints of the king's death (the removal of Saddam) and sees the pawns, those ranking low in the hierarchy and by extension the people of Iraq, to be the real checkmated ones in this conflict and in the subsequent events of the uprising, where the Republican Guards' full-scale revenge operation will checkmate the rebellious Iraqis and reduce them to being the *homines sacri* of this war. Mālik's innocent expression functions as an ominous prediction of the real massacre yet to come.

Consumed by shock, anger and sadness, the narrator is perplexed to see that in this war it is those who were coerced and taken to the front by force who are left behind and alone in the desert when the important personalities depart secretly and in a cowardly fashion. He feels that he, his friend Mālik and all the lost soldiers they meet in the desert share the fate reserved for the camels, the dog, the worms, the lice and the rats playing in the desert. If they have not been killed during the conflict, they are now in a precarious position and are exposed to the many possibilities of death in the desert: they can be captured, mistreated, killed or die of thirst, fatigue or landmine.

Finally, after enduring different challenges ranging from sand storms, fatigue and thirst to the threat of death while crossing areas sown with landmines, the lost soldiers' wandering in the desert comes to an end when they eventually come face to face with 'America' and are taken prisoner. From prisoners of the desert, they become prisoners of war in the hands of 'America', which hands them over to the Saudi forces.

The lost soldiers' encounter with the Americans comes with insults, warnings and threats. Concerning this long-overdue confrontation, the narrator, in his habitual way, is rather sarcastic and ironic: 'It was a decisive moment, the most violent confrontation in our loss' (p. 130). Nevertheless, meeting the enemy, even if it means being taken a prisoner of war, is a real event that instantiates and substantiates the full weight of the defeat in this virtual war:

We were shocked. As we clung to one another, we kept staring at a black female soldier. She started insulting and threatening us from behind her gun, which she kept aiming right and left, pointing it at our heads . . . A military man of officer rank emerged from an armoured vehicle saying. 'Come,' he said, 'this is America.' He put his hands together on his head, so we understood that he wanted us to do that . . . It was a decisive moment, the most violent confrontation in our loss.

America was no longer the nightly declarations made by Bush, Cheney, Powell and Schwarzkopf. It wasn't missiles, fighters and helicopters. At this instant, America was now a visible enemy . . . America had become arms pointed at us.

. . . That's why we felt the heavy weight of defeat and humiliation (p. 130)

The fate of these soldiers who end up as prisoners is certainly less tragic than the fate of another unit placed on the same 'unnecessary front', Ḥafr al-Bāṭin. Even after total surrender, they faced a horrendous end: an American unit buries them alive in the trenches where they are hiding and begging. This harrowing end is shown in Najm Wālī's *Baghdad Marlboro*. Set in the period after the 2003 invasion and when the sectarian war is in full swing, this novel digs deep into buried episodes of previous wars, in particular the 1991 war. In the novel, one of the characters, Daniel Brooks, an American veteran of the Gulf War, visits Iraq to seek pardon from the families of the victims he participated in burying in the desert. He has never recovered from this memory and has been both sick and sad for a long time. The narrator remembers the episode, delving into the pain and dilemma felt by this American veteran: how he was entrapped at Ḥafr al-Bāṭin and forced by his major to help dig the mass graves where Iraqi soldiers who had already surrendered were buried alive. Son of a Vietnam War veteran, Daniel Brooks, nicknamed 'Smiley Man', is a pacifist who was originally working in the supply unit on the American base in Dhahrān, Saudi Arabia. During Desert Storm, his job was to provide the troops with necessary goods such as shoes, shampoo and food. By the end of major operations in the war, however, his commanding officer had abused him and sent him into the desert to dig. When the major saw Smiley Man's shock and absence of enthusiasm for the task, he became angry:

'Who do you think you are? Nathan the Wise? . . . Continue Smiley Shit . . . fifty graves, . . . dig, you, bastard . . . Do you know why I chose you?

> . . . I do that to make you a real soldier . . . Do you understand, soldier, you have to kill the enemy there.'[43]

In the midst of a sandstorm, nineteen huge excavators dug fifty graves, to bury a total of close to a thousand Iraqi soldiers. Daniel had to execute orders:

> Excavators, digging and digging in the desert, and not too far away, maybe twenty to thirty metres away, a crowd of soldiers crammed up against a wall, some kneeling, others standing, most of them half-naked, with dusty hair, looking like zombies out of their tombs, as if they were coming from a bygone age. (p. 183)

The image of these men still remains burned deep in Daniel's memory:

> Some of them raised their hands; some put their hands on their heads, those who had a white handkerchief, or a piece of white fabric, any fabric, as long as it was white so that it could be raised; some fell on the ground mumbling, 'Please don't kill me' . . . How many were they? One thousand or two, perhaps three or four, why not five, six, or seven thousand? (p. 176)

The burial of these surrendered soldiers while they are still alive resonates with the killing and burial of the rebels during the Shiᶜa uprising after the war, discussed later in this chapter.

Rationalising the Mass Killing in the 'Turkey Shoot'

> Had anybody been concerned with the accurate use of words, the destruction of Iraq and the slaughter of an unknown number of Iraqis . . . might have been more precisely described as *a police raid*, as the violent suppression of a mob as an exemplary lesson in the uses of *major-league terrorism*.
>
> Lewis H. Lapham, 'Trained Seals and Sitting Ducks'

> The history of our time is studded with unrecorded holocausts.
>
> Eqbal Ahmad, in Phyllis Bennis and Michel Moushabeck (eds), *Beyond the Storm: A Gulf Crisis Reader*

Among other new things, the Persian Gulf War ushered in a totally new era in the history of military censorship and control of media information that contributed efficiently towards the creation of an impression of the unreality and de-realisation of this war. With the new strategy of implementing and imposing 'pre-censorship' on journalists and reporters, it 'inaugurated the creation of something like an originary silence', Margot Norris has argued, 'a partially blank space of discourse and representation whose absence can only be inferred'.[44] Censorship mostly impacted the act of killing, the sight of dead bodies and the body count. It helped create the illusion of a clean war and a bloodless win, making it acceptable to the American public and the world. The disavowal of the basic activity of war and the taboo that surrounds the dead body are coupled in American discourse on the Gulf War with a 'technological utopianism' made visible in the loud celebration of and fascination with the new machinery and the smart weaponry of high technology.

Norris finds the Pentagon's enthusiastic attitude toward and exhibitionist discourse about the precision of smart weapons 'perverse' and argues that it calls to mind the idolatrous attitude toward and glorification of the killing machine in Franz Kafka's novella *In the Penal Colony*.[45] Indeed, the technological discourse gets muddied and tarnished during the war in at least two notorious episodes in which technology is precisely turned into this Kafkaesque killing machine, oblivious to the pain and suffering that it inflicts on the human body. The bombing of the Iraqi troops from Kuwait City who were retreating to Basra along what was called the Highway of Death and the targeting and bombing of a bunker used by civilians as a refuge in Baghdad exposed the fiction of a bloodless war and pointed to the salient activity of war – the killing and injuring of the human body. The targeting of the returning Iraqi troops from Kuwait is considered to be the closing episode of the ground phase of the war; it produced a carnage that strangely connects the Persian Gulf War more to the First and Second World Wars than to a supposedly bloodless war. Paradoxically, despite the strictly enforced rules of censorship, this last chapter in the war was covered extensively and received immediate attention in the media. Why then was access permitted to the devastation and carnage on the Highway of Death? And how does the Iraqi writer or poet describe the reality of this extermination operation?

In this section, I argue that the targeting of non-combatant retreating troops, as it is portrayed in works of fiction, robs the postmodern war's rationale and shows that the political functions of war, whatever its type and nature, cannot be achieved or served better than by dead human bodies. Thus, the Persian Gulf War in the closing episode of its ground phase resorted to the familiar necrological methods and practices of the two earlier world wars. I also compare the 'Killing Box' – both a virtual and a real space where the massacres of non-combatant troops were committed – to a modern extermination camp. Finally, I argue that, despite the mass killing of thousands of Iraqis, the purposeful lifting of censorship from this particular operation was intended to reveal not the horror of war or the wrongness of the Americans' actions but the moral aspect of the Americans' victory over the 'immorality' and the 'evil' of the Iraqi troops, who were perceived as a bunch of looters.

A Little Bit of History

On 23 February 1991, Iraq agreed to unconditionally withdraw its forces from Kuwait, and Saddam Hussein ordered his men to return home. On the same day, the green light was given for the ground war (Operation Desert Sabre) that with air support was to last just one hundred hours. Even though the Iraqis had already been dealt a heavy blow during the air campaign, in which they had been pounded for thirty-eight days, American generals nevertheless still looked for a visible grid of targets. Some even regretted a lack of targets: 'The Iraqi forces were beat down and devastated by the time the land campaign started. We had so much capability and so little to use it on . . . We were resource rich, not target rich,' writes General Buster Glosson.[46]

To makeup for this lack of target opportunities, a sovereign decision was made ahead of the ground campaign itself to resort to targeting and killing as many of the Iraqi forces in Kuwait as possible, especially those who, according to General Glosson, had committed war crimes – even though targets such as the Basra water-purification plant were ironically spared out of humanitarian considerations, and even though there was no way they could know if any of the soldiers targeted had committed such crimes. Perhaps as a way to make up for the lack of targets the general had regretted earlier, he proudly records the decision he made:

> I made a decision before the Iraqi forces in Kuwait even started their withdrawal that we are going to destroy as much as possible when they attempted to run. This was because of the brutality they had wreaked on the

> innocent people of Kuwait and the way they had brutalized the city and the people for more than six months.
>
> ... *I wanted to make sure that we killed as many of those Iraqi security and military thugs as we could.*[47]

With the knowledge that the Iraqis were getting ready to pull out of Iraq, the American strategy was, as General Glosson writes, 'to keep the Iraqis from moving for any reason'.[48]

General Glosson claims that he had asked 'to make sure that the President or his Sec Def, if they go on TV [,] they say that retreating combat forces will be attacked ... because we are going to try to stop or destroy all the Iraqi security and military forces coming out of Kuwait City'.[49] This decision is reiterated several times in Glosson's book *War with Iraq* and was apparently not something improvised at the last minute. After an intensified round of Russian diplomacy, Baghdad Radio announced Iraq's acceptance of a cease-fire proposal and an unconditional retreat of its troops in compliance with UN Resolution 660. The troops in Kuwait were ordered to withdraw to positions held before 2 August 1990. Amidst chaos and in uncoordinated panic, Iraqi troops started their withdrawal from Kuwait on 26 February 1991 with whatever vehicles and tanks they could find. Many officers and commanders found the order for withdrawal from Kuwait hard to believe. Some considered it one of the most dangerous and complicated phases of battle. Extreme weather conditions were simultaneously helping protect the retreating troops from Coalition airpower and impeding their movements. The withdrawal from Kuwait City began on Highways 8 and 80 and was in full swing by evening. Around midnight on 27 February, the first US bombing of retreating troops started. 'U.S. planes trapped the long convoys by disabling vehicles in the front, and at the rear, and then pounded the resulting traffic jams for hours,' writes Joyce Chediac, a Lebanese American journalist. 'It was like shooting fish in a barrel,' one American pilot said.[50] Hundreds of Iraqis jumped from their cars and their trucks, looking for shelter. American pilots used whatever bombs happened to be close to the flight deck, from cluster bombs to 500-pound bombs.

The massacre is well documented in all its apocalyptic glory in the diary of one of the returning soldiers: the poet ᶜAli ᶜAbd al-Amīr. Hadiyya Hussein includes this material in her novel *Māba'd al-ḥubb* (*Beyond Love*). Brief, dense, and Kafkaesque in its horror, the diary of the returning poet-soldier, who has survived the targeting and massacre of troops, captures an absurd and unique scene. Familiar in its classical structure of the hunt for the enemy, this scene could in fact have belonged to an operation in either the First or Second World War, but in this case the enemy was no longer adopting a combatant position, and the columns of vehicles and soldiers were soft and easy prey. In its lopsidedness, the 'Turkey Shoot' was thus absurd, obscene and empty of any existential meaning. It was unique in the way it combined ultramodern technology with a methodological, efficient structure for killing: what in the jargon of the new American war was referred to as 'the Killing Box'. American planes cut the head and tail of retreating Iraqi military columns along Highway 80 between Kuwait City and Basra. By immobilising the convoys of the returning troops, the Coalition aircraft were able to hold them in a temporary strategic position where they could firebomb and exterminate them within the confines of designated three-dimensional territory along what came to be known as the 'Highway of Death'.[51] The Americans thus virtually re-enacted and re-appropriated the camp as a technique, a structure and a space where massacre and extermination were permitted. In the efficient strafing of non-combatant soldiers, they created what we might call the 'virtual postmodern camp', producing an orgy of carbonised bodies and scattered limbs blown from bodies.

From Inside Hellfire

In *Beyond Love*, Ḥusayn stresses the horror of the one hundred hours of the ground offensive and its end result involving the massacre of the retreating troops. Although she clearly condemns the targeting of the defeated troops, she is also revolted by President Saddam Hussein's stubbornness.

> A hundred anxious and horrifying hours under the most violent bombing under the military of thirty countries . . . It was hellfire and the Iraqis were the firewood . . . On February 26, 1991, troops had headed down a wide desert road. They had returned in failure and defeat. On the road they had been the target of the enemies' planes despite the withdrawal order . . . they had been returning home frustrated. Under fire they had melted into their

> vehicles' steel and their bodies had been carbonized. The fortunate ones had walked hundreds of miles, torn with hunger and humiliation, and many had fled to the Saudi border looking for escape.[52]

To give substance to her condemnation, the author gives voice to one of the returning soldiers, who is no less than the Iraqi poet ᶜAli ᶜAbd al-Amīr. In *Diary of a Soldier Returning from the Defeat*, the poet-soldier records the return of the troops and the massacre on the highway. For the narrator of the diary, who turns out to be a veteran from the Iran–Iraq War, the flight north on the road back to Basra stirs up the painful memories and geography of another front that took away years of his life. The same can be said of thousands of Iraqis:

> This was the same road that has taken up a great deal of my life during the eight year war with Iran: the Battles of East Basra between 1982 and 1984, Majnun, al-Nashwa, Buhayrat al-Asmaak, Al-Faw and . . . and . . . and . . . and here again were the hands of death taking me and thirty other soldiers in a vehicle through the darkness in silence. (p. 135)

The surviving soldier's diary reveals an apocalyptic landscape where the lawlessness of the harrowing scene is paralleled only by the gruesomeness and obscenity of the killing of the men in flight. Some leave their vehicles and the main road in order to continue the journey, their steps sinking into the mud all the way to Basra. The survivor's testimony describes vividly the panic and chaos caused by what he calls the 'Campaign to destroy the Iraqi people':

> Back from death, balls of fire, shrapnel, burning vehicles, and cluster bombs, I was back from moving death, where the lines of retreating vehicles had become an excellent target for airplanes. The vehicles burned along with the bodies. The storm of explosions had thrown soldiers onto the roads, dead and mangled or wounded and helpless. They remained grim faced, looking toward the horizon and waiting for their death. It was only by accident that I escaped the massacre. (p. 131)

Not only are the columns of returning troops targeted along the highway but from the survivor's testimony it seems that, even after they arrive at famous landmarks in Basra – Saᶜd Square and al-ᶜIshār, one of the lively centres of the southern town – or when they are trying to cross the river Shaṭṭ al-ᶜArab, the soldiers continue to be attacked in scenes of panic and chaos, where sidewalks, streets, squares and bridges are choked with soldiers and vehicles:

> The chaos rose to a fury as soldiers on the sidewalks and between cars crowded into parallel lines, trying to cross a temporary bridge set up over Shatt el-Arab. The hundreds of vehicles were barely moving. What a massacre there would be if an airstrike attacked us right then! No sooner did I think this than the thunder of an approaching plane incited a panic. *Like terrified worms* on the ground we jumped from the vehicles to the streets nearby or under the small bridge. Some soldiers threw themselves on the riverbank. (pp. 133–4, emphasis added)

The diary is punctuated by repeated scenes of aeroplane and missile attacks taking the soldiers by surprise even when they are crossing palm tree orchards and other short-cuts away from the main road, with the procession stopping for random, unknown reasons and thus exposing the soldiers:

> The vehicles were motionless in a long line on the road, . . . I sensed the smell of death close to us. I yelled to those who were with me 'Get down quickly!' From a gap in the clouds obstructing a bright moon, two planes appeared . . . the explosion resounded; shrapnel flew above my head . . . Fire devoured the unmoving line, but our vehicle seemed safe . . . Morning came with the effects of fire all around us. (pp. 135–6)

Surreal in its horror, the scene strikes the reader most not regarding the number of 'bodies drilled with shrapnel', carbonised and mummified in their vehicles, or the devouring of the cadavers by stray dogs or even the 'many fragments of bodies scattered in the middle of the road', but rather regarding the sight of those frozen in the instant between life and death, 'drenched in blood' and dangling from their vehicles:

> I will never forget the sight of one young soldier seated on the edge of the road with blood covering his shoulders and his back. He was looking toward the horizon and the stretch of mud and grass, moving his head in a familiar regretful way . . . As we passed him, I looked through the window and followed the slow movement of his trunk back and forth . . . was it the

> rhythm of the body's death? His hand was still pointing to the horizon, and his back was turned to the killing. (p. 138)

Unable to finish the journey to the safety of their own homes and not yet among the carbonised or bloody dead, the living dead are left at the side of the road, dangling in the void, waiting for their death. Those who survived the Apache attacks abandon their remaining vehicles and join the retreat north on foot.

It is the destruction of the men who committed the crime of the invasion and made it palpable and tangible that will concretely incarnate and substantiate the action of the war and the reality of its outcome. The destruction caused by the air campaign was apparently not real enough as a punishment for the invasion of Kuwait, and the real punishment had to be inscribed on the very bodies of troops who had been forced to comply with their commanders' orders both on the way into and on the way out of Kuwait. The ultimate price for that evil action had to be paid for with the very bodies and lives of the troops, even if they were no longer playing a combatant role but were instead trapped in the most vulnerable position on their way back home. For the Coalition, disappointed by the fact that they could not destroy the Republican Guard and unsuccessful in spotting and eliminating Saddam Hussein, there remained only the biological lives of the retreating troops on which to exercise their sovereign right over life and to substantiate their supremacy. What surfaced in this perverse operation was clearly war's most defining trait, visible in its lust for bodies. But what was excised from the American narrative of a clean win and a bloodless war finally finds a central place in the language of the dead body in the Iraqi narrative. Thus, in the diary of the returning soldier, the dead body, with its multiple open injuries is both staring at us and being stared at. Dismembered, drilled, carbonised, devoured by straying dogs, or drenched in blood, the body is made visible and present to encompass and reflect in its destruction the very earth itself:

> Bodies drilled with shrapnel were thrown on the side of the road; the scorched corpses reeked in a day devoid of life . . . Burned or destroyed vehicles lay here and there. Slumbered bodies drenched in blood dangled from their sides. Other bodies had been abandoned on the streets. The earth

> itself seems to have recoiled, ready to jump, to join us, another body about to be destroyed. (p. 136)

In its lust for the body, this extermination of the troops makes the post-modern war look like any other war. The targeting of the retreating forces was carried out systematically at the last minute before an official cease-fire took effect. It is important to note how Washington postponed the timing of the cease-fire from 5:00 a.m. to 8:00 a.m. on 28 February so that the total number of hours in the ground offensive would reach the round figure of 100. In *Beyond Love*, the survivor's anger escalates to fury when he learns of the time of the cease-fire and realises that many soldiers have been separated from life by only a few minutes: 'I learned that a cease-fire would go into effect at 8:00 a.m. – in just two minutes. How could they have been killing us only five minutes earlier? Five minutes had separated many young men from life' (p. 139).

The postponement underscores the total disregard for human life. The number of lives taken does not seem to matter, and a few more hundred dead is nothing; what matters more is reaching a round figure of hours in the ground offensive, a number that would be easy to record and remember.

With deep sadness, the survivor reports how after the cease-fire those troops who made it to safety were welcomed by the local population of the small southern towns of Iraq with bitter signs and rituals of defeat and humiliation, recalling Shi^{c}a massacres as well as old and recent wars.

> Crying together we left the fire behind along with the remains of our brothers. We wailed in mourning when we entered the gates of the small southern towns whose people came out at our sudden appearance . . . Many women scattered sand on top of their heads, and others beat their chests with their hands in a historical reenactment of the killings that had always taken place here. (pp. 139–40)

The 'Turkey Shoot' massacre in the closing episode of the ground war is crucial because the fallen bodies of the troops permit the war's outcome to be located not in the losing side's lack of options to contest the outcome but in the reality-conferring capacity of the body, especially the open body. As Scarry explains in *The Body in Pain*,

> the outcome of war has its substantiation not in an absolute inability of the defeated to contest the outcome but in a process of perception that allows extreme attributes of the body to be translated into another language, to be broken away from the body and relocated elsewhere at the very moment that the body itself is disowned . . . The force of the material world is separated from the fifty-seven thousand or fifty million bodies and conferred not only on issues and ideologies that have as a result of the first function been designated the winner, but also on the idea of winning itself.[53]

A Police Operation and the Virtual Camp

The Apache bombing of the retreating Iraqi troops along the Highway of Death strangely resonates with a bombing operation in Germany during the Second World War described by Carl Schmitt as a 'police action' in his book *The Nomos of the Earth*:

> Bombing pilots use their weapons against the population of an enemy country as vertically as St George used his lance against the dragon. Given the fact that war has been transformed into *a police action* against trouble-makers, criminals and pests, justification of the methods of this 'police-bombing' must be intensified.[54]

The hunt for the returning soldiers, now branded as criminals, looters and thieves who had to be punished for their crimes, transformed the Persian Gulf War from a clean, surgical, bloodless war into an ignominious police action worthy of a Hollywood film, justified and conceived to establish and protect a new world order.[55]

One of the most critical voices pointing to the reality of this war as a police operation is Giorgio Agamben, who in 1991 wrote a short essay about the war entitled 'Sovereign Police':

> The most *spectacular* characteristic of this war, perhaps, was that the reasons presented to justify it cannot be put aside as ideological superstructures used to conceal a hidden plan. On the contrary, ideology has in the meantime penetrated so deeply into reality that the declared reasons have to be taken in a *rigorously literal sense* – particularly those concerning the idea of *a new world order*.[56]

Examining what is meant by the term *police action/power* in the context of military intervention, Michel Dean retraces historical occurrences, uses and definitions of it in dictionaries and other sources. Among the definitions of 'police action' he found is the following in the *Oxford English Dictionary* (2004): 'military intervention without formal declaration of war when a nation or group within a nation is considered to be violating international law and peace'.[57] According to Dean, an earlier famous precedent that illustrates the 'broad and elastic' use of force characterising 'the exercise of an international police power' is found in the Monroe Doctrine, complemented by the Roosevelt Corollary, in the case of the US defence of Latin American countries against European intervention.[58] Proclaimed in 1823 and 1904, respectively, these doctrines make no mention of Middle Eastern countries as places where the doctrines can be extended and applied in case of wrong-doing. But given the stakes in the Persian Gulf region, stretching and adapting these doctrines to include it apparently presented no challenge.

Despite its domestic connotation related more to internal matters of state rather than to foreign affairs, what is meant by 'police' in the phrase *police action* is in fact the broad, elastic power of government and the discretionary use of force combined with the sovereign capacity to decide on the exception in emergency situations and exceptional circumstances. It is this important idea of the sovereign character of the war conceived and conducted as a police action that is underscored and explained in Agamben's essay. Agamben stipulates that the Gulf War clearly illustrates the slide of the concept of sovereignty,[59] characterised by the 'indistinction between violence and right' and 'the capacity to decide on the exception' by suspending the validity of the law, into police action, which becomes the locus of this contiguity between violence and law, enabling it to function within a similar state of exception. The police force acts as a sovereign in the way it operates by extra juridical command and within the decision on the state of exception ('Sovereign is he who decides on the exception', as Carl Schmitt points out):[60] 'The rationales of "public order" and "security" on which the police have to decide on a case-by-case basis define an area of indistinction between violence and right that is exactly symmetrical to that of sovereignty'.[61]

The case of the Gulf War, a reaction to what was considered a violation of international law and order and with no formal war declaration, seems to fit the definition of police action as a military intervention, and, as Agamben explains, 'such an operation is not obliged to respect any juridical rule and can thus make no distinction between the civilian population and soldiers (or in the case of the Iraqi troops between soldiers out of combat units) as well as between the people and their criminal sovereign, thereby returning to the most archaic conditions of belligerence'.[62] In taking the decision to bomb the retreating troops because they were now seen as a bunch of looters and thieves, the Coalition generals in charge acted like the police, in all sovereignty, excepting their actions from the law. It is this discretionary decision based on the exception, this elastic and broad power that characterises the police, that makes Agamben speak of the war as a police operation, which is even more clearly observed in the targeting of the retreating troops, as reflected in the *Diary of a Soldier Returning from the Defeat.*

The state of exception, under which the sovereign police operation of the manhunt and the extermination were carried out during the flight of the troops on the Highway of Death, opens up a space and structure in which the most absolute *conditio inhumana* was realised: this space is what Agamben defines as 'the camp'. For Agamben, the camp is 'a piece of territory that is placed outside the normal juridical order'. It is only because the camps constitute a space of exception – a space in which the law is so completely suspended – that everything is truly possible in them, where power confronts nothing other than pure biological life without mediation.[63] According to Agamben, this structure does not belong to the past but functions as 'the hidden matrix and *nomos* of the political space in which we still live'.[64] This resonates with other manifestations of the camp such as Guantánamo Bay and Camp Bucca, which will be discussed in Chapter 4.

Stripped of their war status as retreating units in a non-combatant position, reduced to the status of criminals and thieves, and trapped and immobilised in their long convoys, the Iraqi troops were wholly reduced to 'naked life' in the space of the virtual camp within the confines of the Killing Box; they faced the horror of cluster bombs and hellfire with only their biological lives.

When established, a Killing Box is designed to allow lethal attack against surface targets without further co-ordination with the establishing commander and without terminal attack control. As a methodological lethal technique, the

Killing Box was developed in the late 1980s and was used first during the Gulf War and later during the 2003 war. It was massively used in the ground war in 1991, in particular during the aerial assault against retreating troops. This targeting was at odds with international law, in particular the Geneva Conventions, which stipulate that 'persons taking no active part in hostilities, including members of armed forces who have laid down their arms and those placed hors de combat by sickness, wounds, detention, or any other cause, shall in all circumstances be treated humanely, without any adverse distinction founded on race, color, religion or faith, sex, birth or wealth, or any other similar criteria'.[65]

Behind the highly sophisticated military and technical characteristics of this methodological technique is the basic straightforward idea of pure extermination. The name 'Killing Box' combines a function (to kill) and an object (the box) used as a location, a method, and a technique for the killing to be carried out effectively. It resonates with the horror of other infamous lethal techniques, such as the cremation oven and the extermination it caused.

Checkmated and Buried Alive

As described in *Beyond Love*, when the surviving troops arriving in Basra display the signs of humiliation, defeat and shame, unfamiliar scenes catch their attention. The narrator of *Diary of a Soldier Returning from the Defeat* notes that some soldiers discharge their anger and frustration by firing at government buildings, military units and symbols of the Ba^{c}ath Party. The narrator is stunned when he notices what is already happening in Basra:

> Just ahead of us, a clamouring tank suddenly stopped and turned to the right, discharging a heavy shower of bullets at a huge portrait of the president. I was floored by this act. 'Something is going to happen here,' I said to myself' . . . We continued walking between burned vehicles looking at propaganda portraits and official murals on the façade of the military road units. They had been sprayed by bullets from close range. (pp. 133–6)

The troops and the population are united in their feelings of humiliation and shame, which lead to the uprising:

> The feeling of humiliation was shared among the army and the people who had no hope of relief except through revolt. The first spark started in

> Basra and spread to the other provinces . . . This is how it was: vanquished people and angry demoralised troops who had left behind them burned corpses and damaged machinery came together. (p. 74)

According to Anthony Cordesman and Ahmed Hashim, there were several reasons why the uprising broke out in the south. Among other things, they stress the importance of 'the political and military vacuum' in this region that resulted from the destruction of transportation and communication networks during the aerial phase of the war. In addition, the south paid the highest toll and suffered the most devastation not only during Desert Storm but also earlier during the Iran–Iraq War, without receiving appropriate recognition or compensation, thus creating a feeling of marginalisation and deep frustration among a population representing the majority of the country that was being ruled by a privileged minority. Combined with the scenes of returning troops, all of these factors triggered the *intifāḍa*: 'The uprising began when defeated and disgruntled infantry soldiers streamed back into Basra from the front, bringing back with them harrowing tales of defeat at the hands of a superior foe and mismanagement of the war by their own government'.[66]

In addition to the defeated troops and local populations, many exiled Iraqis hurried to join in the initial scenes of the rebellion. These were mostly Shiᶜa Iraqis who had previously found refuge in Iran during the Iran–Iraq War. At the conclusion of the Gulf War, they poured into the south of Iraq, some of them crossing through the marshes from Iran. Some of them were affiliated with the underground Islamic Daᶜwa Party, but others were not, such as Khiḍr, the free war deserter, whose story is told in Naṣīf Falak's novel *Khiḍr Qad and the Drab Olive Years* (see the discussion of this novel in Chapter 1). He leaves Iraq a free man and returns also free in order to take part in the uprising and pursue his dream of removing the monster Bahḍām (Saddam).

Leaving the Iranian camp where he has spent years as a refugee, this quixotic hero lives in delusion, for not only does he believe that Bahḍām will fall but also he is confident that it will be he, Khiḍr, who will accomplish this long overdue dream. Just as he was mobilised by a sweeping enthusiasm and hope when fleeing Iraq to take refuge in Iran, which turned out to be just a smaller Iraq, on the way back to his country through the marshes Khiḍr is fired up and confident: 'Everybody lost hope in the possibility of getting rid of him. They turned their back and left me alone . . . I will chop off the head of the snake. Let happen what may. Anything would be better than Bahḍām remaining in power.'[67]

For this returnee, an overwhelming feeling of guilt is unavoidable when he pours blame on himself and all those exiled Iraqis who fled Iraq and left it moaning and bleeding: 'Fleeing the country was a destructive mistake. We left it to its fate, dying one cell after another . . . Hundreds of thousands of runaways' (p. 154).

In fact, Khiḍr stands symbolically for the Iraqi people and all those who will be massacred in the uprising and collectively turned into *homines sacri*, the sacred men whose killing will not be considered a murder and will go unpunished. Khiḍr's profound secret is nothing more and nothing less than the deep secret buried in all Iraqis' hearts: 'What if,' Khiḍr wonders, 'all Iraqis carry in their hearts the same secret as I: as soon as they put their heads on their pillows, they think or dream of a way to save themselves from the engineer of calamities' (p. 164). Like many expatriate Iraqis who have crossed from Iran through the porous borders, Khiḍr ends up in the town of al-ᶜAmāra. The majority of those who have re-entered from Iran are Shiᶜītes. Unlike them, Khiḍr is a free man who has rejected all kinds of affiliation, whether ethnic, religious or political. His desire for life 'inherited from his ancestors in the form of genius cells defying death and destruction' (p. 160), with a hint at Sumerian mythology, entrusts him with the most ambitious, dangerous yet utopian adventure: 'It's either the survival of my species,' Khiḍr vows, 'or of the shit smellers' (p. 160), here referring to the Baᶜathists (see the discussion of this novel in Chapter 1). Khiḍr is not just a simple war deserter: he is an artist, an intellectual and an independent activist, but one without allegiance to any group or any organisation; he reaches the point where writing is no longer enough, and he needs to take action: 'I am tired of writing. I was active on paper like one engaged in a marathon, breathless all my life, but now I will move on into action' (p. 161). During the uprising, he takes part in attacks on police stations and a Baᶜath Party building, destroying many murals of the president, fighting the Baᶜathists alongside his cousins, fleeing the heavy artillery of the Republican Guard from one corner of al-ᶜAmāra to another and from one roof to another. The army, despite its humiliating defeat in 'the Mother of All Shame', as he sarcastically refers to the Mother of All Battles, is now trying to redeem itself and regain its prestige by crushing the country's civilians. 'Despite dishonour and cowardice, this army intends to defy its own people. It will use the weapons of its shameful defeat to burn towns and villages in Kurdistān and then advance towards the south' (p. 166). Falak's depiction of the Ba^{c}ath agents' police operation in hunting down people and the confrontation between the Republican Guard and the rebels is epic, with vivid images of violence and pitiless killings. 'Everything is dead, only the language of bullet is alive . . . Corpses of women, babies, and children everywhere' (p. 170).

As for Khiḍr, he is caught when he tries to save a lost baby who is the only survivor in his family. When Khiḍr is caught, the baby is dealt with very quickly and cruelly, thrown violently against a wall, his brain exploding and streams of his blood running down the wall. The narrator reports that hundreds are captured – some summarily executed, but others taken in pick-up trucks and thrown collectively into a deep hole. They are half alive, half dead in this hole, some going into a coma and others, such as Khiḍr, still aware, still feeling and hearing what is around them. The gratuity of the massacre reaches an absurd level when, unaware of the dangers, Sallāma the shepherd, Khiḍr's lover, is taking a stroll with her goats when she is kidnapped and thrown in the same hole: 'Sallāma saw herself falling on top of a bald man, with a thick moustache and all in blood . . . She didn't understand what was going on: Who are these people piled up on top of each other? How did they end up as human debris in this big hole?' (p. 177).

In this mass grave, Khiḍr, the alienated artist, dreamer and war deserter is finally united with Sallāma in an irony of fate and war. He defies this ineffable death with his mystical and poetic refrain, 'I was with, not by, myself,' a phrase that accompanied him during his flight for freedom into Iran through Kurdistān. 'I was with, not by, myself' unites Khiḍr with Sallāma in a macabre scene. It finds its full meaning as a refrain for love and humanity and a cry against the Ba^{c}ath's heinous crimes and barbarism.

In *Beyond Love*, there is no escape from killing; 'those who were trying to escape death via the outlying roads were trapped by helicopters that poured white oil on them and then threw firebombs on them, reducing them to ashes' (p. 76). Here, not only is their killing not considered murder but also they are treated even more savagely when they are dumped and thrown collectively into the same grave or when it is forbidden for them to be buried so that their rotten corpses in the street will serve as a lesson to other people. Hadiyya Hussein denounces the fact that many corpses were left exposed in the streets of Karbalā for days in order to scare the population and to teach a lesson to those who still wanted to defy the regime. In the novel, those who try to collect these corpses and give them proper burial are immediately shot:

> With horror falling upon the houses, Karbala became a ghost city filled with the smell of decay. Its streets were empty except for tanks, the regime's armed men, and the bodies that no one dared to bury. The authorities had forbidden their burial so that they would serve as a warning to others. The corpses remained disfigured and rotting for many days until they were buried in unknown mass graves. (p. 76)

Ḥusayn calls the massacre of Karbalāʾ 'the new battle of Karbalāʾ', clearly alluding to the centuries-old bloody massacres that had happened in this very place.[68] This massacre, coupled with those at Basra, al-ᶜAmāra and al-Ḥilla, took place under the watchful eyes of the American forces, which stood by and did nothing, adopting as blameful a position as that of the regime:

> At the same time [that the Iraqi helicopters reduced people to ashes] American helicopters hovered in the skies, watching the event of the new battle of Karbala, where children were exterminated along with their mothers and the elderly. (p. 76)

The Republican Guards' extermination of the civilian populations in the uprising is in fact a continuation and extension of the massacre committed by the American forces against retreating Iraqi troops. The Iraqi forces were unable to mount any kind of response against the aerial bombing in the first phase of the war and did not respond to the extermination of their returning troops. But, even so, they were still capable of suffocating the uprising and exterminating the rebels.

According to Cordesman and Hashim, the failure of the uprising was due to a lack of organisation and ideological vision. 'The focus on Shiite Islamic extremism alienated secular and nationalist Iraqi Shiites, most opposition groups outside Iraq and the members of the U.N. Coalition. It also produced a viscerally hostile reaction of the regime's elite, the Sunni Arabs and many members of the Shiite middle class.'[69] The idea of an Iranian-backed regime coming to power was a scary idea not only for secular Iraqis but for the Sunni monarchies of the Gulf region as well.

Conclusion

With the end of Saddam Hussein's censorship and the beginning of a new-found 'freedom', but now in the context of the postmodern war and a discourse marked by de-realisation and media polemic, Iraqi authors have been countering the dialectic of abstraction with one of tangible human experiences. The accounts discussed in this chapter are soldiers' tales about what the Gulf War was like for the Iraqi soldiers, told by the men who were there. Despite the many particulars given in these accounts about coercion, propaganda and suffering, we still 'don't know what an Iraqi taking part with a chance of fighting would have been like', as Baudrillard said.[70] In the accounts given in the novels discussed, the Iraqi soldier is portrayed in his availability to be killed and massacred in the desert or in the virtual camp as well as in his capacity to be thrown in a mass grave both by the Americans and the Iraqi army. Although a limited representation, and given the relative scarcity of written materials on this important conflict in the history of modern Iraq, the selection of novels discussed here has the merit of covering some of the most important phases in the Gulf War, offering us an Iraqi viewpoint focused on the *homo sacer*, not on technology. It gives us an idea of the scale of destruction and the reality from the ground, where we finally learn about those who were left out of the media narrative and official coverage as the conflict was happening. The Iraqi narrative of the Gulf War developed in these novels offers a perspective centred on the Iraqi soldier and on the manifold losses incurred during this war. It portrays the war as a police operation in its sovereign, broad and elastic use of force and shows that in the end it was also a war like any other war in its lust for bodies. With the postmodern war, the Iraqi soldier enters a new era: he becomes useless and irrelevant.

Notes

1. ʿAbd al-Karīm al-ʿUbaydī, *Ḍayāʿ fī Ḥafr al-Bāṭin* (Loss in Ḥafr al-Bāṭin) (Baghdad: Muʾassasat Masārāt, 2009), p. 61.
2. Najm Wālī, *Baghdad mālbūrū* (Baghdad Marlboro) (Beirut: al-Muʾassasa al-ʿarabiyya li-al-dirāsāt wa al-nashr, 2012), p. 61, my translation.
3. Kanan Makiya, Cruelty and Silence: War, Tyranny, Uprising and the Arab World (New York: Norton, 1993).
4. miriam cooke, *Women and the War Story* (Berkeley: University of California Press, 1996).
5. See ibid., p. 266.
6. Nuha al-Radi, Baghdad Diaries: A Woman's Chronicle of War and Exile (New York: Vintage Books, 1998).
7. Raʿd al-Ḥamdānī, *Qabla an yughādiranā al-tārīkh* (Before history leaves us) (Beirut: al-Dār al- ʿarabiyya li al-ʿulūm, 2007).
8. Batūl Khudayrī, *Kam badat al-samāʾ qarība* (A sky so close) (Beirut: Arab Institute for Research and Publishing, 1999), translated as Betool Khedairi, *A Sky so Close* (New York: Anchor Books, 2001).
9. M. Klare, 'High-Death Weapons', in Mordecai Briemberg (ed.), *It Was, It Was Not: Essays & Art on the War against Iraq* (Vancouver: New Star Books, 1992), p. 41.
10. James Der Derian, *Virtuous War* (Boulder, CO: Westview Press, 2001), pp. 64–5.
11. 'The High-Tech War Machine', *Business Week*, 4 February 1991, p. 38.
12. For the first term, see Mary Kaldor; for the second, see Paul Virilio, *Desert Screen: War at the Speed of Light*, trans. Michael Degener (London: Bloomsbury Academic, 2005); and for the third, see Klare, 'High-Death Weapons', p. 41.
13. Chris Hables Gray, *Postmodern War: The New Politics of Conflict* (New York: Guilford Press, 1997).
14. Virilio, *Desert Screen*, pp. 46–7.
15. Briemberg, preface to *It Was, It Was Not*, p. i.
16. All three essays appear in Jean Baudrillard, *The Gulf War Did Not Take Place* (Bloomington: Indiana University Press, 1995).
17. Ibid., p. 17.
18. See Christopher Norris, *Uncritical Theory: Postmodernism, Intellectuals, and the Gulf War* (London: Lawrence and Wishart, 1992), p. 23.

19. Baudrillard, quoted in Norris, *Uncritical Theory*, pp. 193–4.
20. Norris, *Uncritical Theory*, pp. 27–9.
21. cooke, Women and the War Story, p. 79.
22. Quoted in cooke *Women and the War Story*, p. 79.
23. Virilio, *Desert Screen*. pp. 41–2.
24. Al-^{c}Ubaydī, *Ḍayā^{c} fī Ḥafr al-Bāṭin*, p. 61, my translation.
25. John Balzar, 'Video Horror of Apache Victims' Deaths', *Guardian* 25 February 1991, p. 1, quoted in Gray, *Postmodern War*, p. 36.
26. Christopher Coker, The Future of War: The Re-enchantment of War in the Twenty-First Century (Malden, MA: Blackwell, 2004), p. 6.
27. Christopher Coker, *Waging War without Warriors: The Changing Culture of Military Conflict* (Boulder, CO: Lynne Rienner, 2002).
28. Coker, *The Future of War*, p. 73.
29. Samuel Hynes, *The Soldier's Tale: Bearing Witness to Modern War* (New York: Penguin, 1997), p. xvi.
30. Quoted in ibid. p., xvi.
31. Al-^{c}Abbās is the son of Imām ^{c}Ali ibn Abī Ṭālib; he is revered in Shi^{c}a Islam.
32. Al-^{c}Ubaydī, *Ḍayā^{c} fī Ḥafr al-Bāṭin*, p. 30. Page references are given parenthetically in the text after this point; my translations throughout.
33. Elaine Scarry, *The Body in Pain: The Making and Unmaking of the World* (New York: Oxford University Press, 1985).
34. Ibid., p. 89.
35. Ibid., pp. 86–7.
36. Ibid., p. 87.
37. Ibid., p. 84.
38. Ibid., p. 89.
39. Baudrillard, *The Gulf War Did Not Take Place*, p. 61.
40. Ibid., p. 69.
41. See Lewis H. Lapham, 'Trained Seals and Sitting Ducks', at http://harpers.org/archive/1991/05/trained-seals-and-sitting-ducks/.
42. An interesting connection here is that the Arabic phrase *al-shaykh maat* (the king is dead) is the origin of the term *checkmate*.
43. Wālī, *Baghdad Marlboro*, pp. 185–7. Page references are given parenthetically in the text from this point; my translations throughout.
44. Margot Norris, 'Military Censorship and the Body Count in the Persian Gulf War', *Cultural Critique*, 19 (Autumn 1991), p. 225.
45. Ibid., p. 233. *In the Penal Colony* describes a torture and killing machine that

inscribes the sentence of the condemned on his body before letting him die slowly.

46. General Buster Glosson, *War with Iraq: Critical Lessons* (Charlotte, NC: Glosson Family Foundation, 2003), p. 253.
47. Ibid., p. 249, emphasis added.
48. Ibid., p. 253.
49. Ibid., p. 265.
50. Quoted in Mickey Z., 'Highway of Death, 22 Years Later (What We're Up Against)', Uruknet, 20 February 2013, at http://www.uruknet.de/?p=m95393.
51. Derek Gregory, *The Colonial Present: Afghanistan, Palestine, Iraq* (Malden, MA: Blackwell, 2004), p. 165.
52. Hadiyya Hussein, *Beyond Love*, trans. Ikram Masmoudi (Syracuse, NY: Syracuse University Press, 2012), p, 74. Page references are given parenthetically in the text from this point.
53. Scarry, *The Body in Pain*, p. 124.
54. Carl Schmitt, *The Nomos of the Earth*, quoted in Michel Dean, *The New Police Science* (Stanford, CA: Stanford University Press, 2006), p. 19, emphasis added.
55. 'The Iraqis wanted to haul ass back to Basra and then be on television talking about what all they did and didn't do. Horner called them "plunderers". I called them ruthless thugs and killers and I intended to ensure they never had the opportunity to totally disregard human life' (Glosson, *War with Iraq*, p. 265).
56. Giorgio Agamben, *Means without End: Notes on Politics*, trans. Vincenzo Binetti and Cesare Casarino (Minneapolis: University of Minnesota Press, 2000), p. 103, emphasis added. Michael Hardt and Antonio Negri also refer to the same idea in their book *Empire* (Cambridge, MA: Harvard University Press, 2001).
57. Quoted in Dean, *The New Police Science*, p. 190.
58. Ibid., p. 191.
59. 'The sovereign is the point of in distinction between violence and the law, the threshold on which violence passes over into law and law passes over into violence' (Giorgio Agamben, *Homo Sacer: Sovereign Power and Bare Life*, trans. Daniel Heller-Roazen (Stanford, CA: Stanford University Press, 1998), 30). To maintain justice and law, the police or the army (sovereign power) has the authority to resort to violence (killing) by excepting themselves from the law.
60. Schmitt, *The Nomos of the Earth*, quoted in Agamben, *Homo Sacer*, p. 25. One inevitably thinks of Guantánamo in this context.
61. Agamben, *Means without End*, p. 104.
62. Ibid., p. 106.

63. See also Agamben, *Homo Sacer Sovereign Power and Bare Life*, pp. 170–1.
64. Ibid., p. 37.
65. Geneva Conventions of 1949, common Article 3.
66. Anthony Cordesman and Ahmed Hashim, *Iraq, Sanctions and Beyond* (Boulder, CO: Westview Press, 1997), pp. 100, 101.
67. Naṣīf Falak, *Khiḍr Qad wa al-ʿaṣr al-zaytūnī* (Khiḍr Qad and the drab olive years) (Baghdad: Manshūrāt al-Jamal, 2006), p. 157. Page references are given parenthetically in the text from this point; my translations throughout.
68. This is a reference to the Battle of Karbalāʾ, which took place in 680 between al-Ḥusayn, the grandson of the Prophet, and his group of supporters, on the one side, and the forces of Yazīd the Umayyad caliph, whom al-Ḥusayn did not recognise as caliph. The battle ended in the massacre of al-Ḥusayn and his supporters, including al-Ḥusayn's six-month-old son.
69. Cordesman and Hashim, *Iraq, Sanctions and Beyond*, p. 102.
70. Baudrillard, *The Gulf War Did Not Take Place*, p. 61.

3

Bare Life in the 'New Iraq'

The 2003 war in Iraq spawned a decade of violence, chaos and suffering. The so-called end of hostilities with the fall of the regime of Saddam Hussein opened a new era that will last for several years in which the politics and the policies of democratisation and pacification of the country will function in fact as a continuation of war. Beneath the intentions and the actions of pacification implemented in the form of building a new Iraq with democratic institutions, many battles raged, and violence is still lurking, involving different antagonistic groups and giving rise to more warring parties. All of this has perplexed and frustrated the Iraqi people, shattering their hopes for a better life, dignity and security, and revealing to them the contradictions and the paradoxes of the American occupation. It seems as though the promise of a peaceful, democratic Iraq was pitched so high that it couldn't be reached before the country sank deep into waves of violence and corruption that would lead to an uncertain future and a present that looks no less dehumanised and dehumanising than the awful face of the former regime.

Today, eleven years after the invasion of Iraq and almost three years after the end of the American occupation, Iraq is still in the throes of not a war in the conventional sense of the word but a cycle of violence and non-violence, where the end of a war that was supposed to establish the ground for peace and to realise the aspirations for law and order was only a fertile breeding ground for more killings and more human rights abuse. These realities of the occupation with its promises, its paradoxes, and its failures have been only partially and unevenly reflected on and debated in the news, military analysis and policy reports. Iraqi authors have also started to come close to reflecting in fiction the intricacies of the events of these years. Their perspectives offer a better understanding of the different experiences in a multifaceted war, the strategies of life in the 'new Iraq' and the choices for the future.

In this chapter, the analysis of selected novels shows how during the occupation the Iraqi people were entrapped in an unsafe, dangerous space. They were caught between the claws of the politics of the occupation and its war on terror, on the one hand, and the abuse of the lords of a sectarian war, on the other. These novels portray the ordinary Iraqi man with not much of a choice: he either kills or is killed. The category of *homo sacer* can potentially be extended to anyone, anywhere, anytime; one can be killed whether in the Green Zone or in the Red Zone; all the occupied space is alienating and produces 'bare life'. Novels such as *al-Minṭaqa al-khaḍrāʾ* (The Green Zone, 2009), *Baghdad mālbūrū* (Baghdad Marlboro, 2012), *al-Ḥafīda al-Amrīkiyya* (2009, *The American Granddaughter* (2012)), and *Ruʾūs al-ḥurriya al-mukayyasa* (The freedom of the bagged heads, 2007) clearly show the continuation of war and the return to its classical duality and even its privatisation. I look in particular at the first three novels named here and examine how they shed light on the power relations between the occupier and the occupied and the privatisation of the business of war, which led to its proliferation and to the emergence of the private warrior on both the American and the Iraqi sides. In these fictional narratives, central to the understanding of the occupation are the management of the occupied space and the different tensions between the different actors inside this space, including the marines and the Iraqi translators, the colonel and his local aids, the raiders and the Iraqi family, the kidnapped American and the militia, and the translator who is torn between the militia and the marines and solves his dilemma by becoming a suicide bomber.

In these fictional accounts, all of these different entities are portrayed in their conflicts and entanglements in such a way that only fiction can achieve, using an aesthetic that problematises and dramatises the human experiences of the Americans and the Iraqis in their existential struggles with life and death.

Shākir Nūrī's novel *The Green Zone* rightfully refers to the continuation of war in the form of the uninterrupted battle that goes on beneath the surface of the civil order. The novel is set in the area named the 'Green Zone' by the Americans and selected to be their safe haven and a citadel of law, order and culture. Five Iraqi translators cross daily into this zone and have to be screened twice every day when entering and exiting, where they work with a colonel, a chief translator and five marines. The novel builds on the relationships between these figures, which are ambiguous and fraught with hypocrisy and suspicion. Friendly on the surface, they are dominated by silent tensions and hatred. Focusing on one translator in particular, Ibrāhīm, *The Green Zone* highlights the choice that some Iraqi individuals in this position have made: to respond violently to the occupation.

The second novel discussed in this chapter is Najm Wālī's *Baghdad Marlboro* (2012), a fictional exploration of the past three decades in Iraq and the friendship of two war veterans – one American and one Iraqi. The American war veteran (Daniel Brooks), who had served in 1991 Gulf War and killed many innocent Iraqis, comes to seek forgiveness from the families of the victims and to meet the narrator and hand him a relic he had found in the Iraqi desert with the narrator's name and address on it. When militiamen abduct Daniel, the narrator is confronted with an awful choice: either to kill this American or be killed. Tirelessly trying to evade the fatality of this alternative and hunted by the militia, the narrator sacrifices his house, his life, and his hometown to escape war-torn Baghdad and the lords of the sectarian war. This novel and *The Green Zone* offer two different approaches to dealing with violence, but I argue that neither of these responses is satisfying to build a safer Iraq and that Iraq remains no place to live a life of integrity for the Iraqi subject.

Finally, Inaᶜām Kachāchī's *The American Granddaughter* portrays Zayna, an American of Iraqi origin, who travels back to Iraq as an embedded translator working for the Americans. Like Ibrāhīm in *The Green Zone*, Zayna feels torn between loyalty and duty and is abused by the marines as she tries to do her job. She, too, ends up disillusioned about the American occupation. I use her experience as an international translator in Iraq as a counterpoint to Ibrāhīm's experience as a local translator who gets radicalised and becomes a private warrior.

In the first section, I explore the geography of the occupation and the organisation of the occupied territory opposing two paradigmatic spaces: the city (the Green Zone) versus outside the city – the inside/outside division of space under the occupation. I examine the depictions of the city, the paradoxes the occupation creates and the humiliating practices it involves and show how these practices deepen the divisions and inspire more violence. The second section looks at the portraits of the occupier and the occupied and the different relations between the two parties. The third section focuses on the violence in the country and the *homo sacer* in the 'new Iraq'.

The contrast between the choices made by Ibrāhīm in *The Green Zone* and the narrator of *Baghdad Marlboro* highlights the fraying of the path of hope for the end of the spiral of violence that still engulfs the country. This section also examines how, as Zygmunt Bauman puts it, 'places no longer protect, however strongly they are armed and fortified. Strength and weakness, threat and security have now become, essentially, extraterritorial (and diffuse) issues that evade territorial (and focused) solutions'.[1] Using an anthropological analysis and approach, I conclude the chapter by examining the background and secular politics of the suicide bomber, focusing on the character of Ibrāhīm as translator/suicide bomber.

The Eternal Return of Occupation

> 'Good morning! Do you know that this is the twelfth time that Baghdad has fallen?'
>
> Then he went on counting its falls throughout history.
>
> Najm Wālī, *Baghdad Marlboro*

> Genghis Khān is here anew, but this time around he is wearing a military garb and boasts on his arm the American flag.
>
> Shākir Nūrī, *The Green Zone*

> What hurt him most was that the invaders were lowly, and he couldn't get along with them. They didn't rise up to his history or to his ancestry. This was a painful paradox.
>
> Shākir Nūrī, *The Green Zone*

As noted earlier, in Shākir Nūrī's *The Green Zone* five Iraqi translators cross into the Green Zone daily and have to be screened twice every day when entering and exiting it. This is where they work with Colonel David, Ms Betty (a chief translator who has earned not just a job in the zone but also the heart of the colonel in charge of it), and five marines. The marines – who like rap music and find themselves performing tasks they don't necessarily believe in – have the job of checking and clearing the translators. They also conduct with the help of the translators different home raids of suspected Iraqi terrorists. Although the marines are friendly with the translators on the surface, their relationship to them is dominated by silent tensions and hatred.

As the tensions in the novel build and culminate with raids, killings, kidnappings and death threats, we witness the emergence of the private warring parties. Ibrāhīm, the protagonist, who is one of the Iraqi translators working in the Green Zone, enjoys a good deal of trust from the colonel, David, and a good margin of mobility. Ibrāhīm can cross over from one space to another.

Ibrāhīm's meditations and reflections on the new invaders of his country 'They didn't rise up to his history or to his ancestry' are ambiguous as he is tormented by the return of the occupation and by the lowliness of the new occupiers. Is he to remind the Americans of the centuries-old history of Iraq, the cradle of civilisations, or to remind the Iraqis of a painful history made of successive and bloody invasions and occupations? The answer is a double 'yes': while Ibrāhīm, the narrator of the story, tries to boast a long history, he is aware at the same time that it is a painful history that whips him with the re-enactment of the blows of mythical and perennial invasions. Iraq's history goes back to Ur, but the American colonel in the Green Zone in Baghdad, in his ignorance and arrogance, mistakes the remains of Ur for a military base and is ready to demolish it until he is reminded of its historical importance by an enlightened co-worker: 'The American colonel was completely ignorant about the land he was walking on'.[2] The remembrance of the mythical age of the beginnings in his country is a source of mixed feelings of pride and pain that weigh heavily on the conscience of Ibrāhīm, who is humiliated by his job as a translator working for the American occupier. Two iconic dates are among the most painful, one echoing the other in a kind of a mythical re-enactment of the past: the 2003 invasion and fall of Baghdad brings back the bloody memory of the resounding fall in 1258. Ibrāhīm recounts that it is these two dates that frustrated drunkards inscribe on the pillars of al-Rasheed Street on their way home late at night and then pee on until they have erased them. From Ur to Hūlāgū to Tamerlane to the British to the Ottomans, the Iranians, the Hashemite and the more recent bloody coups, 'the idea of the eternal return' of the same imposes itself forcefully on the narrator:

> We were governed by the idea of the eternal return . . . The war wanted to take us back to Ur as if we were governed one more time by the myth . . . the myth of the war this time around. The idea of the eternal return has repeated itself nineteen times, and history keeps repeating itself, and Baghdad is besieged. (p. 72)

The Inside/Outside Divide

> I did not imagine that the country was really divided into two: the Green Zone and another area that I cannot name as it is outside human life.
>
> Shākir Nūrī, *The Green Zone*

> In the beginning there was the fence.
>
> Jost Trier, quoted in Carl Schmitt, *The Nomos of the Earth*

> The only safe place was inside the walls. That's why they called it the Green Zone.
>
> Rajiv Chandrasekaran, *Imperial Life in the Emerald City*

> The colonial world is a world cut in two. The dividing line, the frontiers, are shown by barracks and police stations.
>
> Frantz Fanon, *The Wretched of the Earth*

Historically and symbolically it is the wall that defines a city by drawing a clear geographical demarcation between the inside and the outside, as the myth of the creation of Rome tells us. 'There is no Rome without the walls.'[3] From its beginning, walls marked the US occupation of Iraq. Blast walls, roadblocks, military checkpoints and barbed-wire barriers were used to surround the Green Zone in Baghdad. With the election of the Green Zone as a safe haven, a place for law and order, and with the erection of walls and security devices around it, the spatiality of the occupation first manifested itself in the assertion of the inside/outside divide that separated the city from the lawlessness and the disorder of the outside. This separation evoked an old and similar distinction that separated the Old Continent (Europe) and the 'New World' of the colonies, a distinction developed in Carl Schmitt's *The Nomos of the Earth*.[4] According to Schmitt's concept, the Amity Line created a distinction between the realm of law (Europe) and the realm of nature (America). Similarly, during the years of the occupation, 'the new world' was now Iraq, where the legitimacy of American military actions knew no limits to target the 'barbarians' of the 'rogue state', which was expected to absorb all kinds of violence and abuse, so that Iraq and the world could be free of the evil of terrorism. The history of the area elected by the occupation authority to be the locus of power and law did not start with the American takeover of Baghdad. It was a part of the city that bore the marks of a spatial divide in Baghdad and had already been surrounded with walls during Saddam's time. *The Green Zone* gives us insight into the history of the palace of the Green Zone, Karrādat Maryam.

The palace was initially built west of Baghdad in the Hārithiyya neighbourhood in the late 1950s; it was later used and expanded by Saddam Hussein in the early 1990s. On the banks of the Tigris, this area, including the Republican palace, became home to the American and British embassies. The area was connected to the opposite bank of the river with a bridge called 'the Hanging Bridge', which in Saddam's time provided open access between the two sides of the river. The Americans closed the bridge and closed any other access to the Green Zone.

This place has been there for a long time, but obviously its new name, 'Green Zone', is an American addition that was originally meant to evoke a haven of peace, fertility and hope. Looking for safety and security and finding the commodities and equipment the area offered, the Americans needed only to annex a few more convenient locations, such as al-Rashīd Hotel and a convention centre, in order to make it 'chez soi', 'a place with borders that could be made tight and impermeable, from which trespassing could be effectively barred and entry could be strictly regulated and controlled'.[5] For that purpose, the Americans had to close the bridge, cutting off the zone from the other side of the river, and to fortify the perimeter of the area with 'seventeen foot-high blast barriers made of foot-thick concrete topped with coils of razor wire'.[6]

In other words, the area where the Republican Palace stands and where the elite of Baghdad lived during Saddam's time had already been conceived along an inside/outside division of space in Baghdad – a city inside the city. But 'there is a big difference between the walls of yesterday and those of today' (p. 91), laments Ibrāhīm. The Americans appropriated the established division and emphasised the separation with even more walls, more guards and a sophisticated technology. How then did this appropriation of the old divide and its reinforcement inaugurate a new era and announce a rupture from the past? Ibrāhīm wonders how these segregating principles upon which the Green Zone was founded can promise democracy in the new Iraq. He is keen in reminding us of the history of walls in Baghdad, such as those found in the Kaljiyya neighbourhood, which go back to the Mongolian invasion and are named after their soldiers. The area of Kaljiyya was instituted as a red-light district by the British and was surrounded by high walls during the monarchy to hide the sight of the prostitutes from the people. In other words, walls were placed there to hide an ugly reality:

> The idea of the walls goes a long way back and today walls separate the neighbourhoods of Baghdad to segregate the population . . . The Mongols built the area of the brothel, and so do the Americans today. What a contradiction. But the Mongolian were more courageous than the American soldiers; the Americans never leave their tanks, while the Mongolians would dismount from their horses to look for their victims and arrange them into piles. (p. 83)

This brings us face to face with the first contradiction in the building of a 'new Iraq' on the dividing principles of the past and on more segregating devices such as the walls and the different checkpoints that separate the different areas and neighbourhoods in Baghdad.

> The American Generals felt that they inherited this area to establish in it their power, calling it the Green Zone. At every intersection, huge Abrams tanks secure the protection, while tens of convoys of armoured cars patrol protected by concrete blocks scattered in the middle of the roads in order to block car bombs. On the roof of the buildings, the snipers stand with their guns, and in the skies the helicopters hover. (p. 95)

The Americans' occupation takes hold of what is known among Baghdadis as Karrādat Maryam or the Republican Palace, cutting it off from the outside world by erecting more walls and implanting new security devices and guards in order to make it a peaceful locus of order, law and culture. This law and culture have their origins not in the word, which builds bridges between the people, but in the fence, re-enacting the old idea of the fence as security and separation.

The culture that is built on fences and walls segregates and creates an atmosphere of fear, suspicion and mistrust across the divide. In the novel, the relations between the Americans and the Iraqis who work in the Green Zone (the translators, for example) are tarnished with deeply rooted fears and feelings of suspicion despite the different opportunities of connection through common interests in language, music and dance. The American soldiers make Iraqi rap music and create songs, and the Iraqi translators are invited to the Americans' tango parties in the marble ballroom at the palace. But all these expressive possibilities fail, and the language of violence and fire is the only code that passes between the two parties. As a consequence, the spiral of violence becomes full blown with the rise of attacks on the Green Zone and terrorist hunting raids. Ibrāhīm is amazed at the organisation and order of the Green Zone. Everything in it – the lifestyle and social life, the government and business models – is modelled according to patterns in use in the United States, so much so that many call the Green Zone 'Little America'. This comparison evokes the image of a larger America – the early America that was the land of wilderness and lawlessness inhabited by the barbaric, as John Locke formulated it: 'In the beginning, all the world was America'.[7] But the land of wilderness and chaos is now Iraq, where the Green Zone is just an island. With the occupation of Iraqi land and the new spatial organisation, it is as if the Americans have taken with them their mythology to re-enact the history of their continent during their civilising and ordering mission in the heart of the Middle East, thousands of miles away from home.

'For the inhabitants of Baghdad just to get close to the Green Zone could mean their immediate death with a bullet' (p. 93). No one can access this fortified citadel with its high walls, recounts the narrator, except with a permit issued from the highest level of the occupation authority and after one is subjected to fingerprinting and eye scanning as part of the dramatic and radical security measures, especially after it became common for some people to deceive the security with false identity cards and false permits in order to breach the zone's wall.

From a formerly luxurious neighbourhood where Iraqis could take a stroll, the Green Zone becomes an alienating place for everyone entering and living in it. And the only Iraqis accepted in this area are those working with the occupation. Ibrāhīm tries to take his feelings of alienation off his chest by confessing them:

> I used to enter this area as if I were going to another planet, an isolated planet standing alone on the summit of the mount of fear, suspicion and caution, although it used to be nothing but a luxurious neighbourhood where we could boast taking a stroll . . . Everyone living inside these walls faces the indisputable feeling that he is a stranger and an alien for the others and for himself. (p. 44)

In addition to its heightened security apparatus, its walls and its gates, what distinguishes the Green Zone and catches the attention of everyone who lives and works there is the presence of alcohol, the number of bars and night clubs, the area occupants' nightly drinking behaviours and the presence of music. There are seven famous bars where the law forbidding soldiers to drink is broken on a nightly basis.

In the geographical ordering of the space under the occupation, the civilised world of the Green Zone stands in stark contrast with what is dubbed the Red Zone – the residential and dangerous neighbourhoods of Baghdad 'where the mob, the populace and the filthy terrorists live' according to the Americans (p. 14), and where security is poor, the traffic is always jammed, insurgents are everywhere, and lawlessness and chaos are the norm. The erection of fences, walls, boundaries, checkpoints and police stations and the production of hierarchies make the spatial geography of colonial occupation. Accompanying the marines to a Sunni village to look for potential terrorists, Ibrāhīm feels as if they are crossing into a totally different country completely at odds with the Green Zone. There is no traffic pattern, the streets are full of potholes and cars maintain a distance from the Americans' Humvee. In this lawless space, nothing protects the Iraqis, says Ibrāhīm, except the American soldiers' use of 'the killing force' (p. 131). This account evokes Frantz Fanon's description of the space or the town of the colonised and its disorder and lawlessness:

> The town belonging to the colonised people . . . is a place of ill fame, peopled by men of evil repute. They are born there, it matters little where or how, they die there it matters not where, nor how. It is a world without

> spaciousness, men live there on top of each other . . . The native town is a town on its knees.[8]

In *Baghdad Marlboro*, the Red Zone is not just the dangerous neighbourhoods of Baghdad in contrast to the area of the Green Zone, but the whole country and the chaos into which it has sunk, its trash piling up in every corner and threats of killing and kidnapping everywhere. In his flight from one town to another, hiding from the militia who have invaded his house and threatened to kill him, the narrator of *Baghdad Marlboro* comes to a conclusion about the depth of the chaos:

> He who leaves the capital of trash, killing and kidnapping, whether he heads south or north, east or west, will see trash piling up on the streets, mountains of trash flooding residential neighbourhood so that the spill reaches over the sidewalks . . . as if the whole country has become a ruin, a garbage can unique of its kind.[9]

The distinction between the Green Zone and the Red Zone also calls to mind the old medieval Islamic distinction of space with the political duality between Dār al-Islam and Dār al- Ḥarb. In this Arabo-Islamic distinction, Dār al-Islam is the territory where Islamic law, peace and civilisation reign. 'Dār al-Ḥarb, on the contrary, is a lawless territory; it is the abode of the barbarians and is characterized by a permanent state of war'.[10] Dār al-Ḥarb is in a permanent state of war both with itself and with Dār al-Islam. In the geography of occupied Iraq, the story is changed: the words *Islam* and *salām* and *ḥarb* are euphemised and replaced by the use of the colours green (a symbol of fertility, hope and peace) and red (a symbol of danger, blood and war), with no allusion to religion. The duality is stripped of its religious connotations. The opposition in the occupied space of Iraq is now between Little America (the abode of peace), where law and culture reign, and Baghdad – formerly Dār al-Salām (the Abode of Peace) but now Dār al-Ḥarb (the Abode of War) – which is in a state of war internally and externally, with lawlessness ruling the day. As Ibrāhīm wanders in his city meditating about his country and its new fate, he summarises the past and the present:

> A city that apparently no one wants to continue to call the 'Abode of Peace' since for decades it was prepared to be the 'Abode of War', and it ended

being an occupied city. We cannot speak about it in a relaxed way, and it is in a coma now, completely wounded and defenceless to the invaders, as to the stupid politicians, without walls protecting it, a city disputed by history in the past and by politics in the present, while it was burnt twice but is still fighting for life. (p. 96)

Following the old distinction between Dār al-Islam and Dār al-Ḥarb in radical political Islam, the relationship between the two worlds is called 'jihād'. The new relationship between the two worlds redefined as the Green Zone and the Red Zone is now reduced to a security issue. US politics of security replace jihād with the 'war on terror', a new concept that equates the old and the new distinctions despite the dropping of the old religious connotations. As Bulent Diken and Carsten Bagge Lausten put it,

In this context there is a significant kinship between religious fundamentalism and the politics of security, which may be understood as a new religion because it also reduces all political problems and issues to a 'fundamental' problem of security. What unites Islamic terror and the war against terrorism today is that in both a cosmic battle between order and disorder is at the forefront.[11].

Nūrī acknowledges through his protagonist that, in contrast with the tightened security of the Green Zone, Baghdad's frontiers were left wide open from all sides to the other newcomers, 'the fundamentalists', as Ibrāhīm calls those who entered the 'land of the battle' and spread to all corners of the city, whose sky now 'is full of helicopters hovering like insects with their huge noses, as the Baghdadis like to describe them, and controlling the city tirelessly' (p. 92).

During the invasion and in the first days of the occupation, Baghdad was left to its fate and was in the throes of unprecedented levels of violence and chaos, where looting and the lack of basic services such as electricity and water made the major headlines. The looting of the museum of Baghdad, which is home to some of the oldest art collections testifying to the birth of civilisation and knowledge, right under the US marines' noses was one of the mysteries of the invasion. Ibrāhīm is bewildered and perplexed by the way events unfolded. He asks:

What happened, what fly has stung the Army of the United States and paralysed it before these gangs and groups of thieves? Baghdad, like Babylon before it, used to be the centre of the universe. People came to it from all over the world. And now what are those marines who came from far away doing? Is it possible for America to plunge into barbarism two millennia after the spread of Christianity in the Near East? (pp. 94–5)

In an article in the *New York Times*, Thomas Friedman went as far as talking about the predominance of the Hobbesian state of nature in Iraq after Saddam's fall: 'The Iraqi people were "in a pre-political, primordial state of nature". For the moment Saddam has been replaced by Hobbes, not Bush.'[12] As Derek Gregory argues, however, this state of nature was not an eternal state of nature; it was of course produced: '"Bush" begat "Hobbes"'.[13] But no one is better placed than Ibrāhīm to give us an insider view with the appropriate language and the right metaphors. He knows this city very well:

The city looks as if grabbed by an iron fist, just like it used to be before the fall of the regime. It is bathing in endless chaos. Nothing has changed in essence because the old power is still alive and was not totally killed off, as it may have seemed in the beginning. There is a mixture of Saddam's loyalists, nationalists who joined the resistance, and Islamists both Sunni and Shiᶜa, gangs and militias; all of them found in this time an excellent opportunity and good luck. Everything is permitted for ᶜAli Bābā: forbidden traffic of all kinds – weapons, cigarettes, drugs, money and valuable artefacts. (p. 92)

ᶜAli Bābā, a character from *A Thousand and One Nights*, takes on a particular meaning in this context. The reference to him conjures up the robberies of the forty thieves who accompanied ᶜAli Bābā. By extension, it alludes to all those who enjoyed a free hand and took advantage of the absence of law in the early days of the occupation: 'those who attacked everything and ransacked shops, taking alcohol, perfume, tobacco, watches, jewellery, computers in all immunity, without being charged or condemned' (p. 95). The occupation forces' unwillingness to establish civil order, to prevent pillage and theft, and to provide security for the population was seen as a major failure that angered and frustrated the people and eventually turned opinion against them.

Another character from *A Thousand and One Nights* invoked in the narrator's reflections about his city and the chaos into which it has been plunged is Scheherazade. In her capacity as witness, she can testify to the majesty and splendour of Baghdad in its golden age. Scheherazade, whose statue in Baghdad was miraculously spared from bombing, is persistent in her desire to live on: 'For the second time she escaped a decreed death', exclaims Ibrāhīm, but 'no doubt she must be witnessing a totally different and alien life for Baghdad' (p. 96).

The contrast is total, as the narrator observes, between the past and the present of the city, between the Abode of Peace and the Abode of War, where the doubted newcomers divide up the space and define it anew according to their own interests and calculations, and where some end up dancing the tango in the marble ballroom of the palace in the Green Zone, while others are locked up in mobile prisons (discussed in Chapter 4) spread throughout the desert, a new American invention for the occupation and the war on terror:

> The city of *A Thousand and One Nights* whose minarets used to compete with the moon sleeps tonight doubtful, with all the suspects who landed here. The Green Zone seems safe, and its bars, its restaurants and its small markets give to the night a false meaning and an artificial flavour just like the ambience of a black and white movie. (pp. 46–7)

These two popular figures, Scheherazade and ᶜAli Bābā, symbolise the two paradigmatic forces, evil and good. Evil and violence in the form of ᶜAli Bābā are let loose in the Iraqi society under the occupation, but the desire for life and order is envisioned in the figure of Scheherazade, who, defying death and war, persists as a good omen.

Letting the country initially plunge into lawlessness and chaos would ironically justify the colonial mission – in a replay of the first colonisation in the nineteenth century – by allowing the occupying forces to take Iraq 'from darkness to lead it into light', as former lieutenant general Jay Garner, the first civilian administrator of occupied Iraq, put it and as Colonel David formulates it in *The Green Zone* when he tells Ibrāhīm that they are there to kill the barbarians, those strange, uncivilised creatures 'Gog and Magog', clearly betraying with this discourse the ideological and irrational underpinnings of the occupation: 'We came to fight Gog and Magog' he says, 'yes, the strange creatures that appeared here, or so we understood' (p. 53).

Tango: The Dance of the Occupation

In *The Green Zone*, Shākir Nūrī uses dance as a paradigm for the relationship between the occupier and the occupied, where the local elite are supposed to mimic the movements of the Americans and learn from them how to become good governors. The author has carefully chosen the tango, which is not even an American dance, because of the duo it requires and the partnership it implies (after all, it takes two to tango, as the saying goes). Beautiful and elegant, the tango is also the symbol of the harmonious steps and movements between the dancers. It is quite curious that Nūrī chose tango instead of rock 'n' roll, which is a properly American form of art, but perhaps he did so because dancing to rock 'n' roll doesn't require a partnership between the performers but rather emphasises freedom of expression. As Colonel David exclaims, the local elites working with the Americans seem to have quite a lot to learn from them despite the fact that many of them lived in the West for many years. In the eyes of the occupier, they remain unprepared to lead the dance and, by extension, to lead their own country: 'Colonel David pokes fun of the new leaders because they didn't learn how to dance in Europe or in America despite their long stay there. Do you know that Colonel David is an excellent dancer?' (p. 114).

These local elites and native intellectuals, some of whom were exiles and returned to Iraq with the American occupation, are motivated to mimic and learn from their occupiers. One of the marines is of Argentinian origin, says Ibrāhīm, whose position as an insider allows him to observe these facts. This marine has to train the future leaders of the Green Zone to learn and master tango. 'All of them hurried to the ballroom because they received instructions to learn tango so that they can celebrate the seventh anniversary of the occupation'. As Colonel David says,

> He who doesn't know how to tango doesn't know how to govern. It is the dance signalling the marriage between the Iraqis and the Americans because the occupation of any country needs two dancers, and dance cannot be performed without them, just as the occupation cannot be accomplished without the occupier and its client. (p. 115)

These new leaders of Iraq accept the occupation and its mission, and they are ready to co-operate and play a positive role in this dance that takes two to be performed.

> Colonel David wanted to make of the tango between the marines and the Iraqis, the dance that connects with the ties of marriage the occupied and the occupier, a marriage between tango and local rhythms of an army divided into sects and factions. Every weekend they streamed into the marble room: you would find ministers, advisers, assistants and generals all accompanied with wives or mistresses and sometimes their female soldiers for some. They rehearsed and practised for the big party. (p. 116)

Ibrāhīm and his fiancée, Viviane, who has gained Colonel David's trust, are invited to the tango parties, but very quickly the couple feel uncomfortable hanging out with the 'beau monde' of these parties made of ministers, high advisers and heads of security companies. Viviane refuses to dance: 'I don't want to be part of the dance of the occupation. They dance as though they have possessed the country in this dance', she objects (p. 117).

The Occupier and the Occupied: The Portrait of a Couple

If Viviane, Ibrāhīm's co-worker and fiancée, is opposed to dancing tango in the ballroom, Ms Betty (Bāsima Francis), another Iraqi woman working in the Green Zone, is all for it. She even performs the most beautiful and sensual duo with Colonel David himself. This woman attracts the attention of all the translators, including Ibrāhīm:

> I didn't expect an Iraqi woman, even if she was a Christian, to perform that dance with such elegance, as if her legs were made of plastic and not bones . . . She twisted her leg and passed it in between the Colonel's legs without touching his; she was able to bow to the back, and her hair reached the ground without touching it. She surpassed the Spanish and Latin American dancers with her agility and her skills. (pp. 115, 117)

Ms Betty is noticeable not only because of her dance skills but also because of her behaviour and her relationship to the occupier. She incarnates the figure of the occupied, in particular of the minorities and the role they might have played in the occupation.

Ms Betty is a local agent. She knows the ins and outs of the business of recruiting local interpreters. In addition, the colonel finds in her not only a helpful agent, thanks to her exceptional knowledge of the geography of Baghdad, but also a beautiful lover. Their story becomes like a 'Romeo and Juliet in the Green Zone' (p. 54). Ms Betty left her Christian neighbourhood of al-Battāwīn and established herself in the Green Zone.

> Ms Betty didn't have any political interests before, but with the arrival of the Americans she knew how to snatch the opportunity to enter the Green Zone through its largest door: the heart of Colonel David, who did not hesitate to designate her first as a translator, then as a secretary, and finally as the head of the security of the translators. (p. 56)

It is this 'infernal duo', Colonel David and Ms Bāsima Francis, says Ibrāhīm that pulls the strings of the security business and the translators' jobs inside the Green Zone. Using her local knowledge, Ms Betty is responsible for the security of the translators not for their own sake but to ensure the security and safety of the American forces in the Green Zone.

> She stays up late looking up the records and organising the duties of the translators and their daily schedules . . . [S]he sent off every translator to accompany the marines' raids according to sectarian and ethnic divisions. For example, she used to send a Sunni translator to a Shiʿa neighborhood and a Shiʿa translator to a Sunni neighborhood and the Kurdish translator to the Arab areas . . . She wanted to prevent any possibility of any sympathy or compassion we might have for the people we raided. (p. 119)

These ways of dealing with the translators and assigning the jobs comes to the translators' attention only months after they have signed their contracts. Taking part in the daily raiding operations with the American forces is the only 'stroll' outside the Green Zone these translators can take; otherwise they are imprisoned in their work cubicles inside the zone (pp. 119–20).

> Ms Betty had doubts about everybody; she scrutinised our names and sent informants to dig up our past and check our backgrounds in the neighbourhoods where we used to live. In this she relied on the guards of the buildings, informants, mayors, advisers and intellectuals. She feared that

> some of us might just be tools in the hands of the resistance, trying to infiltrate and mislead the American forces. The lie detector to which we were subjected every three months was not enough for her; as she used to say, 'Iraqis are able to deceive the demon, let alone a lie detector; that's nothing for them'. (p. 56)

In his portrait of this couple, Colonel David and Ms Betty, Nūrī points to the ethnic and religious divisions in Iraq and indicates that high-profile security positions with the American forces were more likely to be assigned to ethnic or religious minorities, such as the Christians and the Kurds. The relationship between Colonel David and Ms Betty is a good example of the mimicry relationship between the occupiers and the occupied described in Fanon's book *Black Skin, White Masks*, especially in the chapters 'The Woman of Color and the White Man' and 'The Man of Color and the White Woman'.[14] This unequal relation between the colonel and Betty during the occupation raises many questions, especially regarding the fact that, as the narrator recounts, Ms Betty

> used to sit in her office like a Babylonian goddess on her throne, and she wanted the colonel to sit under her feet . . . I thought about the philosophical dimension of their relationship, which brought together a powerful man with an attractive woman, a master and a slave and not a man and a woman because love under the occupation has its own circumstances and its own rules. And for more than thirty years Ms Betty was dreaming of this man who came from the outside to take her on the rug of *A Thousand and One Nights*, so they met. (p. 56)

Different divides mark the relationship between the colonel and Ms Betty. It is not only a relation between the occupier and the occupied or between master and slave, as Ibrāhīm puts it, but a relation between races (a white man and a non-white woman). Through this relation, there might be gratification and a 'subjective consecration' of the Christian minority or of the minorities of Iraq in general, many of whom for decades had been excluded from positions of power. With the war and the occupation, some of them now enjoyed the trust of the Americans. In this regard, we might wonder, as Louis T. Achille rightfully did,

> insofar as truly interracial marriage is concerned . . . to what extent it may not represent for the colored spouse a kind of subjective consecration to wiping out in himself and in his own mind the color prejudice from which he has suffered so long.[15]

In the case of Ms Betty, of concern are not just the color prejudice but also the ethnic and the religious prejudices as well. The love and the trust Ms Betty enjoys from the American colonel rehabilitate her in her own eyes and in the eyes of her fellow Christian Iraqis, many of whom want her favours and ask for her intercession in religious matters. Nevertheless, Ms Betty remains, as the narrator observes, a slave to her master, Colonel David, because, no matter how romantic their love is, it remains unequal and is subject to the terms and rules of the circumstances of the occupation.

Imagining the American

Who is the American occupier? How is he reflected in the fiction about the occupation? And how do the Iraqis see him and refer to him? In *The Freedom of the Bagged Heads*, Jāsim al-Raṣīf uses one word to refer to the Americans, *al-ᶜimyān*, 'the blind ones', because of the blind raids they conduct and their savage and random kidnapping of innocent people.[16] The term *al-ᶜimyān* refers not only to their not being able to see what they're doing and what's going on around them but also to the blindness of their hearts. The Americans are blind to their own actions and to the fear and the panic they cause wherever they go. In the raids they conduct, 'the blinds' make sure to blindfold the kidnapped and to cover their heads with dark plastic bags and then take them to secret locations for torture and abuse.

The Green Zone depicts the Americans in Iraq from the perspective of Ibrāhīm, the translator who is a retired professor of English and a librarian. Although Ibrāhīm is an educated layman who comes across as someone who is open-minded, his references to the Americans are not free of stereotypes and preconceived ideas. However, because he is someone who sees the group of five marines working at the security gate every day and who hangs out with them at night in the bars of the Green Zone, his depictions of these five soldiers sound balanced and at times humanised. He humanises the soldiers and talks about them in terms that raise more understanding than anger or hatred. However, his feelings and perceptions of the Americans are sometimes confused and contradictory. According to his observations and reflections, the average American soldier is someone who doesn't know much about Iraq except for the word *Babylon*; the soldier doesn't even know why he is in Iraq or what caused the war. He appears to be from a poor social background and without much education. He is in Iraq to do a job, obey orders and make money.

> He didn't ask how this war broke out. And he didn't want to know about its causes. It was none of his business. He was told 'fight', so he came to fight; 'kill', and he started killing: 'these people are evil, and you ought to fire at them before they fire at you'. At the end of the day, he joined the marines because of the attractive salary, and he was tired of living without a job in the African neighbourhood of Los Angeles. (p. 23)

Even though Ibrāhīm admits that he does not like stereotypes, nevertheless he views the Americans with standardised images and talks about them using stereotyping words. Americans, these creatures formerly seen only on the TV screen, with their own cultural behaviour, are best kept in the imaginary, far away from the real, yet they become an unexpected, painful and disturbing reality:

> What's an American? One wonders. He is a cowboy who fills his stomach with hamburgers and quenches his thirst with Coca-Cola and has no other God than the dollar. This is how we imagined Americans when we were kids . . . I did not expect to see them except on a TV screen, and here they were, flesh and blood before my eyes; they never tired of searching us. (p. 8)

Ibrāhīm profiles the five marines working at the security gate of the Green Zone using colourful racial terms: there is Neil, a black from a Muslim background; Johnny, a yellow Asian; Richard, an Irish Red; Bachelor, a white fat boy like a piece of chuck; and Batista, with his Latin features. The novel focuses most closely on this group of five. Their cultural experiences are limited to watching violent movies on TV. Their job requires them to clear those entering and exiting the Green Zone, and they are ready to kill all kinds of deer both figuratively and literally because the area is home to the former president's many deer. Some of them like music and compose Iraqi rap, music that explicitly calls for the end of the war, because they believe that music alleviates the violence of the barbarians even though they resort to violence themselves – but only as a defence mechanism, according to their logic. They form a band, calling it '4th 25'. Ibrāhīm finds them 'less barbaric than the others' because they hope that their music will bring about the end of the war. They want to transform their music into something explicitly against the war, like what Jimmy Hendrix did for the Vietnam War, but Neil and his amateur musician friends are paradoxically able both to play their music instruments for peace and at the same time fire their rifles:

> They composed songs insulting the war, but they don't fall short of killing at any time: 'What can we do? We cannot defend ourselves with the guitar' . . . Here everything gets mixed up – the meaning of music and the meaning of killing. (p. 32)

Neil and his friends even sometimes look in their boxes for CDs that will encourage them to execute their attacks on armed terrorists. Sometimes they see in the passers-by a potential terrorist who ought to be killed, and at other times they reject killing these innocent Iraqis who just happen not to understand instructions in English: 'I don't see terrorists,' says Neil.

> 'I only see normal pedestrians crossing the streets at night and those who do not understand English and don't stop their cars because they do not understand the instructions. Should we kill these people just because they don't understand what we tell them? Should we kill them because they walk the streets of their own homeland?' (p. 37)

However, this statement is in stark contradiction with another:

> [They think] of those who are in the streets [as] nothing but terrorists who ought to be captured like rabbits; they have nothing to do but charge their rifles and guns with gunpowder and hit the trigger to just execute one order: to kill in order to live. (p. 42)

Ibrāhīm is perplexed by this ambiguous side of the five soldiers, who embody a contradiction, being at war and doing their jobs but at the same time making and playing rap music: 'Music was one of the secrets of the human beings who came to fight us. But music calms the barbarity of man, and these five guys were indeed less barbaric' (p. 35). It is this humanised side of the five marines that makes them amiable to the group of Iraqi translators, particularly to Ibrāhīm, who engages in small-talk and jokes with them after work, when they meet in the General Electric bar in the Green Zone. The novel provides a humanised portrait of the soldiers. Neil, for example, isn't able to fire at others; Johnny 'doesn't have enemies in this country', but he 'just kills in order not to be killed' (pp. 24–5); Richard is a timid person who 'doesn't know why he is here' (p. 25); and Bachelor day and night 'curses his officers and the leaders of his unit, feeling that he has been captured in the trap of the marines' (p. 25). As for Batista, 'even when he kills, he says his prayers and draws the symbol of the cross on his chest' (p. 25). These five soldiers all hope and dream to return home safely. They share the same fate at security gate number 2. But sometimes they have to go on raiding patrols so that they can keep up their fighting skills:

> This is how the marines take turns in securing the safety of the Green Zone: every five soldiers are assigned together to the security task for a limited time . . . At this checkpoint, they are independent and sovereign: they decide everything. They are responsible for the safety and security of all of the Green Zone. (p. 25)

In addition to music, alcohol is an outlet for the soldiers' frustration and doubts. After long days, they spend their evenings in the different bars of the area, where their fears, their dreams and their sadness surface with alcohol. Ibrāhīm perceives these five marines as victims of the infernal machinery of capitalism. When he first sees how they treat the people at the security gate, he thinks of blowing them up, but he pushes away this idea:

> They were not necessarily criminals. They were caught in the mechanism of this big machine thirsty for blood and money; without this, these demons would not have come to fight us. It's good that I waited because killing them would have made me sad anyway. Their love for music freed me from the idea of exploding them. (p. 18)

The other image that Ibrāhīm and other Iraqis hold of the American is scarier. It is of those working with the security companies in the Green Zone and the private contractors such as the infamous Black Water, Dini

Group and Sandline International, among the three hundred private companies assuring the security of the American and the British forces, their embassies and their interests in Iraq. Security counselling and services are also offered to the Iraqi police and Iraqi government. These private security contractors living in the Green Zone come to the narrator's attention because they are among the privileged regulars of the area's many bars and taverns. They are noticeable because of their drinking habits and their lavish spending in the bars. Their daily wage is one thousand dollars, which is the equivalent of the monthly salary of an Iraqi translator. 'They are an army inside the army and more ruthless than the American army itself; they don't hesitate to kill anyone simply if they have doubts about their looks' (p. 29).

All Wars Considered: Terror and Sectarianism

> I did not understand why pedestrians were the preferred targets for American soldiers. Perhaps it was because of their silent walking, which rendered their movements strange, like the movements of ghosts who had to be made to disappear with precise bullets. And that was their fate . . . The gate of death is open to us and to all passers-by.
>
> Shākir Nūrī, *The Green Zone*

For the Iraqis who experienced the Gulf War in 1991 with its invisible soldiers fighting at a distance and its hit-and-run attacks, the war during the occupation was different. It took weary Iraqis back to the age of real battles on the ground, with the return of visible soldiers made of 'flesh and bone' attacking the insurgents and other militants and, above all, with the overwhelming presence of the injured body that no longer could be hidden. The narrator of *The Green Zone* puts it this way when he explains Ibrāhīm's opinion:

> He got tired of wars, and he was not ready to welcome a war where the invisible warriors were transformed into real soldiers made of flesh and bone, with their military suits, their machine guns and their equipment. They are no longer dropping their bombs from high in the sky and then safely returning to their bases; they are now occupying our streets and government buildings, looking us in the eye and killing us as they please. (p. 64)

With the occupation, the sky is no longer the theatre for operations, and the essential and classic antagonism and duality of the war are back; they are now re-inscribed in the paradigm of the war on terror and the militia war, with its kidnapping and slaughtering of hostages. Although we clearly know the identity of those who occupy Iraq, we don't really know who the lords of the sectarian war and the different militias are. The narrator of *Baghdad Marlboro*, whose house is invaded by militiamen, reflects exactly on this new striking reality of the sectarian war: 'Those who occupy Iraq', he says, 'we know who they are, but those who occupy my house and other houses, nobody knows who they are'.[17] In *Baghdad Marlboro*, the sectarian war is described as something even beyond the classical duality of the war, involving the primitive condition of multiplicity, an exacerbated state of nature, in which everybody is killing everybody, and where, thanks to information technology and the Internet, the kidnapping and the killing can sometimes be as fake as the resounding Islamic names of the organisations carrying them out and just staged to abuse people and extort ransoms: 'Everybody is killing everybody,' says the narrator, 'and I am running away from men who wanted me to be one of those for whom killing has become like a daily exercise or a live entertainment' (p. 262).

The landscape of the sectarian war is even more complex and volatile to describe because the identity of the war actors is blurred and difficult to track. What we know is that the lords of this war are gangs looking for money and opportunities, as the story of the kidnapping of Daniel Brooks shows. This man who visits Iraq looking for forgiveness for the killings he committed in the 1991 war (even though his commanding officer forced him to do it) comes loaded with dollars he has saved in America and wants to give to the families of the victims. His abductors take all this money, and this is why they do not ask the narrator for more money; they just ask him to kill Daniel. These private warriors are like ghosts. Nameless, with covered faces, they are just referred to as 'the veiled ones' in *Baghdad Marlboro*. They hide their real identities behind resounding Islamic names they give themselves. These unknown, armed men storm into the narrator's house, offering him a deadly alternative. Their methods are in fact modelled on the dealings of the American occupier, as the narrator says, with the only difference being that the American occupier's identity is known, whereas these men's identity remains unknown. After they invade the narrator's house, they blindfold him, and take him to a secret location, giving him an ultimatum to kill Daniel before they let him go:

> They blindfolded me after they took me with them and led me to the car. Thank god, they did not cover my head with a plastic bag, which was widespread in those days. The Americans used it before the kidnappers started using it with their victims. They only blindfolded me with a piece of dark fabric. (p. 236)

The depth of this sectarian war that fills the newspapers is frightening to the narrator of *Baghdad Marlboro*. After he runs from those who have threatened him, he eagerly looks for any news about the American hostage Daniel Brooks, following the news of the sectarian war and the widespread kidnapping in the newspapers, on television, as well as on video footage and websites that specialise in showcasing the daily killing and beheading of hostages and victims.

The new war is now staged on the screen in the form of recorded footage, whether it is real or fabricated, just for the purpose of extorting money, as in one 'tragicomic kidnapping' story related by the narrator:

> Since the month of April and after the first anniversary of the fall of Baghdad, kidnapping, which was unknown in Iraq, was on the rise to the point that those groups not only gave themselves Islamic-sounding names to cover up for their real objective and abuse for money but started fabricating stories of kidnap, such as the news of that tragicomic kidnapping when an Iraqi organisation claimed that it was keeping an American soldier hostage and threatened to kill him. The paradox is that the footage that was posted on an Islamic website attracted the attention of the marketing co-ordinator of Dragon Models Company, who confirmed that the soldier on the footage and the gun used are in fact plastic toys manufactured by the company. (p. 260)

The victims of this sectarian war are not only Iraqis but also the Americans working in Iraq, the foreign journalists, the visitors and the innocent random people. After following this war in the media for a while, the narrator gets tired of it and stops looking for news about Daniel.

> I didn't want to read what was just confirming the same events over and over. What is the point reading newspapers that do not relate anything except for slaughtering, killings and explosions, while death pours from every mouth? I said to myself, you take a bus or walk on the street, buy this or that merchandise, sit in a café or at the doctor's office, go into a hotel lobby or say hello to your neighbour, you don't hear anything except different news of killing . . . [W]here did this violence come from? (p. 262)

In both novels, *The Green Zone* and *Baghdad Marlboro*, the Red Zone as the zone of disorder, deadly attacks and death gains more and more space, covering most of Iraq – in particular what was called the Sunni Triangle and all the Sunni areas, with the exception of Kurdistān. In fact, organised and spontaneous forms of insurgency and resistance to what was seen as a colonial occupation did increase in number and intensity as people's feelings of abuse and humiliation grew. The situation became more complex when attacks against the occupation forces were doubled by internal fights and targeted actions among rival warlords of different sects as well as by attacks targeting those among Iraqis who helped, worked with or dealt with the occupying forces, including members of the Iraqi Governing Council. All this called for decisive action on the part of the occupation forces. The insurgency and the new forms of violence and organised terror gave the war on terror a fully fledged legitimacy and existence. In addition to trying to re-establish order, the strategy of invoking the war on terror had the advantage of boosting the American mission in Iraq and diffusing the real burden of the occupation, as Derek Gregory argues: 'The generic invocation of "terrorism" was an attempt to rehabilitate one of Bush's central arguments for the war, to obscure the reality of occupation and to try to rescue the American mission in Iraq by reflagging it as another front in the continuing "war on terror"'.[18]

The politics of security adopted by the occupation forces in an effort to stem the violence failed to pursue human rights as a measure and a method of pacification. Instead, the Americans committed horrific abuses and in this way produced the reverse of pacification, increasing feelings of resentment and more vengeful violence. The adopted strategy transformed a politics of security into a politics of insecurity and terror.

Of the novels examined in this chapter, *The American Granddaughter* and *The Green Zone* offer two testimonies of the new antagonism in the war on terror that delve into the Iraqis' emotions in face of the politics enforced by the American army. Zayna and Ibrāhīm, two translators working with the occupier, give us first-hand accounts of how the aspiration to stifle the violence in Iraq was in its methods and strategy productive of more violence – an open-ended kind of violence. Zayna's and Ibrāhīm's jobs with the Americans don't involve just translating documents, interpreting or 'cultural advising', as Zayna puts it,[19] but are stretched beyond the requirements stipulated by their contracts: both have to be part of raiding operations, storming into the houses of Iraqis suspected of plotting against the occupation. Ibrāhīm and Zayna are witnesses to the abuse of basic human rights and humiliating treatments. Their jobs are not just about translating words. Ibrāhīm confesses that sometimes the translators have to denounce people's emotions and feelings and read their minds:

> Some of the translators are wicked; they intentionally translate the feelings of the people we raid and interview – like, for example, when we say 'he is angry' or 'he is happy, sarcastic or sad'. Translating these feelings exposes the people and endangers their lives . . . We have to be very careful as some of them [the Americans] know Arabic quite well. (*The Green Zone*, pp. 110–11)

Sometimes without waiting for the translation, the raiders attack the people just because they protest against the way the marines stormed into their houses. 'It is not easy', comments Ibrāhīm, 'to see an American soldier hitting an old man who might be your father, your uncle or your grandfather' (*The Green Zone*, p. 111).

Ibrāhīm has to do these tasks wearing a mask all the time lest the people whose houses he raids with the soldiers recognise him. As for Zayna, she is American anyway and not known to the community, but she has to lie to her grandmother and hide from her the fact that she is working with the occupier of her country of origin. The hard missions starts after 10:00 p.m. when she is working and living in Takrīt:

> We were told he [the person targeted] was an evil son of a bitch . . . [A]s long as he and others like him were free, Iraq could not rise up and give its rendition of the hymn of democracy. It was midnight when we headed in

> three vehicles to the house of that contemptible man . . . It was my first real raid. (*American Granddaughter*, p. 93)

Breaking into the houses of innocent Iraqi people and breaking their doors, the soldiers are 'like panthers', according to Zayna. They are armed to the teeth, using their weapons to terrorise the women, the kids and the elderly, humiliating them and abusing them when no one is proved guilty of anything; only suspicions based on wrong intelligence data hover over them. 'And what does it mean to accompany American patrols?' asks Ibrāhīm, who is saddened and puzzled by these kinds of assignments that he has to perform as if in a nightmare.

> It means that I have to ask the people to keep to their calm and to accept the occupation. There is a voice that comes from the depths of the people whom we raid in their homes asking about their men. Are they not entitled to hold on to the old wisdom that says, 'Kill the informer before you kill the occupier'? *It is the Americans who make the terrorists; they incubate them in their laboratories.* As for us [the translators], we are no longer translators, but informers; *we offer them the heads of other people on a silver platter.* Has the translator become a strange creature? They uproot us like trees without mud, and they plant us in the Green Zone and ask us to provide them with intelligence, and this is not in accordance with the contract we signed with them. We are not informers; we are translators. (*The Green Zone*, 109–10, emphasis added)

Every time insurgency reaches a peak or every time there are attacks against an American in one of the cities where a translator comes from, that person, says Ibrāhīm, comes under suspicion and attack. In *The Green Zone*, the village of Tal al-Yāqūt, where Ibrāhīm comes from, is one of the strongholds of resistance and militant activities against the occupation, and this is enough for Ibrāhīm to be invited to the colonel's office to be rebuked, as if he shares the responsibility and the guilt:

> Every time an American was killed in the vicinity of his [Ibrāhīm's] village, Tal al-Yāqūt, Colonel David invited him to his office and subjected him to an interview. He even threatened to put an end to his rebellious village that harbours terrorists, causing the death of the biggest number of American soldiers with explosive devices. (p. 108)

Ibrāhīm witnesses in the patrols in which he takes part how the marines would eagerly look for the terrorists in the streets of Baghdad and with their loudspeakers ask them to come out of hiding, and how they would curse themselves and the fate that brought them there out of fear of car bombs and improvised explosive devices:

> The driver of our tank whistles in the streets as if he were calling the population to come out and expose their bodies to bullets because empty streets do not satisfy his killing instincts . . . He would shout, 'These bastards play hide and seek with us'. (pp. 132–3)

Through the lenses of these two translators, who had to do more than what their contracts said they would be doing, we gain insight into how terrorists are made by the politics of the occupation. The politics of security provides the appropriate conditions to hatch and grow the terrorist mind and the terror act. In the case of Iraq, it triggered more violence and more killing and led to an open-ended form of war on both sides of the equation.

Infamous battles to eradicate militant actions and insurgency – the battle of Fallūjah, for example – show that the techniques of attack involved the targeting of human dignity and human rights as well as dehumanising practices such as the use of extremely loud and deafening music to terrorise, distract and make the insurgents lose control. It is a surreal scene, observes Ibrāhīm, to hear loud heavy-metal music and rock 'n' roll in the empty streets of Fallūjah under siege.

Loudspeakers are attached to rifles, tied to the soldiers' belts, hung from the towers, and tied to the Humvees:

> The American forces exploded the bells of hell with rock 'n' roll music so that it would enervate the militants and at the same time relax the marines by creating a light atmosphere of laughter and good humour among them . . . They did not hesitate to play clips of children crying and men shouting and even symphonies of cats' moaning and dogs' barking and other metal-piercing sounds. (p. 112)

With the fighting shifting to and taking place on the ground, and during confrontations such as the battle of Fallūjah and in the raiding operations, the body takes centre stage and becomes visible with its injuries, its wounds and its mutilations. And if there is a problem in the body count, it is not because the count is obstructed by instructions coming from above, but because of logistics, in particular the scarcity of space where the cadavers are stored. The sight of bodies piled up beyond the morgues' capacity is a new feature in the Iraqi war novel.

Accompanying the marines to look for the body of one of their fellow soldiers, Ibrāhīm is frightened and shocked by the sight of all these bodies at the morgue, where he also meets with lines of Iraqis looking and enquiring for the bodies of their relatives. In these circumstances, the translator is embarrassed; he feels ashamed and more like an informer than a translator. The bodies of Americans are immediately retrieved from Iraqi morgues and flown back home, whereas the bodies of the Iraqi people have several possible fates: either they are lost, dismembered and sold in pieces, or they remain piled like sardines for almost two months due to the lack of space, but more precisely due to the very high number of deaths in attacks. In these conditions, counting the bodies is a challenge:

> Cadavers don't lie. Each body tells its own story. Lucky are those who found the cadavers of their loved ones. As for lost bodies, they remain a worry for their families. They departed, leaving their families suffering in pain. Some of the bodies become food for the fish in the Tigris and the Euphrates. (p. 135)

In these scary locations, Ibrāhīm is startled and feels out of place, as though not in his country, but in an Iraq that does not resemble itself at any time of its history:

> I did not imagine the existence of such a place in my country. Not now and not at any other time: bodies were piled up in huge fridges spread out in corridors, some were underground, in basements – or rather these were parking lots for cars turned into places to store dead bodies. (p. 134)

In the war on terror, not only does the body become visible but it also comes to our attention as a commodity subjected to different kinds of smuggling and trafficking, merchandise on the black market. *The Green Zone* reveals how the central morgue becomes the place for strange procedures, the circulation of human organs retrieved from the place of the explosions, and of 'cadavers without identity, without names, and without faces' (p. 135). These practices are common in the midst of daily explosions and suicide operations – to the point that Iraq becomes 'the cheapest market in the business of human trafficking' (p. 136).

As for the American body, it is beheaded, slaughtered, showed on video and discarded in random places. For example, Daniel Brooks's body is found near a small bridge on the Euphrates River, says the narrator of *Baghdad Marlboro*, who reads the news of Daniel's beheading in a newspaper:

> He was found slaughtered on a small bridge in a small village west of Baghdad . . . with his head separated from the rest of his body . . . [I]t is true that the Americans didn't know about his missing until very late, but until his death they didn't receive any video or any letter asking for a ransom . . . [E]ven when the peasant found the corpse and informed the police, who informed the Americans, nobody paid attention to his corpse. He was the only American for whom it remained unknown what date he went missing because his entrance to Iraq wasn't registered with the American embassy. (pp. 313–14)

Other American bodies are flown back home, but they are surrounded by no less mystery because most of them are put in welded metal boxes because of severe mutilations, and even the families are forbidden sight of the body – which in turn raises the doubt and anger of the families, especially the mothers of the victims. In *The Green Zone*, Ibrāhīm notes how Bachelor's mother is angry and doubtful that her son's body is truly back because what she gets back is locked in a welded box. She says:

> 'This is the saddest day in my entire life . . . [T]hey placed [Bachelor's body] in a steel box welded on all sides and told me that it's impossible to open it because the body is mutilated . . . But I am not sure' – says Bachelor's mom – 'that there is a cadaver in this cold steel and disgusting box. Does America now put the bodies of its fallen soldiers in closed metallic boxes? We didn't see this during World War II or during Vietnam, when the military laws stipulated that the cadaver should be placed in a wooden coffin with a small glass opening at the head position to see the face of the dead. Where did this tradition go? Did Bush swallow it?' (p. 139)

The fallen American soldiers flown back home are honoured with small wooden crosses planted in places such as the sandy beaches of Santa Monica as a way to memorialise the death and the sacrifice for the homeland, and some mothers entertain the hope that their fallen sons are still alive somewhere: 'Is this all that the soldiers deserve? Shaky crosses planted in the middle of the sand? . . . "I still think that my son Bachelor might be still alive somewhere and that he cannot reach me"' (p. 140).

Individual choices:

How does the Iraqi novel respond to the challenges and abuses of the politics of security enforced by the Americans and to the sectarian violence engulfing the country? What are the alternatives and the choices offered in the novels to navigate the complex labyrinth of life in a landscape filled with death? Is there a way to escape the violence?

Two different responses are formulated in two of the novels examined here: one responds to violence by engaging in the cycle of killing and the other by escaping the non-alternative of death or death. But neither response, as we will see in the analysis, is satisfying, and neither helps solve the dilemma in which Iraq finds itself. Ibrāhīm, a translator working with the Americans, ends a suicide bomber in the Green Zone; his answer to the violence and the abuse he suffers from both the Americans and the militias is to kill himself and to commit more killing. He becomes the private kind of warrior that proliferated in Iraq during the heyday of the occupation and continues to this day. His choice contrasts with that of the main character of *Baghdad Marlboro*, who rejects all violence and after two years in hiding from the sectarian war ends up leaving the country altogether and finding refuge in the United States after he falls in love with the widow of one of his friends. Neither response offers an adequate or humane solution to the problem of the proliferation of killing: either one stays in Iraq and is a potential *homo sacer* or one leaves the country.

The Making of a Suicide Bomber

In *The Green Zone*, Ibrāhīm might have felt satisfied with a translation job with the Americans and housing offered in the Green Zone. But the reality is far more complex because he feels bad that he is working with the occupiers of his country and abused when his work pushes him to become an informant. He feels imprisoned in the Green Zone, as if he is silently witnessing a crime from afar.

The most painful aspect about the translator's job for Ibrāhīm is that it puts him in the position of a negative spectator; he feels guilty, like a silent witness to a heinous murder, unable to stop it from taking place or to report it to anyone. He describes his predicament using the metaphor of the voyeur he feels he has become in the alienating space:

> Why did I put myself behind these high walls, peering like a spectator through a small hole? It is as if I was observing a crime take place in a closed room, like any coward voyeur. These feelings never left me, but they got worse with those concrete walls that were covered with traces of bullets and the graffiti of the rebels. (p. 51)

For Ibrāhīm, accepting the translator job means wearing a mask to be able to accomplish the tasks he has to do and to live in the Green Zone, where the colonel offers him accommodation. He painfully realises the meaning and the weight of this mask:

> Everyone is wearing a mask. He who doesn't wear one becomes easy prey for the militants or the resistance. But here they hate to use the latter expression. Instead, colleagues advise us to use the expression 'terrorists'. (p. 58)

The mask he is wearing is a double one. There is the real mask he has to wear to protect his identity when he is out on raids with the soldiers, and there is the figurative mask, which has a deeper effect on Ibrāhīm, taking over his real face, his moral features and his soul. When he looks at himself in the mirror, he does not recognise himself. The figurative mask has deeply altered his features:

> He couldn't believe his eyes. 'Oh my god, my face has completely changed' . . . He touched the mask that ate his entire face and devoured his features as if it wanted to hide it forever. The traitor had no face except for what others saw since the moment he shook hands with Colonel David and became one of the inhabitants of the Green Zone. 'Oh my god, I am fighting for America', realised Ibrāhīm, when he understood what his job with the Americans really meant. (p. 52)

Worse, he calls himself a 'double traitor' not because of lack of sincerity in doing his job, which Colonel David warns him against ('The lack of devotion in translation is like treason' (p. 53)), but because he is disloyal twice, first to his country and second to the work of translators in general: 'If translation in and by itself is an act of treachery, then I am a traitor twice' (p. 53).

In addition to wearing a real mask, the translator may need to have a different name in order to hide his or her identity to avoid being targeted by the militias. These Iraqi men and women working in the Green Zone need to have a working name – 'Mark, John, Jimmy, Roger, Rashīd, Kāmil and Viviane' (p. 57). Sometimes, if need be, the translators have to change names, identity cards, even the way they dress in order to escape death threats.

> Everyone who entered the Green Zone had to change his name and to pick a nickname because names are compromising; everybody wants to stay away from their real names, and everybody is wearing a mask to say I am the other, as if we were at a costume ball. (p. 44)

For example, Viviane, Ibrāhīm's co-worker and fiancée, hides her real identity behind two kinds of shields. First, she both wears a Muslim headscarf and has a Christian name to confuse the militias.

> Her real name is ᶜAlya and not Viviane . . . Viviane is some kind of mask that ᶜAlya is wearing for fear that people in the neighbourhood where she lives might find out about her job with the Americans . . . as if the headscarf and the pseudonym might give her another stretch of life. Who knows? Our lives are in the hands of the resistance or the terrorists or our own hands . . . Everyone is threatening everyone else, and nobody knows the strength of the other, but it is the number of guns, bombs and explosives that makes this or that militia strong. (p. 58)

But Ibrāhīm has no other name than his real name: *Ibrāhīm*. He refuses to have any other working name or another identity. Confused and torn between feelings of guilt and necessity, he is tortured; he becomes prey to contradictory thoughts. He has to provide for his family, but he feels like a traitor serving the occupier and helping him in his war by 'offering his country and his countrymen on a silver platter' (p. 52). In addition, he is overwhelmed with humiliation as on a daily basis he is subjected to a thorough security clearance before entering and exiting the Green Zone. The friendship between the translators and the marines does not interfere with their job, but for Ibrāhīm there is still a feeling of humiliation and bitterness when he sees the behaviour and the arrogance of these soldiers who

> never tire of searching us every time we cross the checkpoint . . . We used to wait for a hand sign, a word, or a nod from a soldier to get the permission to enter to a dear part of our city, which they locked and surrounded with gates and guards . . . Every time we crossed this checkpoint, Neil and his friends searched us from head to toe; and sometimes we didn't understand their reactions or didn't understand them at all. Neil would yell at us, asking for our IDs; he would examine the signature of Colonel David and rub our IDs against his butt to dust off our photos, saying: 'I don't want to see your ugly photos before lunch'; then he would throw them to us, and sometimes they would fall short of our hands, so we had to bend down in order to pick them from the ground, and he would affect a hypocritical smile, saying: 'We are friends, but orders are orders. (pp. 14–15)

Whether crossing into the Green Zone or into the Red Zone, Ibrāhīm can't hold his head high because on both sides stand electronic devices, soldiers, barracks, checkpoints, electronic gates by which he needs to be cleared so that he can either cross or evade the eyes of the resistance and militant factions. To escape the feelings of humiliation and of being a voyeur imprisoned in a room, peering at the crime taking place outside, Ibrāhīm resorts to alcohol. Naturally, he frequents the different bars and taverns of the Green Zone along with his Iraqi translator friends and with the American soldiers who have become his 'friends' – Neil, Jimmy and Batista. It is not only the translator who resorts to drinking to find some relief, but almost all the inhabitants of the Green Zone: 'If it weren't for this bar, we would have died long ago', says one of the American soldiers (p. 27). The translators also enjoyed hanging out in the bars of the Green Zone because they can't go back home:

> We used to spread ourselves throughout the seven bars of the Green Zone . . . Some friends preferred the sports bar, some the British bar and

> some the roof bar managed by General Electric or the marble dancing room, where only those working with the Americans had access. (p. 27)

The narrator insists on the presence of bars, taverns and alcohol in the Green Zone. We are told, for example, that this is where parties and happy hour take place every night and where contractors, deal makers, soldiers, marines and translators meet around alcohol. However, Ibrāhīm's drinking habits are not limited to the Green Zone; he sometimes goes to local bars to quench his thirst and drown his sadness and frustrations with cold beer, where the effect and the bad quality of this local beer mixed with Valium is even more sickening, adding to his frustration and his pain.

Caught between the American forces and the resistance, the Iraqi translator lives in the nightmare of a dilemma. Between the threats and the warnings from the militia and the resistance, the humiliation meted out by the Americans and the absence of protection outside the Green Zone, the translator is exposed and threatened. He can die at any time, and anyone can kill him without his murder being considered a homicide in the lawless space of occupied Iraq. This zero degree of protection makes the Iraqi linguist a perfect candidate as *homo sacer*. The militiamen play with the translators' nerves, Ibrāhīm says. 'They have put on their list nine thousand men to liquidate, a terrifying number if we add the families' (pp. 64–5).

> The translators who used to leave the Green Zone to go back to their homes were surrounded by danger because there were those who were watching them behind the walls. I was lucky that I was living here [in the Green Zone] despite the fact that it is a city without a heart and everything in it is artificial, calm on the outside but boiling inside like a volcano that might explode at any time. (p. 128)

First, there are the ominous warnings that become a familiar reality in Iraq to terrify and disarm those who are working with the occupier. Despite being a target, Ibrāhīm still uses the term *the resistance* to refer to these terrifying men of the militia and their threats:

> The warnings made it right to our homes. The men of the resistance used to play with our nerves, undermining our morale as they slew black dogs to scare those who help the occupation and threw the dogs' heads at their

> doors as a threat, leaving a leaflet that read: 'Next time it will be the head of your traitor instead of the dog'. Terror used to plant itself in our hearts like weed, killing any other good plant in the midst of the threats from the armed resistance and the 'terrorists', as they like us to call them here [in the Green Zone]. All of us were frightened when we saw black dogs at night transforming themselves into bad omens. (p. 64)

The Americans do not offer any protection outside the Green Zone to the local linguists working with them. Worse, they might even carelessly expose them sometimes: 'Inside the bases, they used to look at us as traitors or perhaps as terrorists. The administration looked at us as of less importance than the international translators' (p. 65).

The local translators' salaries are ten times lower than what an international translator earns, whether American citizen or a Green Card holder, who receives for the year no less than $140,000. And, according to Ibrāhīm, the international translators don't have to leave the Green Zone or to accompany the marines in raid operations. But we know from Zayna, the 'American granddaughter' and international translator working in the Green Zone, that she does have to accompany the marines in nightly raid operations.

> International linguists don't do anything except translating documents in the comfort of their offices, while our lives are exposed accompanying the marines and raiding dangerous neighborhoods. We even got to learn slang and insults from the different linguistic backgrounds of the Black, the Spanish, the Irish and the Asian American soldiers and words like 'asshole', 'mother fucker', 'fucking asshole' and 'shit' became familiar for us. (*The Green Zone*, p. 65)

In the face of the daily humiliating treatment, the suspicion surrounding them and the discrimination in terms of salaries, the local translators feel powerless when they have to take part in or witness the targeting of innocent Iraqis. The mask and the bullet-proof jacket cannot protect them from their feelings of powerlessness in the face of the random killing of innocent people in the streets or in their homes. As Ibrāhīm says,

> The anti-bullet jacket and the mask were necessary; without them, we couldn't take part in patrols and raids. I didn't understand why it was

> usually pedestrians who were the victims of the American soldiers; perhaps it was their silent walking that rendered their movements strange, like the movements of ghosts who had to be made to disappear with precise bullets. And that was their fate. In these situations I felt powerless because I couldn't intervene. As the captain used to say, these were military orders where I had no right to interfere because I am a simple linguist, but when they apply the law, they consider me a soldier. If an explosive device were to explode in my face on the road, I would suddenly be considered and treated like one of them: a soldier. I might die, but without the same rights, without rights altogether. The most that my family could claim would be my cadaver without any compensation because I am a local translator and I have no rights. During that moment, the gate of death is wide open for us and for all passers-by no matter who they are, as long as they are the enemies they look for in the streets. They enjoy and celebrate their bestiality and the fact that their patrol didn't go out in vain because they targeted a number of victims whom they register in their records as terrorists. (*The Green Zone*, p. 132)

Double standards are applied in that the translator remains a simple linguist-civilian when it comes to the law and its application, but, if he happens to die on duty, he is considered a soldier. With his in-between status, he dies without the same benefits or without any benefits. Murād, Ibrāhīm's friend who is also a linguist working for the Americans, is wounded along with a few marines; he loses one of his limbs in a raid operation. Whereas the wounded marines are sent to Germany and the United States to receive electronic limbs, Murād is sent to Amman to get a wooden limb, but the result is far from satisfying. Unemployed and mutilated forever, for Murād

> there was no guarantee for health benefits or any compensation in the work contract in its Arabic and English versions, unlike [for] the imported linguist, who in this case can obtain artificial electronic limbs in Germany or in the United States. (pp. 151–2)

Overwhelmed by feelings of discrimination and suicidal thoughts, Murād is left handicapped and able to provide for his family only through the fund-raising his friends organise for him. He wonders whether 'America deserved that he lost his leg for it' (p. 152).

For Ibrāhīm, such feelings and his failure in trying to free Viviane, who is kidnapped and then killed by militiamen after they are married, eventually lead him to his own act of war, which he commits from his privileged position as someone who has access to the Green Zone. He becomes determined to kill himself and others.

In the Manichean discourse underpinning the war and the occupation of Iraq and espoused by both sides, good and evil fight it out until good triumphs. This simple and narrow way of thinking is tempting and contagious for Ibrāhīm, who feels resentment regarding the dehumanising ways the marines treat the people. Driven by this Manichean division, the idea of exploding these soldiers crosses Ibrāhīm's mind from the time he accepts the job as translator, but he gives it a wait; he tries to get to know and develop a friendship with the marines, given that they are already facing many challenges outside the Green Zone:

> When I saw their ways of dealing with the people entering and exiting the Green Zone, I thought of blowing them up, these evil bastards. In their own world, there is only good and evil, a stupid and disgusting division of things, as if they were blinded and lost the sense of all other colours except for black and white. Their miserable sight carrying tens of kilograms of military heavy equipment made me wait before moving ahead with my idea to turn them into flying dust; there were already other people hunting them outside this place. (p. 17)

Ibrāhīm's intention to kill Americans matures throughout the novel, however, and peaks with the growing pressures he faces from Colonel David and the militia who kidnap Viviane. The novel frames Ibrāhīm's act in folkloric and mythological terms that escape a rational explanation and prepare the reader to understand his action and empathise with him in his predicament. It is in his ancestral village and its folklore that Ibrāhīm finds his inspiration. His natal village, Tal al-Yāqūt, situated in the province of Nāṣiriyya, is where millennial history meets the myth and the imagination and where ancestral heritage and culture meet folkloric practices. In the novel, Tal al-Yāqūt perhaps stands for what is known today as Tal al-Muqayyar, a region located in the heartland of Mesopotamian civilisation and where the patron deity of the ancient city of Ūr, Nana, was adorned in the shrine of the Ziggurāt. In the novel, it is in this chosen site that the insurgency against the occupation is the strongest. When the colonel rebukes Ibrāhīm for this connection as if he had a share in the attacks, he is asked to spy on his own people, but he cannot do that: 'The people of your village have the highest record in targeting and killing Americans . . . You have to realise, Ibrāhīm, that your people are responsible for the deaths of tens of American soldiers' (pp. 172–3). Although the colonel doesn't know what to do with Ibrāhīm, whether to keep him as a translator or to dismiss him from his job, he warns him and remains convinced that all those who live outside the Green Zone are terrorists. On a visit back to his village, which he had left many years ago, but now hoping to reach a deal with Viviane's kidnappers, Ibrāhīm is welcomed by the people of the village with a peculiar festivity drawn from traditional folklore: the Zīrān dance.

It is in the inspiring moment of the dance that Ibrāhīm finds not only motivation and determination but also ecstatic feelings. This traditional and folkloric dance is quite widespread in many places in the Middle East, such as Saudi Arabia, Morocco, Tunisia and Iraq. It is performed barefoot on fire and burning coal, the sound and rhythm of the drums slowly taking the performer into a state of trance so that he is not burned. He repeats words such as 'Allah is Truth' until he loses consciousness and reaches an ecstatic condition of purification and liberation from his body, or sometimes until he is liberated from a jinni who presumably has possessed him. But what is new in Nūrī's use of the dance is that with the occupation the villagers of Tal al-Yāqūt turn it into an instrument of galvanisation and encouragement to inflame the people and to rise against the invaders and push them out. The evil jinni is the occupier that they want to exorcise from the country to purify its soul. The dance is elevated into an imaginary of freedom and liberation. Ibrāhīm wonders:

> Is it possible that the people of his village turned into human beings walking on fire at night in order to plant explosive devices on the roads at dawn? The American occupation made them recycle these dance gatherings, which they had forgotten about until the invasion, and now American

> patrols called them 'the Red Feet'. The rule was that if someone walked on fire at night, he would perform a suicide attack at dawn. Everything changed in the dance, and the jinni had no place in it any more. They transcended reality and exploded their bodies without feeling anything. They united with fire and purified their bodies and minds . . . The Zīrān dance became a way to train the soul to get ready for the adventure, make a foray and cross into death through incantations, prayers, dance and purifying fire. (pp. 187–8)

Welcomed by a Zīrān dance party on the night of his arrival at his ancestral village, Ibrāhīm is fascinated by the fire and captivated by the dance and the performers' defiance.

> So is this how they welcome me, with the dance on coal? I asked one of the attendants sitting next to me, and he whispered into my ear: 'Every time our men dance this means that they are considering a great action' . . . One of the villagers whispered to me: 'Do you want to walk barefoot on fire?' and this meant that I would pledge to perpetrate a suicide attack at dawn and get ready for that. (pp. 186–7)

Earlier Ibrāhīm had made a deal with the militia who kidnapped Viviane. He was supposed to facilitate the entrance of a suicide bomber into the Green Zone, at which point Viviane would be freed. But after being convinced that the militias were playing him and that Viviane was left to die from hunger and thirst to punish her for working with the Americans, he decides to take matters into his own hands by transposing the Zīrān dance from one space to another, from his village Tal al-Yāqūt to the tango ballroom in the heart of the Green Zone, where he will mix tango with Zīrān in an act of transgression and blow himself up. Ibrāhīm, who has nothing more to lose and feels he must stand up for his dignity, conceives of this act as vengeance and a sacrifice for all those who have died, all the victims, whether they are innocent Iraqis or innocent Americans. It is for all the victims that Ibrāhīm in the Green Zone – named after the prophet Ibrāhīm (Abraham), who was ready to sacrifice his son according to God's commandment – claims his action:

> This time, for the sake of Viviane, I decided to bury my cowardice forever. I will not go to the ballroom shaking and empty-handed like any rat. I will

> shed my humiliation for once, hold my head high and avenge all the victims: Murād and Richard, who lost their limbs; Bachelor, who died from a splinter; and Viviane and all the corpses piled up at the central morgue. (p. 200)

Ibrāhīm's act is also the last chance for him to recover his dignity and to cleanse himself of the impurity that clings to him because of his job. This is how he urges himself right before he goes to the tango party: 'Don't forget that the exam of dignity passes by here, from the Green Zone, *so make it red* with your own blood so that it may become green again for others' (p. 202, emphasis added).

When he is ready to act, though, he gets confused. In his head, tango music gets mixed up with the sound of the drums. He suddenly discovers the depth and the strength of his dark side: 'That I possess a basis and a ferment that enables me *to be the greatest terrorist in the world*' (p. 203, emphasis added).

But what is a terrorist? wonders Ibrāhīm in all his lucidity. Trying to define a terrorist, he makes the analogy to the condition of being a homeless because, for him, just as nobody is homeless in essence, nobody is born a terrorist but rather *made* into one when

> Americans kill the father of a son in front of his eyes or rape a girl before her father's eyes or smash the head of an old man or put an innocent in a steel container until he dies and kill innocent pedestrians and accuse them of being terrorists . . . They make the terrorists in their labs. (p. 203)

Ibrāhīm's suicide is not framed in the vocabulary of martyrdom and jihād. There is no trace in the novel of the vocabulary of Islamic militancy. Nevertheless, his suicide does have a sacrificial dimension in that Ibrāhīm considers that he is avenging all the innocent people who have died during the occupation and all the bodies he has seen piled up in the morgue of Baghdad.

It is not an Islamist motivation that pushes Ibrāhīm to his final act. He is a secular-minded linguist who loves literature and the English language, drinks alcohol and goes to dancing parties. It is obvious that he does not fit the stereotype of the suicide bomber we see in the news and or on Internet videos. Ibrāhīm belongs to a different category of suicide fighter that disturbs old patterns because his religious subjectivity is the biggest blank in the portrait drawn of his character throughout the novel. Rather, the novel focuses on Ibrāhīm's growing political subjectivity until his act materialises in the attack. His politics is absolutely secular: we do not know anything about his religious and ethnic affiliations, whether he is Sunni or Shi^{c}a or whether he is a Kurd or an Arab. The author purposely keeps these facts outside of the reader's reach because he doesn't see in them any relevance to the situation in which Ibrāhīm finds himself. In addition to Ibrāhīm's secular politics, Nūri insists on portraying his character time and again in bars, where he often takes refuge after work – in this way stressing the facts of his non-religiosity and secular orientation. Ibrāhīm never attends mosque or speaks of Islamic militancy. This forces us to eliminate the Islamic or religious motivation as a justification for his act and to look at his suicide as devoid of any metaphysical consideration. Although conceptualising his act as vengeance for those who have died wrongfully, Ibrāhīm is not sacrificing himself for his country. He is acting alone, unconnected to any terrorist organisation or militia group. His suicide operation cannot be identified as 'religious terrorism', as this type of act is often described and analysed in the media.

If Ibrāhīm's act is empty of any religious dimension, does he thus embody another example of the *homo sacer*? We saw how he is captive in a zone where he is considered a traitor and a potential terrorist and where he might be killed by the militias, and at the same time he has no expectation of protection by the Americans. The life of this Iraqi translator is subject to death threats from both the inside and the outside. His death is almost decreed, and so he feels like the living dead man, in between two worlds where he is neither fully living nor fully one of the deceased: 'He was no longer able to distinguish between life and death' (p. 202). In these circumstances, where no protection is afforded him as someone working for the Americans, Ibrāhīm falls into the category of the man who can be killed but not sacrificed – the *homo sacer*. Instead of being subject to this fate, however, Ibrāhīm claims back his agency as an individual and as a political human being by acting on his own life. He prefers to kill himself in sacrifice for all the war victims rather than being killed by any militia. The sacrificial dimension of his act redeems his death and his terror act. By acting on his life, he recaptures his sovereignty over his own fate and body, seizing back the responsibility for his own life and death from both the Americans and the Islamist militias as well as from the resistance groups who represent no less of a threat to his life. The sacrificial dimension of his act saves him from being a *homo sacer* by dedicating his action to all those who died wrongfully in the war and occupation.

In the case of Islamic militancy, suicide operations are claimed as martyrdom, and the suicide bomber is called a martyr. May Jayyusi analyses the category of the martyr as the exact opposite of Agamben's *homo sacer*:

> If *homo sacer* is he who can be killed and not sacrificed, then the martyr inverses this relation to sovereignty, transforming himself into he who can be sacrificed and not killed. Many testaments of martyrs are signed with the words 'the living martyr'[,] 'ash-shahīd al-ḥayy'. They can be sacrificed but not killed, the Koranic verse 'Do not count those who are martyred for the sake of God dead but alive with their lord' is the signature of every bayān.[20]

Ibrāhīm's act has no signature, and he leaves no testament except that in his act he wants to avenge Viviane, his wife, his friends who died or lost limbs and all those who have ended up in the morgue in this occupational war. If, according to Agamben, *homo sacer* is 'life that may be killed but not sacrificed',[21] and if the martyr, according to Jayyusi, is 'he who can be sacrificed and not killed', Ibrāhīm's act makes him he who can be killed *and* sacrificed. His sacrifice redeems him, just as the martyr is redeemed by his faith and his belief, but with the difference that Ibrāhīm does not claim to do his act with the expectation of any metaphysical rewards or of being still alive with his lord. His act is truly devoid of any metaphysical connotations.

With Ibrāhīm's destructive act, the marble ballroom is turned into dust. It is not just the life of the suicide bomber that is destroyed but also the lives of all the guests of the tango party – 'ministers, presidents, generals, officers, businessmen and advisers, and also leaders of the Iraqi Ṣaḥwa [awareness groups]' (p. 199). They, too, can be said to have become 'bare life'. Ibrāhīm's terror act transgresses the order and the security inside the Green Zone, and it defies all the walls and all the gates and blurs the frontier drawn between the inside and the outside, bringing the fate of the *homo sacer* to the heart of the Abode of Peace. All those who die at the tango party embody the condition of the *homo sacer*; they become bare lives with Ibrāhīm's act.

Here the novel emphasises the idea of the end of the city as a safe social space, and the end of the wall as a protective device. From an enclave of law and order and a haven of safety and peace, the Green Zone becomes red, a locus of the materialisation of the state of exception and a zone of indistinction, an ambiguous zone of order and transgression, law and lawlessness, safety and danger.

Ibrāhīm's case is similar to the cases brought to light confirming the data showing that there is little connection, if any, between suicide-bombing operations and Islamic fundamentalism. As the study by Robert Pape shows, out of the 188 cases of suicide operations perpetrated from 1980 to 2000, the Tamil Tigers, a Marxist–Leninist group that is adamantly opposed to religion, were the leading instigators of suicide attacks.[22] Ibrāhīm's act may then be analysed within the framework of recent research suggesting that suicide operations are in fact an expression of 'the political culture of death that has emerged in modern times in the Middle East',[23] an idea put forward by the political scientist Bruno Etienne, who places suicide operations in the Middle East and North Africa in their context of long histories of violence, whether colonial violence or the brutality of violent dictatorial regimes. In this context, it is possible to look at Ibrāhīm's act as the cumulative effect of the violence he has been subjected to as an Iraqi who has lived under the dictatorship of Saddam Hussein and its successive wars, and who has witnessed first-hand the violence, the contempt and the humiliation of an occupational war with its walls, checkpoints, abuse and disregard for human rights. And this is what Ibrāhīm himself refers to as being the 'basis' and the 'ferment' that has prepared and pushed him not just to be a terrorist but, in his own words, to be 'the greatest terrorist in the world' (p. 203).

Full Circle

> You have a week to make up your mind and take a decision. Remember we are at war. It is either you kill the enemy or you be killed.
>
> Najm Wālī, *Baghdad Marlboro*

> We are in hell, and all that is left to us is to help those who do not make it worse.
>
> Najm Wālī, *Baghdad Marlboro*

What happens to the unnamed narrator of *Baghdad Marlboro* is very surreal and Kafkaesque, as he himself puts it many times throughout the narration. This comparison is not fortuitous because what is really taking place, according to the narrator, surpasses in its strangeness and luridness any fictional reality.

> Who could have imagined that my house could become a fictional place; for sure if Kafka were still alive, he would have been jealous of me . . . If this story didn't happen to me, nobody would have believed it; he would have thought it to be a creative fiction of a novelist who wanted to imitate Kafka, no more and no less than that. (p. 251)

A well-to-do businessman in Baghdad who has just lost his wife in a bombing finds himself one day, out of the blue, entangled with militiamen in the kidnapping of an American hostage. The American Daniel Brooks comes from the United States to visit the narrator in his home in Baghdad and hands him something with the narrator's name on it that he had found in the desert during the Gulf War and had kept for more than ten years. Daniel Brooks has also come with sums of money for the families of the victims he had killed in the war. He is spotted by a militiaman right away, though, and kidnapped. His abductors are easily able to kill him after they take his money, but they instead want the narrator to do the killing so that he can clear himself of the dishonour of having dealings with an American, or they will kill him. The militiamen give him this ultimatum and invade his house to force him to act. Thus pushed out of his house, the narrator has nowhere to go because many would just blame him for not simply accepting the task of killing an American. He leaves town in order to escape the vicious circle of killing. 'All that I thought of was to leave as quickly as possible so that nobody could force me to kill' (p. 248).

> For more than two years I moved from town to town, from one place to another and from one job to another. I didn't know what to do or whom to turn to. The country was sliding into chaos. Chaos became a daily routine. There was no police, no army, only the militias who invaded the streets of the city every day a little bit more. Should I go to the Americans and tell them that my house has been invaded and that there is an American

> hostage? . . . Would they believe me? Would they believe that their citizen is captive number 150 among those kidnapped by the militias during the past twelve months? Or would they think I was playing them and throw me in one of their prisons, like Camp Cropper, their fancy prison near the airport, if not Abū Ghraib? (p. 247)

On the run for more than two years, having to change jobs every time he changes towns, restless and without peace, this character strangely reminds us of the figure of the war deserter who escapes the war front so that he doesn't have to kill. This is how the narrator thinks of himself as being 'like a war deserter; I didn't want to go to the front so that I wouldn't have to choose between killing or getting killed' (p. 247).

The war deserter is a figure associated with the Iran–Iraq War under the Baᶜath and the dictatorship of Saddam Hussein, as we saw in Chapter 1. But why does a man in flight in occupied Iraq compare himself to a figure who belongs to the past and who is supposed to have been buried forever with the fall of the regime that created it? Why is the memory of the war deserter still vivid in the mind of the Iraqi person twenty years after that war? Does this mean that the situation in which Iraq finds itself today is no different from its situation in the years of the Iran–Iraq War, with its coercion, abuse and disregard for human life? For the Iraqi individual, in the midst of the sectarian war and the chaos engulfing the country, the situation has not changed from the days when one deserted to avoid killing. In this regard, the narrator is just like ᶜĪsā, Khiḍr and all the war deserters who either end up captives or find death or, if lucky, are able to find refuge in another country. In ᶜAli Badr's *The Professors of Illusion*, ᶜĪsā lives in hiding in Baghdad, then he is killed; in Naṣīf Falak's *Khiḍr Qad and the Drab Olive Years*, Khiḍr leaves town and becomes captive in Iran before he finds death in the 1991 uprising. Miraculously, the deserter in Muḥammad Ḥasan's *The Descent of the Angels* leaves the country after years in hiding inside Baghdad and finds refuge in Europe. In the occupied Baghdad of *Baghdad Marlboro*, the narrator seems to follow in the footsteps of these war deserters, reenacting the same pattern, as if nothing has changed. The dictatorship has fallen, but the choices offered in the present are no different from the choices presented in the past. In *Baghdad Marlboro*, the past and the present come full circle, offering the new–old alternative of to kill or be killed irrespective of any superficial change in circumstances. It is this fatality that a taxi driver, an average citizen with whom the narrator discusses the situation in Baghdad, underscores. '"The bottom line, sir,"' says the taxi driver to the narrator,

> 'this defenceless citizen – like me or like you, who is armed only with a strong desire for life, who hasn't secured himself in the Green Zone like the politicians of this country, for whom high concrete walls built around their houses block off even the air – this citizen who goes out every day looking for his bread and the bread of his kids, he has to accept his fate and the fatality of a death prepared for him by this "obscure" enemy' . . . 'Death in Baghdad,' continued the driver, 'might strike at your doorstep, in the street, at the bus station or before boarding a taxi, on the highway or in a checkpoint, before entering your workplace or when exiting, in al-Karkh neighborhood or in al-Ruṣāfa. We sleep and wake up with the muzzle of a gun directed at our temples'. (pp. 310–11)

In the sectarian war, the defenceless Iraqi citizen ends up as bare life in the new Iraq, with only a desire for life but without any protection or rights. He is abandoned to death and can be killed by anyone, any time, anywhere. Mark Danner points to this vulnerability in his essay 'Iraq: The War of the Imagination':

> As Iraqis do their shopping or say their prayers they are blown to pieces by suicide bombers. As they drive through the cities in broad daylight they are pulled from their cars by armed men at roadblocks who behead them or shoot them in the back of their neck. As they sit at home at night they are kidnapped by men in police or army uniform who load them in the trunks of their cars and carry them off to secret places to be tortured and executed, their bound and headless bodies to be found during the following days in fields or dumps or by the roadside.[24]

After being away from his home and from Baghdad for more than two years, the narrator hears of the death of Daniel Brooks and decides to return home and confront the militiamen who invaded and took possession of it. He buys a weapon, as all Iraqis have done, but every day he surprises himself by postponing the confrontation. He is close to committing suicide because of his indecision and his lack of determination when he finally gives up everything, the house, life in Baghdad and the killing that it entails to be there. He decides to leave the country after he discovers he is in love with the widow of his friend.

The Iraqi deserter in the 'new Iraq' rejects violence and chooses to leave the country as the only way out of the spiral of killing in the sectarian war and the war on terror, as if to suggest that the new Iraq after the American occupation is no place for life and no place for safety and peace and that the only way for Iraqis to live in peace today is to leave their country. Here we come face to face with Iraqis' only alternatives: either they become suicide bombers, killing themselves and others, or they reject killing and desert not just a war but the country. Is it possible for the Iraqi subject to live and remain in Iraq without having to kill or to be killed?

Neither *The Green Zone* nor *Baghdad Marlboro* is able to answer this simple question positively in the war-loaded landscape of the new Iraq.

Conclusion

Using different fictional representations to portray the experiences of the occupation and the sectarian war, this chapter about 'bare life' in the 'new Iraq' shows two men trying to navigate existential tortuous paths amid terror, kidnapping and death threats. Feeling besieged, these characters try to recover their freedom and their agency by choosing two antagonistic routes. Both become bare life and embody the fate of the *homo sacer*, who can be killed by anyone without his killing becoming a murder. Feeling abused, Ibrāhīm of *The Green Zone* choses to kill himself in a suicide operation. The narrator of *Baghdad Marlboro* becomes like a war deserter, fleeing Iraq and thus re-enacting a strategy (desertion) of the past. The past and the present are equally dehumanising, and the only choices left in these situations of abuse during war and occupation are narrowed down to desertion and suicide bombing. With these choices, is it possible for the present in Iraq to see a future less frightening than the awful past?

Notes

1. Zygmunt Bauman, *Society under Siege* (Cambridge: Polity Press, 2002), p. 88.
2. Shākir Nūri, *al-Minṭaqa al-Khaḍrā*ʾ (The Green Zone) (Dubai: Thaqāfa li al-nashr wa al-tawzīᶜ, 2009), p. 71. Page references are given parenthetically in the text from this point; my translations throughout.

3. Jost Trier, quoted in Bulent Diken and Carsten Bagge Lausten 'The Camp', *Geografiska Annaler, Series B, Human Geography*, 88, 4, 2006, p. 444.
4. Carl Schmitt, *Nomos of the Earth in The International Law of Jus Publicum Europaeum* (New York: Telos Press, 2003).
5. Bauman, *Society under Siege*, p. 88.
6. Rajiv Chandrasekaran, *Imperial Life in the Emerald City: Inside Iraq's Green Zone* (New York: Vintage, 2006), p. 14.
7. Quoted in Giorgio Agamben, *Homo Sacer: Sovereign Power and Bare Life*, trans. Daniel Heller-Roazen (Stanford, CA: Stanford University Press, 1998), p. 36.
8. Frantz Fanon, *The Wretched of the Earth* (New York: Grove Press, 1963), p. 32.
9. Najm Wālī, *Baghdad mālbūrū* (Baghdad Marlboro) (Beirut: al-Muʾassasa al-ʿarabiyya li-al-dirāsāt wa al-nashr, 2012), p. 257, my translation.
10. Bulent Diken and Carsten Bagge Lausten 'The Camp', *Geografiska Annaler, Series B, Human Geography*, 88, 4, 2006, p. 445.
11. Ibid.
12. Quoted in Derek Gregory, *The Colonial Present: Afghanistan, Palestine, Iraq* (Malden, MA: Blackwell, 2004), p. 217.
13. Ibid., p. 220.
14. Frantz Fanon, *Black Skin, White Masks* (New York: Grove Press, 1967).
15. Quoted in ibid., p. 71.
16. Jāsim al-Raṣīf, *Ruʾūs al-ḥurriya al-mukayyasa* (The freedom of the bagged heads) (Beirut: al- Muʾassasa al-ʿarabiyya li dirāsāt wa al-nashr, 2007).
17. Wālī, *Baghdad Marlboro*, p. 234. Page references are given parenthetically in the text from this point; my translations throughout.
18. Gregory, *The Colonial Present*, p. 237.
19. Inaʿām Kachāchī, *al-Ḥafida al-Amrīkiyya* (Beirut: Dar al-Jadīd, 2009), translated by Nariman Youssef as *The American Granddaughter* (Doha, Qatar: Bloomsbury Qatar Foundation, 2012).
20. Quoted in Talal Asad, *On Suicide Bombing* (New York: Columbia University Press, 2007), p. 48.
21. Agamben, *Homo Sacer*, p. 83.
22. Cited in Asad, *On Suicide Bombing*, p. 54.
23. Bruno Etienne, *Les combattants suicidaires*, cited in ibid., p. 50.
24. Mark Danner, 'Iraq: The War of the Imagination', *New York Review of Books*, 21 December 2006, p. 84.

4

Bare Life in the Camp

Through the novels *The Green Zone* and *Baghdad Marlboro*, Chapter 3 gave us a fuller and more complex picture of the widespread violence and the extent of the abuse Iraqis have suffered in the politics of security enforced by the American occupation and in a sectarian war where people can be raided, arrested, kidnapped and taken to secret locations to be tortured and killed – all at random. In Ibrāhīm's suicide operation in the heart of the Green Zone, we saw how walls no longer protect and how the safe haven of the Green Zone itself is also threatened by the same logic of terror that has replaced the city as a social space, according to Giorgio Agamben's analysis. Agamben finds in this logic that extends terror to all citizens the paradigm or 'the structuring principle of the camp as the hidden matrix and *nomos* of the political space in which we are still living'.[1] For Agamben, the camp is not only and necessarily, as its name may indicate, a carceral place where people can be interned and abused; it is also a principle that extends terror, abuse and torture to all citizens. In that sense, we can say that in Chapter 3 we saw the spread of the idea of the camp not only to the whole of the vulnerable portions of the Iraqi population in the unprotected zones but also to the Green Zone itself with transgressive acts such as Ibrāhīm's bringing the fate of the killable, the *homo sacer*, to the very heart of previously deemed safe enclaves.

Where in Chapter 2 we saw a manifestation of the camp in the Killing Box and the extermination of the retreating troops, in this chapter, through the examination and discussion of Shākir Nūrī's novel *Majānīn Būkā* (The madmen of Camp Bucca), published in 2012, we see another dimension of the war on terror: the camp, not only as a virtual camp or as principle and 'a hidden matrix' shaping the political space where Iraqi people live but as a dreadful *reality* that literally materialises in the Iraqi desert under the

American occupation. The camp in this chapter is a *real* detention facility hidden in the depth of the desert and shrouded with secrecy and where 'the most absolute *conditio inhumana*'[2] that has ever existed is again realised in a re-enactment of previous colonial camps. During the occupation, many of the Iraqis whose homes were raided and who were arrested were transferred to secret locations for indefinite periods of detention, without being entitled to a trial and without a formal accusation or indictment. Those who were captured as prisoners of war in the early phase of the invasion of Iraq also ended up in detention camps without even being entitled to their legal status as prisoners of war under the Geneva Conventions. Many were kept captive in the infamous Abū Ghraib prison, but after the scandal that erupted regarding this prison and after its closure the detainees held there were transferred to the newly built detention camps in the Iraqi desert, which did not capture as much media attention as Abū Ghraib or Guantánamo Bay. For years, war prisoners in Iraq, suspected terrorists, other militants of the insurgency and in general whoever was suspected of being active against the occupation forces were secretly detained in desert camps, but the media attention was suddenly diffused after the Abū Ghraib scandal.

Based on the testimonies of camp survivors, Shākir Nūrī's novel *The Madmen of Camp Bucca* is one of the first and rare texts to reveal and address the dreadful reality of secret detention camps built by the American forces in the Iraqi desert after the invasion of Iraq. The novel exposes the vengeful logic underpinning the war on terror and the war on Iraq and reveals the lawlessness of these spaces of exception by showing how the detainees' bodily lives were *made* vulnerable to injury, torture and abuse and how the captives could be and, in many instances, were killed with impunity by their American captors or even by fellow detainees who had been empowered by the Americans. In this novel, the camp is shown as the site or the machine of 'bare life'. While the novel exposes the illegality of these camps, at the same time it points to the absurdity and viciousness of the carceral techniques and the organisation of the camp, denouncing the links connecting the events of 11 September 2001 (9/11), the Iraq War and the war on terror.

The narrator of the novel is one of the camp survivors. He writes a memoir about the years he spent there and is contacted by an American film crew who want to buy the memoir from him to make it a movie about the camp. A former war reporter who served in the 2003 war, the unnamed narrator was captured in the desert by the American forces during the invasion along with members of the unit he was accompanying; they all ended in the camp, finally face to face for the first time with an enemy that for years had remained for them invisible and ghostly.

> This is how the war went: the enemy was showering us with his bombs and fires from the sky and we did not find any cover or refuge from him . . . Then the image changed: the ghosts of the enemy took the form of soldiers moving before our eyes for the first time. At once we felt happy and sad: happy because finally after so many years we discovered these enemies and sad because we did not possess the right weapons to fight them.[3]

The narrator is not the only detainee who wrote a memoir in order to document the existence of a disposable camp of tents and barracks established in a remote, hidden location on the moving sands of the desert; along with him, there were other enlightened and wise men, writers and poets – in particular his friend Nūḥ/Noah, 'the oldest prisoner of Iraq', and the writer and poet Muzhir. Together they share the burden and the necessity of counteracting the action and the erasure of time and space by recording in their hearts and minds many stories of what happened to them – and especially to the detainees who died during the seven years they spent inside the camp.

9/11 and Iraq: A Vengeful Logic

> 'O Bucca, you the twin of Guantánamo! Who can erase these two words from our heads?' . . . this is what the detainees whispered every time they walked by the barbed wire.
>
> Shākir Nūrī, *The Madmen of Camp Bucca*

The title of *The Madmen of Camp Bucca* invokes a reference to a place beyond the frontiers of Iraq, connecting the reality of the prison camp, the war and the occupation of Iraq to the attacks on the World Trade Center and the Pentagon on 9/11. In the novel, when the first group of prisoners is taken to the desert, they do not know where they have ended up. 'Bucca, Bucca!', one of the American guards shouts at them. But the prisoners are perplexed and do not understand what that means. The guard then shouts with a more reassuring tone, 'Um Qaṣr, Um Qaṣr', and then, 'Bucca, Um Qaṣr, Basra', thus inserting the name 'Bucca' into a more familiar topology by giving the prisoners the exact name and location of the place where they have ended up. But the prisoners are more perplexed after one of them explains that 'Bucca' was a fire marshal who died on duty on the day of the attacks on the World Trade Center. This explanation only fuels the captives' confusion: How did the name of a 9/11 victim become the name of a prison camp in a remote corner of the Iraqi desert, not too far from the port of Um Qaṣr in the millennial city Basra? Where is the missing link in this equation?

> 'Bucca' made us more and more anxious and nervous. We wondered why they forced this name here. It is a name bearing the sign of vengeance and revenge, recalling the events of 9/11 and making the soldiers only more violent toward us. What is our fault? As for this city [Basra] it is the place of wonders, the adventures of Sindbād, the city of literature, language, and the *Rain Song*, dates and the confluence of the two rivers. (p. 33)

Supposed to honour the memory of the firefighter, the prison camp's name does not make sense to the prisoners. To them, naming the camp after a brave firefighter who died on duty is an insult to his memory and a crime against his bravery:

> The name Bucca falls on their ears like a strange name, piercing their memory with a knife, cutting their veins and . . . their blood. Oh you, the firefighter whom America committed a crime against, you sacrificed your life to save innocent Americans; America did nothing more than humiliate you by naming after you the worst prison ever in the history of humanity, a prison where the eyes of the prisoners are gouged with plastic bullets. Oh my God, does this man deserve to be insulted every day while his soul still hovers above the place of the crime? And to make matters worse, America invited the daughter of this man to visit the camp and to bless this quagmire that bears the name of her father. (p. 295)

The link connecting the war in Iraq to the events of 9/11 and the war on terror imposes itself on the detainees and the reader as a shocking connection pitting against each other Baghdad, 9/11 and Kabul – the war in Iraq, the war in Afghanistan and the global war on terror – to form a complex relation that explains the presence of the camp in Iraq and its name after a New York fire marshal. Indeed, many scholars have drawn parallels between the war in Iraq and the war in Afghanistan in the way that both wars can be traced back to the events of 9/11,[4] and the connection was fairly clear at the time of the invasion. According to Andrew Hill, to reduce the invasion of Iraq to a simple response to the 11 September attacks would be an oversimplification, but the terms by which the attacks contributed to the invasion of Iraq are worth pursuing: there was the desire to erase the disgrace of the attacks, which called for something more than the assault on Afghanistan.[5] In this context, Hill cites Henry Kissinger in an interview in Bob Woodward's *State of Denial* (2006), noting that Kissinger was a key White House adviser in the run-up to the Iraq War. Asked why he had supported the Iraq War, Kissinger replied:

> 'Because Afghanistan wasn't enough' . . . In the conflict with radical Islam, he said they want to humiliate us. 'And we need to humiliate them'. The American response to 9/11 had essentially to be more than proportionate – on a larger scale than simply invading Afghanistan and overthrowing the Taliban. Something else was essential. The Iraq War was essential to send a larger message, 'in order to make the point that we are not going to live in the world that they want for us'.[6]

Behind the naming of the camp after one of the victims of 9/11 is clearly the logic of revenge, according to the narrator:

> Every time the guards look at the banner with the name 'Bucca' on it, they show their teeth and become even more violent towards us, as if we had exploded the World Trade Center. Cursed is New York who is sending us such people. (p. 36)

And this is exactly what Alain Badiou underscores in his analysis of the war in Iraq when he declares, 'The invasion of Iraq was born out of a culture of vengeance'.[7] But what made Iraq enter into the calculus of the Bush administration's military strategy and become the theatre of operation and the target that could assuage anger and vengeance in the war on terror is a double factor: a history of hostility with Iraq coupled with the fact that Iraq was perceived as a more defined (that is locatable) enemy than the terrorists spread throughout the world. Indeed, scholars have argued that, after the assault on Afghanistan failed to produce its intended outcome when Osama Bin Laden and much of the al-Qaeda leadership remained on the loose, the Bush administration turned to what was perceived as a more straightforward target to assuage its anger and vengeance. In this regard, the long history of hostility between Bush and Saddam Hussein made Iraq the best candidate for that. It was, in the words of David Simpson, 'a simple space– time location at which to claim to fight the war against terror'.[8] This idea is echoed in a statement by Jeremy Black: 'In 2003 the USA focused on Iraq – a definite and defiant target with regular armed forces – rather than on the more intangible struggle with terrorism, which challenged Western conventions of war-making'.[9] Statements putting forward the connections between 9/11 and Iraq were made not later, after the failure of the first phase in the war on Afghanistan, but already only a few days after the attacks of 9/11, as in a letter signed by forty-one neoconservatives and sent to President Bush:

> It may be that the Iraqi government provided assistance in some form to the recent attack on the United States. But even if evidence does not link Iraq directly to the attacks, any strategy aiming at the eradication of terrorism and its sponsors must include a determined effort to remove Saddam Hussein from power in Iraq. Failure to undertake such an effort will constitute an early and perhaps decisive surrender in the war on international terrorism.[10]

This is how 9/11, the war on terror and the war on Iraq were tied together in the Bush administration's strategy. Despite the fact that Iraq seemed to represent a suitable opponent for the United States in its war on terror even before the invasion, things quickly shifted after the invasion with the emergence of the insurgency on the ground and the chaos and terror that engulfed the country, taking the United States yet again back to dealing with a diffuse and ghostly enemy capable of expanding and multiplying, a situation typical of the war on terror and highly different from the conceptions of the enemy of previous wars – for example, the Second World War. One way of dealing with this spectral enemy was to capture suspects and jail them, a programme that the CIA had already started in the 1990s and that intensified after the 9/11 attacks. This programme, which, according to Andrew Hill, was called 'the extraordinary-rendition program', involved 'the snatching of suspects from numerous countries and their transportation either to US-run facilities outside the United States (notably Afghanistan) or their turning them over to foreign security services for detention and interrogation' as a means of circumventing US law on the detention of suspects.[11] It is perhaps to this tradition of extraordinary-rendition programmes and the capturing of suspects to detain them in hotel rooms, warehouses, trucks and aircraft that we can trace the recent and more visible trends of jailing suspect terrorists in the war on terror and in the establishing of detention facilities such as Camp X-Ray and Camp Delta in Guantánamo Bay, Camp Falcon, Camp Cropper near Baghdad airport and Camp Bucca at Um Qaṣr near Basra.

Andrew Hill argues in his book *Re-imagining the War on Terror* that the proliferation of these camps and detention facilities during the prosecution of the Iraq War and the war on terror is

> suggestive of the desire to fix the enemy in place . . . of an acting out derived from the frustration at the inability to identify the enemy – in general – in the War on Terror with a distinct locale or territory . . . This fixing of the enemy in place at the same time suggests a parallel desire to render the enemy permanently visible.[12]

With the establishment of the camp, from volatile and ghostly the enemy is made visible with a corporeal form. He is 'despectralised' and transformed from an indeterminate and unlocatable ghost into a tangible, material, fleshy being who can be held in jail, made to experience pain and killed if necessary.[13]

Shākir Nūrī's novel shows not only how the 'enemy' was created and made visible but also how this was done in a new edition of earlier versions of the camp. This is why in the novel the detainees invoke Camp Bucca as the twin of the Guantánamo Bay prison and make associations between the names 'Bucca' and 'Cuba' as similar and shameful places: 'Bucca, Cuba, two words carrying the same letters and the same hell,' as one of the characters puts it (p. 139).

Imagining the Enemy

The war on terror is founded on an imagined conception of a new enemy, a non-state enemy perceived as savage and barbarian, ignorant and mischievous. He is seen as an evil, a threat and a danger to the safety of the civilised world and its values, and he must be dealt with – tamed and punished.

Worse, the war on terror conflates the enemy with a monstrous figure, less than human or non-human altogether. This conception of the enemy justified the treatment and the torture of the detainees, whether at Guantánamo, Abū Ghraib or Bucca. This perception is in fact shaped and informed by colonial history. It came to the fore and was very visible in the first speeches of President George W. Bush after the 9/11 attacks and in the imagination of all those who supported the war on terror in Afghanistan and Iraq. It brought to the surface old and new colonialist and orientalist dichotomies of 'us' versus 'them' and justified the withdrawal of all law, national and international, from the treatment of the suspects. In *The Madmen of Camp Bucca*, the narrator uncovers the deeply harboured image of a vilified enemy, envisioned in this geographical environment as a wolf or a mythical and scary monster that deserves to be killed. In one dialogue, the writer Muzhir, the narrator's friend, talks to the narrator about his idea of how the American dehumanises the Iraqi enemy in general and the prisoner in particular:

> 'Do you know that they believe that in the desert any Iraqi can be metamorphosed into a wolf?'
>
> 'Really?'
>
> 'Worse. They think that by just listening to the howling of the wolf and by looking at the moon, the Iraqi can become a ferocious wolf that can devour any creature. They read all these myths at night.'
>
> 'Do you understand now why they brought eight thousand guards to Bucca?'
>
> 'Sure.'
>
> 'Look at their observation towers; they are surrounded with barbed wire like our barracks. Have you asked yourself why this is? It is because they fear the attacks of the wolf.'
>
> 'You mean after we get metamorphosed into wolves?'
>
> 'Yes. You don't know the Americans. I know them through their great literature. They even believe that when the Iraqi becomes angry, his facial muscles shrink, his canines become prominent, and his hand muscles shrink so that his fingers look like claws, and his head gets covered with thick hair. He then becomes half-man half-animal, a monster that enjoys eating human flesh and sucking blood. All this derives from their belief that we are

> the land of myths, and that the metamorphosis of man to a werewolf is a result of a malediction from god
>
> . . .
>
> They are ready to fire at us at any time because they consider us mythical creatures coming from bygone ages and endangering their lives'. (pp. 77–8)

In this illuminating passage, the racial underpinnings of the camp and the exclusion that it is founded upon are explained: we are shown how the enemy is described as a barbarian and an evil threat to the American way of life and values not only in Bush's declaration after 9/11 but even further back than that, in the shared imaginary and gothic literature.

Muzhir also acknowledges that, all things considered, the literature of the Americans is otherwise a 'great literature' but one that is tarnished with misconceptions and misrepresentations caused by a scared and sick imaginary that not only requires that the barracks of the imprisoned enemy be surrounded with barbed wire but also surrounds the guards' towers with the same barbed wire.

'What Is a Camp?'

> The temporary is the permanent and the eternity of the camp is the eternity of the desert and we have no choice except to wait.
>
> Shākir Nūrī, *The Madmen of Camp Bucca*

> There is no law here except for the law of killing.
>
> Shākir Nūrī, *The Madmen of Camp Bucca*

Unlike the virtual camp discussed in Chapter 2, the camp in this chapter is a real detention facility hidden in the depths of a vacant space in the Iraqi desert, far from the attention of public media. This camp is also thus located outside the law and established within the context of a military occupation and a war on terror. For these reasons, it is useful to examine the depiction of the reality of Nūrī's camp with respect to Giorgio Agamben's philosophical and historical reflections/on the camp. In 'The Camp as the *Nomos* of the Modern', Agamben identifies the structure of the camp and formalises it as a lawless space and the incarnation of the state of exception, where law is completely suspended.[14] Drawing on examples of historical occurrences of the camp, whether the *campos de concentraciones* created by the Spanish in Cuba in 1896 to suppress the popular insurrection of the colony or the concentration camps in South Africa where the English herded the Boers at the start of the twentieth century or the Nazi *Lager*, he highlights the connections of the camp to a state of emergency and a colonial war.

The camp according to Agamben is a space where pure sovereign power reigns, facing nothing but the naked life of the prisoners. Sovereignty or sovereign power is to be understood not so much as the exercise of the rule of the law but as the power to make exceptions to the law – or, as Carl Schmitt puts it, 'Sovereign is he who decides on the exception'.[15] Thus, says Agamben, the camp is 'the space that is opened when the state of exception begins to become the rule'.[16] Initially a temporary suspension of the rule of law on the grounds of a state of danger, the camp becomes a permanent spatial arrangement where the exception becomes the norm but at the same time is outside both the law (prison law in particular) and the normal order. This paradoxical aspect of the state of the exception inaugurates a new juridico-political paradigm wherein the norm becomes indistinguishable from the exception. 'It is only because the camps constitute a space of exception – a space in which the law is completely suspended – that everything is truly possible in them.'[17]

Defining the formal structure of the camp as the materialisation of the state of exception allows Agamben to look not only at historical occurrences as anomaly but also at the camp as the characteristic of the political space of modernity itself. His reflections on the camp and its formal structure help us understand and analyse the dreadful practices inside this site as depicted in Shākir Nūrī's novel and the ways the novel opposes to the lawless logic of the camp a different logic of resistance and resilience, which is completely absent from Agamben's hopeless account of the camp and the fate of its inhabitants – the *homines sacri*, sacred men.

Inside Bucca

As mentioned earlier, owing to special media attention and the scandal that erupted around the photographs of the abuse of prisoners in the detention camps, Abū Ghraib prison and Guantánamo Bay Camp emerged as more famous, if not infamous, than Camp Bucca despite the fact that the latter surpasses both locations as the site where the largest number of detainees was registered since the beginning of the American prosecution of the war on terror. But, unlike Bucca, neither of these first prisons has inspired novels or dramas, except for short poems written by Guantánamo prisoners themselves and smuggled outside the prison.[18] However, what is common about the three detention facilities is that all of them emerged more or less at the same time and in the wake of the state of emergency declared by President Bush after the attacks of 9/11. In addition, all three camps were located outside the United States of America and outside national and international law, allowing the indefinite detention, abuse and coercive interrogation of the captives. Detainees at Guantánamo were not granted the status of prisoners of war but were considered enemy and unlawful combatants. This new concept, which emerged after the invasion of Afghanistan, stripped those who were captured in this war of their political rights and their legal status. At Camp Bucca, as depicted in Nūrī's novel, the detainees were also stripped of their rights and legal status. 'For them we were not prisoners of war, but terrorists fighting the American devil; how can we fight him when his soldiers bore on their chests the inscription "Force is Right"' (p. 54) wonders the narrator. Many of the detainees belonged to Saddam Hussein's armed forces, but they were not granted any legal status and were not treated as prisoners of war – a situation that Nūrī portrays through seven generals featured in the novel who were captured during the invasion of Iraq. Other prisoners were suspected of taking part in the insurgency and fighting against the Coalition Provisional Authority in Iraq. This new concept of the 'unlawful combatant' deprived the detainees of their rights to be treated according to the international and legal conventions, such as the Geneva Conventions. Inside Bucca, the prisoners are not explicitly labelled 'unlawful combatants' but are treated as such, being subjected to the same horrendous methods of torture as the prisoners of the Guantánamo Bay detention camp or at Abū Ghraib.

From being a war reporter to becoming a prisoner without accusation, the unnamed narrator of the novel, who is among the first group of captives brought into the desert, falls into a confused state, barely aware of where he has been taken, but he tries to make sense of the physical circumstances where he is entrapped and the material conditions of the space surrounding him. At first, he can only describe what he is able to observe regarding the camp's organisational structure and the different methods of torture and abuse the prisoners are subjected to. But what first strikes him is that, although the camp has an improvised aspect, it has the structure of something conceived to be not temporary, but permanent and unlimited in time. The camp seems simply to emerge as something independent from time and the law. There is no reference to instructions for the emergence of Camp Bucca, just as for the Nazi concentration camps the head of the Gestapo could declare, 'Neither an order nor an instruction exists for the origin of the camps: they were not instituted; *one day they were there*'.[19] The narrator points out,

> In the beginning, Camp Bucca was made out of tents where the detainees were herded together like animals ready to be slaughtered. Some were standing; others were sitting, clinging to one another as there were no walls to lean on, no windows, and no openings. But soon the tents were folded and disappeared, and instead they established wooden barracks made of boards put together in the form of rectangular boxes, like fruit boxes. It looked like they were establishing for us disposable and temporary wooden prisons that they could dismantle any time.
>
> This is why we caressed the idea of the temporary, but our detention was going to be permanent and never ending. (p. 38)

A few weeks into his captivity, the narrator observes that the barracks have multiplied in the desert with the outpouring of truckloads of captives, and then the camp starts to be organised into different groups of smaller camps, each smaller camp including between nine and fourteen barracks, until there are twenty-two camps in total. In each barrack, there are between thirty and thirty-five detainees, and in each camp between seven hundred and one thousand detainees. The camp itself looks like a microcosm of the Iraqi society, encompassing all sects, affiliations and groups. What is remarkable and unique in the organisational structure of Camp Bucca as it is depicted in the novel is that the Americans distribute the detainees into barracks and camps according to their sectarian, religious and intellectual affiliations: there was the camp of the Shiʿī from the Mahdī army, the camp of the Takfīrī, the camp of the Wahhābī, the camp of the Baʿathī and in general all the Sunnī groups, and so on. There is also a camp for the Arab detainees from different nations. Each camp is surrounded by barbed wire to prevent confrontations from erupting between the inhabitants of each group; despite this precaution, there are many violent clashes between the Sunnī and the Takfīrī camps, for instance, as well as between the Shiᶜī and the Takfīrī. A leader heads each group of these different sects inside the camp, with three main leaders: Abū Sajjād heading the Shiᶜī camp; Abū Anas as the leader of the Takfīrī, the Wahhābī and Sunnī groups; and Abū ᶜĪsā, the leader assigned by the Americans to be the head of the Ṣaḥwa (awareness) groups and the rival of Abū Anas. In addition to these subdivisions, the barracks are divided into four different categories according to the level of threat the detainees represent: the green barracks with captives free of any accusation (an irony considering that they have been detained in the first place), the yellow barracks for those who represent a real danger according to the investigators and the red barracks for the most dangerous of all – members of al-Qaeda and the Islamist extremists. In addition to these categories, there is the barrack without any distinctive colour for the mentally ill prisoners or those who become mentally ill because of torture – 'perhaps because they did not assign a colour to mental illness', as the narrator exclaims (p. 35). The organisation of the camp into small camps and different groups and the marking of the barracks with a colour code reflect a strategy of humiliation and division that will foster internal fights and rivalry between the different groups and a way for the Americans to better dominate and torture the prisoners. The narrator is keen on underscoring the humiliation and the paradoxes of the new situation in which he finds himself feeling like a sheep:

> We who gave the world the Tower of Babel, created languages, and systematised them into codes and symbols, we who conquered the continents, we find ourselves in small cages, accepting the categorisation of the camp's administration into barracks and colours: not only did they colour our barracks, our identities, and our tents, but they also marked our foreheads and our bodies with a tattoo so that they could differentiate us like sheep whose backs are dyed in order to determine their prices. (p. 323)

The narrator observes that the number of prisoners keeps multiplying, reaching twenty-five thousand. For him, what is striking overall as a result of the hierarchical structure enforced in the camp is the atmosphere of fear inspired by the extremist groups who conduct themselves as supervisors and sovereigns over their fellow detainees and the suspicion that the divisions create between the captives. The narrator regrets the splitting of and rivalry between the leaders of each group, the endless fights over the way to conduct prayers and other things that bring to light myriad differences, breaking up the community of detainees.

> The detainees were transformed into different groups as if we had returned to tribal times. There was the group of Abū Sajjād, the group of Abū Anas and the group of Abū ᶜĪsā. We looked like two colonies – the colony of the detainees and the colony of the occupiers: two different worlds separated by a thick wall, a wall of feelings and resentments. We were in hot barracks where the temperature reaches fifty degrees Celsius; we were numbered according to the level of danger of each group. But whether we had a beard or not, whether one was bald or hairy, wearing a *dishdāsha* or a *sirwāl*, praying or not praying, for them we all were terrorists. (p. 101)

All of these Islamic groups tighten their grip on a portion of the prison population and start applying their different understandings of the teachings and rules of Islam, which creates tensions and provokes fights between the groups. The narrator is lucky to be in the green barrack with those who have not been formally accused and who are considered moderate prisoners, including the seven generals, the writer Muzhir and Nūḥ who is nicknamed by other inmates 'the oldest prisoner of Iraq'. The narrator notes with regret and bitterness the reality of the divisions and how the Americans encourage the internal fights between the prisoners, who never stop splitting up and multiplying like 'cancerous cells' escaping and challenging the guards' authority:

> Before we came to this camp, we didn't know what it meant to be a Sunnī, a Shīᶜī, an Arab or a Kurd, a Yazīdī, or a Sabean or an Assyrian . . . Lord, where were these groups hiding before the invasion – between the layers of the earth, in the folds of the wind, or in ant holes? Cursed is this earth, which is full of affiliations, rites and religions! The Americans resuscitated these from the depth of the earth, from the dark tunnels, and provided them with everything they needed in terms of weapons and pushed them into our lives. They literally told them: 'This is the day of your liberation; you are free to multiply, split up and defend your beliefs'. (pp. 323–4)

The narrator notes that the most rigid and dangerous of these camps is the Takfīrī camp, where differences of opinion are not permitted and where accounts are settled among the prisoners themselves and anything is truly possible from the prisoners' abuse of each other to torture and even killings. The American soldiers have granted the Takfīrī authority and sovereignty over other fellow prisoners. Worse than that, we learn that the Americans use the Takfīrī camp as one of the ways to enforce punishment and torture – for example, by assigning a prisoner to this camp, where he can be abused. Such is the lot of an unfortunate Egyptian detainee:

> One of the worst punishments possible for a detainee was to be placed among the Takfīrī, and they placed an Egyptian man in camp number fifteen; they strangled him, and when he lost consciousness, they hanged him because he didn't have the same ideas and did not pray like they prayed. (p. 325)

All this happens under the watchful eye of the American guards.

Paradoxically, in addition to compartmentalising the prisoners according to their religious and sectarian affiliations, the soldiers 'refused to call us by our names, which were erased and disappeared even from our heads as we no longer needed them . . . and in time we became just a number' (p. 38).

The detainees are subjected to different kinds of torture and abuse. Among the most common are beating, sleep and food deprivation, imposed nudity and other various cultural shocks. When the prisoners are first taken to the camp, they are hooded and beaten until they lose consciousness, only to be awakened with extremely cold water dumped on them. At times, they are denied access to a toilet so that they are finally forced to soil their pants. Other times nakedness features among the most common punishments to humiliate and instil shame in order to push the detainee to confess or provide valuable intelligence. The detainees are kept naked together; they are forced to shower collectively, with all the shame and humiliation this treatment means for them. They are deprived of any privacy when they have to go to the latrines, which are kept open to view and where they have to empty their bladders and bowels under the eyes of female guards and other fellow prisoners. The narrator calls this kind of torture 'cultural torture' because the torturers know what it means to subject an Arab or a Muslim to this kind of humiliating and shameful nakedness. When they are brought to the camp, they are showered collectively with chemical products, like animals, as if to 'clean' them of any contagious diseases they might have.

Next to these introductory methods of punishment and torture, the novel focuses mostly on two major techniques of torture used inside Bucca that have the most injurious effects: the sun and music. Reflecting on the structure of torture and war in her book *The Body in Pain*, Elaine Scarry establishes a parallel between the destructive force and the deconstruction of war and torture. In torture, she asserts, there is an imitation of the destructive power of war:

> War and torture have the same two targets, a people and its civilization . . . Torture imitates the destructive power of war: rather than destroying the concrete physical fact of streets, houses, factories and schools, it destroys them as they exist in the mind of the prisoner . . . [W]hereas the object of war is to kill people, torture usually mimes the killing of people by inflicting pain, the sensory equivalent of death, substituting prolonged mock execution for execution.[20]

In the natural environment of the desert, the one element that is most likely to be easily turned into an annihilating weapon, to secure a mock and prolonged execution, is the sun. At Camp Bucca, the guards place the detainees into containers or barracks without roofs, exposing them for hours to the scorching heat of sun to push them to make confessions. The 'red barrack' is reserved for the most dangerous detainees, says the narrator, those suspected of having connections to al-Qaeda. The narrator compares the punishment of the red barrack with the electric chair:

> The sun used to strike at our heads, as there is nothing else at Bucca except for its blazing fire. No rain, no cloud, no thunder, no lightning, only the fog of December that visits us every year, giving us a glimmer of hope in the dark horizon. It seems that they replaced the electric chair with the red barrack, where the detainee stands all day long under the burning rays of the sun for long days. And perhaps the electric chair used in the United States for the death penalty has more mercy than sunstroke because the electricity circulates in the body of the prisoner, and he dies immediately, whereas he who is sun stricken does not die immediately; he suffers dryness, redness, and skin burns, headaches and stomach aches caused by diarrhoea. The sunstroke circulates in the body of the prisoner, and he spends long

> hours of agony as the sun hits his head and the fire settles in his brains before he finally passes away. (p. 157)

Another lethal technique used for torture at Bucca is deafening rock music to break the prisoners' will and push them to confess. This technique is referred to in the novel as the 'disco'. In this torture technique, music is converted into a maddening instrument and an agent of pain: the detainees are placed in steel containers where they are exposed for twenty-three hours to loud, deafening heavy metal music that destroys reality for them by breaking their will and driving them into a state of madness:

> How ironic the designation of 'the disco' was! This name was so familiar to us, we the generation of the '70s. But in their disco they uproot our ears and paralyse our brains with their loud and killing music. We used to go to the disco after classes to dance with girls, a dance that we did not master . . . But, here, the disco is nothing other than a steel container or a metallic cage where they confine us before they close it. It looks like a giant sardine box. We spend twenty-three hours inside it, where we pee on ourselves and discharge our bowels while listening to hard rock music . . . They used to select a group of us to be tortured in these steel, closed containers so that this would teach a lesson to other prisoners: loud music that explodes the brains and makes one lose one's balance and fall into a deep endless silence. (p. 45)

The disco is used to confine the most dangerous prisoners and is also known as 'supermax confinement'; as Michelle Brown states, 'The guiding principle of supermax centers upon isolation and exclusion, including the restriction of all communication and face to face contact with staff and visitors for security purposes'.[21] This technique was also used in prisons such as Abū Ghraib, but what was new about its use in Bucca was apparently its coupling with extremely loud music.

In this torturing technique, music, a domestic construct of civilisation, is deconstructed and converted into a hurting instrument, and in this conversion it becomes what it is not.

Following Scarry, we can say that at Bucca music is *unmade* by being made what it is not: a weapon. 'Civilization is brought to the prisoner and in his presence annihilated in the very process by which it is being made to annihilate him.' [22]

The labelling of an intensely painful form of torture with a word usually used for entertainment and joy, *disco*, produces a circle of negations of man and civilisation, as Scarry argues in the chapter 'The Structure of Torture'. Following her analysis, we can perhaps say that in the case of camp Bucca detainees tortured in the disco, 'there is no human being in excruciating pain'; that is only a disco; there is no disco; 'that is merely a means of destroying a human being who is not a human being', that is only a disco, that is not a disco but merely a means of destroying a disco.[23]

> The double negation of a human being and a symptom of civilization combine to bring about a third area of negation, the negation of the torturer's recognition of what is happening, a negation that will allow the first two to continue. The torturer's idiom not only indicates but helps bring about the process of perception in which all human reality is made, no matter how screamingly present invisible, inaudible.[24]

In the novel, the music companies whose music is used in this way condemn such use and press charges against the camp's administration. The detainees find out bits and pieces of this news in the thrown-away newspapers that they get their hands on:

> 'Do you know that the music companies have pressed charges against Bucca?'
>
> 'Why?'
>
> 'Because they use the music they produce to torture us.'
>
> We used to think about the dances performed by partygoers in the discos of the world. Only the musicians who created this music realised the damage their music could produce without their intention. (pp. 45–6)

In this process of torture, there is not only an annihilation of the prisoner and his world but also the annihilation of the world and of civilisation through the unmaking and the deconstruction of a domestic instrument (music) turned into a lethal weapon. Scarry explains:

> Civilization [embodied in this case in the disco] is brought to the prisoner and in his presence annihilated in the very process by which it is being

> made to annihilate him . . . [T]his records the fact that the unmaking of civilization inevitably requires a return to and mutilation of the domestic, the ground of all making.[25]

The narrator states that the use of extremely loud music is not confined to the punishment in the disco but also spread throughout the camp with loudspeakers everywhere; the camp itself is the equivalent of a loudspeaker, the narrator observes, projecting a deafening and nerve- breaking music. The narrator also compares 'the disco' with the metallic balls in which prisoners were placed in the Middle Ages in the French prison of Mont St Michel and which were then hammered repeatedly. 'At Bucca they traded the metallic ball for the steel containers and the hammers with metal and rock music' (p. 45).

Resisting Torture

Against the torture and the unmaking of the prisoners' world, Shākir Nūrī's novel proposes a dynamic that might save the captives from total annihilation. Unlike the soldiers' imaginative speculations about their enemy and his possible transformation into a wolf or any other dangerous creature, the prisoners of Camp Bucca can, according to the narrator, metamorphose into anything but ferocious wolves. For instance, they can transform into a camel, that resilient and patient animal of the desert, as they embark on a spiritual meditative path that will help them transcend their condition and cope with the physical and mental torture. With prayers and meditations in the desert and use of soothing natural elements such as the moon, the stars and the sky, the prisoners can transcend the torture and the physical pain of their bodies and reconstruct their destroyed world. They owe the sanity of their minds and their spiritual resilience to their capacity to dream and to meditate, especially after Nūḥ, a prisoner nicknamed 'the oldest prisoner in Mesopotamia', joins them.

In the novel, Nūḥ is finishing in the new camp a ridiculous sentence of 1,215 years. He is transferred to Bucca after the scandal and the closure of Abū Ghraib prison. This prisoner symbolises the fate of oppressed men everywhere and the perpetuity of the prison since time immemorial. In the war on terror, some prisoners could accumulate multiple sentences and were condemned to infinite and senseless sentences that would require them to be jailed for eternity and beyond. This is why Nūḥ's fellow prisoners comment on his name, saying that, like the name of the prophet Nūḥ/Noah, '[Nūḥ] is the most suitable name' for this eternal prisoner, who will nevertheless die in Bucca and will be outlived only by his ridiculous sentence. In the novel, Nūḥ attracts attention with his physical and moral qualities and his charismatic personality. He is a tall wise man who refuses to wear the yellow jumpsuit like the other detainees and keeps his white clothes. Like a prophet, he teaches the prisoners how to meditate, how to contemplate the sky and how to pray silently and faithfully. He is praying in a different way from the fundamentalist groups, which stirs the anger of their leaders.

> Every day he would dedicate one hour to us, when we would sit together around him silently to meditate. We would sit in the position for prayer, looking forward, without moving a wink and without moving our bodies; we travelled with the clouds beyond the fences of Bucca. It was a prayer full of silence and of the taste of the desert, a prayer looking for the paths to divine energy and hope. But soon the news of this prayer spread and reached the three leaders of Bucca; they immediately considered him a Kāfir, a non-believer, because his prayer was different from theirs. (p. 86)

Nūḥ is pious without performing the ritual prayers in the conventional way; he teaches other prisoners how to keep their mental sanity, rise above their instincts and transcend their pain through meditation and prayers. He introduces to the prison a new kind of prayer distinct from simple ritual – a meditative prayer based on spirituality and faith and mixed with contemplation and silence. The prisoners find in his spirit and in his myth a source of inspiration and hope that allows them to dream and rise above their physical pain. 'We needed the myth of Nūḥ to fight the American jailers, and his hour was empowering us to fight the monsters, the dinosaurs and the barbarians' (p. 100). The single hour that the detainees spend gathered around this prisoner-prophet for the meditation rite stands against the twenty-three they are forced to spend in the red barracks exposed to the scorching heat of the desert or confined in the disco, hammered by loud and deafening metal music.

> He used to repeat that the meditation hour would keep us from becoming instinct-driven creatures. He was like a wise man coming from a bygone

> age. That hour made us defeat all other hours; it was like a magical rite, and we called it 'the hour of Nūh', which gave us hope and made us fly very high, away from the barbed wire of the prison . . . But this hour became a danger for us because it angered the other detainees, who threatened to strangle us if we did not pray like them. (pp. 99–100)

In the novel, the figure of Nūḥ is invoked not just as a symbol of the perpetuity of prison punishment and oppression but also as a trope to convey the hope of the prophet saviour and for the delivery of the prisoners from torture. Ultimately, this figure conjures the idea of the renewal of life. His name and his spirituality evoke the myth of the flood – the story of the prophet Noah and his miracle. Nūḥ the prisoner provides the detainees with the hope that they can float away from their jail, if only through his words, his prayers and his stories. 'His name alone resuscitated hope into our souls', says the narrator (p. 85). And under the spell of the myth, the detainees imagine that the desert would be transformed into a sea (especially since the prison was not too far from the seaport Um Qaṣr) and that Nūḥ would build for them an ark from the wood of their barracks and save them from their jailers. From inside the emptiness of the desert and out of the suffered physical pain, the prisoners construct a world of the imaginary. Thanks to their imagining, they can cross from a state without objects and with pain to a state with objects and without pain, where the only evidence that they are imagining, as Elaine Scarry puts it, is that 'imaginary objects appear in the mind':[26]

> Every time he invited us to pray, Nūḥ chased away all the gloom from our lives; and we thought that his ark might manifest itself any time on the sand of the desert; some detainees wondered if a boat could cross the desert and if the flood could happen on this deserted land . . . We knew that our time was not a time for miracles; nevertheless we clung more and more to it. Nūḥ instilled new visions in us, making us start our days with a new hope to see the mirage of the sand transform itself into a blue wavy sea that our ark could traverse to the land of safety. (p. 89)

The group of prisoners gather around Nūḥ and dream of the freedom that the flood would bring to them, and they imagine Noah's ark as their lifeboat, on which none of the American jailers and none of the fundamentalist prisoners of the camp would be allowed. They imagine a flood that would cleanse the desert of the shame of Bucca. This group of detainees that includes the narrator, the seven generals and Muzhir the poet, among others, finds in the myth of Noah and the flood a dream of liberation. They stand in stark contrast to the cohort of different factions of extremist groups and other fundamentalist detainees as well as to their American jailers, which together form the pact of evil that would be left behind to perish when the dreamed-of flood happens:

> Alone, we will embark on the ark, and we will leave you behind us . . . You bastards stay in the middle of the sand, which will swallow you with your barracks and metallic containers, your music, your observation towers and your barbed wire. Take the desert, take the disaster and take Bucca. We will not allow your myth another chance to repeat itself. (pp. 89–90)

Nūḥ falls sick and decides that Bucca is the last stop in his long prison sentence. When he dies, he is buried in the prison cemetery, which is then named after him. Before his death, though,

> this man placed hope in our hearts, while before his arrival our life was empty, without imagination. He taught us the myths of this country and opened up a horizon before us, and so we loved this desert that the Americans forced us to suffer its pains . . . He used to say 'the prisoner needs to dream'. He planted in our hearts the love for ships and made us dream about travels, and we started training our hands to scoop the sand as if it were water. (p. 107)

Survival and Testimony

It is this power of the imagination that allows some of the prisoners in the novel to transcend their state of suffering and their condition as bodies capable of experiencing objectless pain. Muzhir and the narrator, for example, stop feeling pain:

> Our sole comfort, Muzhir and I, was that we still preserved the sanity of our minds; as for our bodies, they were nothing more than pieces of wood or sponges as our limbs no longer responded to torture and our ears stopped

> hearing the loud music. As for our heads they no longer feared sunstroke. (p. 322)

Relieved of their capacity to feel pain, these prisoners are transformed into oral creatures capable of circulating words and exchanging dreams and images:

> The sands of Bucca transformed each of us to an oral narrator looking in his memory for the stories of our ancestors – those who knew the desert. Their stories might restore our lost dignity. And perhaps our weapons in the face of our American jailers would be the conversations, the words, the visions, the dreams and all that is in our heads. We even aspired to something else: we wanted to express the ideas and the thoughts taking place in the heads of other detainees who shared the barrack with us. (pp. 130–1)

This is how some of the prisoners such as the narrator and Muzhir the poet resist time at Bucca: they tell stories and exchange words and memories. This powerful movement keeps them alive and sustains them in their humanity. As in *A Thousand and One Nights*, in which words save Scheherazade from assured death, words save the prisoners from the murderous routine of their existence in the desert and keep them from losing their sanity and their dignity. Inside the camp, the detainees have nothing else to exchange except words and stories:

> We have been behind barbed wire since the invasion, waiting to be released, and time is slow inside the barracks; days are longer than nights, and nights are longer than the days; we recount stories and memories, and, as soon as someone starts telling his story, he pulls the threads of more and more stories: a story inside another, and each story leading to yet another story, so that at the end of the day we find ourselves sleeping on a mountain of stories and waking up only with the morning count, which reminds us of our condition of detention. (p. 101)

The war reporter–narrator and Muzhir the poet 'do not have anything except words'; they 'exchange them, polish them and re-pronounce them to counter boredom' (p. 170). Muzhir and the narrator become the thinking heads of the camp after Nūḥ urges them to try to survive so that they can tell the world what has happened inside Bucca. As Agamben puts it, 'In the camp, one of the reasons that can drive a prisoner to survive is the idea of becoming a witness'.[27] Like the narrator, Muzhir has also been imprisoned without any tangible charge against him. He is accused of spying when he worked as a translator for the American prisoners who were kidnapped by the Iraqi forces in Nāṣiriyya, his hometown. The common complaint coming from these enlightened men who seek to record what is happening in the camp, in addition to the lack of paper and pen, is the dearth of solid ground in the camp and the absence of walls where they might leave the mark of their thoughts and reflections or draw a trace with stones or with their nails, as all the prisoners of the world have done.

> At Bucca, we were deprived of the pleasure of writing on walls. That was the condition of the barracks and tents, as if the jailers did it on purpose and decided to keep us here just to deprive us of the pleasure of writing and leaving our traces in this place, this non-place without borders, a wavy sea of sand . . . Bucca didn't offer us any possibility to record anything. It took us back to the world of the oral: that mirage that does not preserve anything . . . We were deprived of walls, of caves and of writing. (pp. 349–52)

Some detainees try to use tea as ink and onion peels instead of paper, but they 'couldn't transform the sand into paper' (p. 352). This is why Muzhir writes on the sand and then erases what he writes, only to restart anew. Sometimes he writes on cigarette paper a codified writing out of fear of censorship because the guards can examine and translate anything he writes to use against him. The guards deny him access to paper and pen until a Swedish organisation intervenes in his favour and grants him this right in accordance with the Geneva Conventions. But the soldiers do not respect the conventions. Muzhir wants to write a novel about the mystery of the seven generals, who have fallen into a state of deep silence that intrigues the other detainees. Lacking appropriate writing tools, he has to formulate things in his head in a short and dense format. Inside Bucca, he becomes a poet, 'a sad poet' because he doesn't have access to paper to record his novel:

> 'I write in my head, not on paper, and whenever I find a sheet of paper I hide it in my pocket so that I can write on it a short passage, such as a Japanese haiku or an Iraqi song or a poem that can flow and doesn't have

> to be memorised. I train my memory to remember and memorise.' He [Muzhir] used to give each of us a passage to memorise by heart. (p. 142)

Through the words they exchange, the thoughts they formulate, the poems they make and memorise and the songs they sing, these prisoners form a network of solidarity, a bond that connects them and helps them survive inside the camp. Their words and their poems are proof of resistance, stubborn life and the reconstruction of the world.

These survivors, who are in the minority simply because they survive and can therefore testify, can be considered 'privileged' in comparison with most prisoners, who do not make it back from the camp, do not survive and can never speak. This is why the testimony of these survivors can be said to contain a 'lacuna', as Agamben puts it. Reflecting on the survivors of Auschwitz in his book *Remnants of Auschwitz* and drawing on Primo Levi's thoughts, Agamben analyses the structure of testimony as essentially something whose value lies in what it lacks. As Levi states,

> There is another lacuna in every testimony: witnesses are by definition survivors and so all, to some degree, enjoyed a privilege . . . No one has told the destiny of the common prisoners, since it was not materially possible for him to survive . . . I have also described the common prisoner when I speak of 'Muslims'; but the Muslims did not speak.[28]

The Muslims – or *die Muselmänner*, as they were called in the language of the German *Lager* to refer to those camp prisoners who never made it out of the camp –would never be able to tell about their experience because no one has ever returned to describe his own death. For Primo Levi, they are the true witnesses:

> We, the survivors, are not the true witnesses . . . We survivors are not only an exiguous but also an anomalous minority: we are those who by their prevarications or abilities or good luck did not touch bottom. Those who did so have not returned to tell about it or have returned mute, but they are the Muslims, the submerged, the complete witness, the ones whose deposition would have a general significance . . . We who were favored by fate tried, with more or less wisdom, to recount not only our fate but also that of the others, indeed of the drowned; but this was a discourse 'on

> behalf of third parties', the story of things seen at close hand, not experienced personally. The destruction brought to an end, the job completed, was not told by anyone, just as no one ever returned to describe his own death. Even if they had paper and pen, the drowned would not have testified because their death had begun before that of their body. Weeks and months before being snuffed out, they had already lost the ability to observe, to remember, to compare and express themselves. We speak in their stead, by proxy.[29]

In the same way, in their attempt to bear witness to the life of the camp and to the fate of the other prisoners who perish inside Bucca, survivors such as the narrator and his friend Muzhir are only pseudo-witnesses. The value of their testimony lies in what it lacks, 'as at its center it contains something that cannot be borne witness to and that discharges the survivors of authority'.[30] The true witnesses in the novel are those who perished – for example, those who tried to escape and were reduced to scary skeletons or the seven generals about whom Muzhir wants to write a novel if he can only get the right tools and who are exterminated inside the camp and never return to speak about their deaths. The survivors speak in the non-survivors' stead by proxy; they bear witness to their missing testimony. In this case, such testimony appears to have two subjects, as Agamben notes:

> To speak, to bear witness is thus to enter into a vertiginous movement in which something sinks to the bottom, wholly desubjectified and silenced, and something subjectified speaks without truly having anything to say of its own ('I tell of things . . . that I did not actually experience').[31]

Concerning the etymology and the origin of the word *Muselmann*, 'which was in common use in Auschwitz', Agamben advances that there are many possible explanations, but

> the most likely explanation of the term can be found in the literal meaning of the Arabic word muslim: the one who submits unconditionally to the will of God . . . But while the muslim believes that the will of God is always manifest even in the smallest events, the *Muselmann* of Auschwitz is instead characterized and defined by 'a loss of all will and consciousness'.[32]

Submission and resignation coupled with the loss of will and consciousness define the various cases of *die Muselmänner* inside Camp Bucca. Many scholars call the *Muselmann* the 'living dead' or the 'mummy man'[33] inhabiting 'the limit between life and death'.[34] It is in this condition that many camp detainees at Bucca are left in Nūrī's novel after they are subjected to extreme torture in the disco and in the red barrack or after they try to escape but are caught and their bodies brought back to the camp to serve as deterrence to the other prisoners:

> The soldiers attacked and recaptured a prisoner who fled the camp into the desert . . . [T]hey brought him back and made his skeleton a décor between our barracks to serve as an example to scare us and deter us from thinking of escaping . . . Americans like to teach lessons. (p. 166)

The same thing happens to Muzhir the writer. He is put in the red barrack, the barrack without roof, under the sun for consecutive days and is tortured in the disco. After such rounds of torture, he is like an animated cadaver, babbling and raving: 'The sun is in my head, the sun is in my head' (p. 157). His friends do not know whether this madness is due to the effects of sunstroke or to any drugs and substances given to him that might have damaged his brain.

> Muzhir became very weak because he was left in the red barrack for many days and the sun affected him . . . His words did not help him in any way, and he is treated like any other prisoner . . . He looked at the sky, lifting his head high. We suspected that they did something to him, or perhaps they gave him some drugs that could have destroyed his brains. Was it the sunstroke or the effects of the loud music that they rehearsed in his ears in the infamous disco? (p. 155)

Another intriguing example of spectral life or living dead at Bucca is given in the story of the seven generals. Many things intrigue the narrator and Muzhir, who wants to write about the generals. The narrator wonders if they had been captured during or after the battles and whether they are prisoners of war or regular prisoners. They are subjected to investigation and torture because of 'what remained in their minds in terms of maps and plans that intrigued the administration of Bucca' (p. 163). The spectres of the seven generals, who have fallen into a deep and mysterious silence, represent another example of the figure of the *Muselmänner* in Camp Bucca. In order to obtain confessions from them, their executioners lead them regularly to the disco, where they cannon them with maddening music for twenty-three hours. Their hands cuffed and tied to their backs and their heads covered with plastic bags, they end up in a humiliating condition, urinating and defecating on themselves.

> They almost became mad and were transferred to the barracks of the mad detainees after music exhausted their brains; they were like drunkards wavering between the barracks . . . Their fault was to be part of the army of the previous regime; they defended their country to death, and then they were captured by the invaders. Can we ever ask someone in all the wars of the world, 'Why the hell do you defend your country?' (p. 214)

Before their death, they fall into a strange condition, the condition of the *Muselmann*, as if they have left this world and gone to another: 'In vain I tried to talk to the generals. They found refuge in their own secrets and mysteries. They joined a different world from ours, and only broken and unconnected words without meaning could come out of their mouths' (p. 213).

All seven generals die during torture, and their deaths would have gone totally unwitnessed if not for the confession of one of the guards, the narrator says. The following paragraph briefly summarises the way the seven generals are secretly put to arbitrary and gratuitous death during or after torture:

> Junayd died during torture. They put him upside down in a bag and attached it from its middle with an electric wire so that the air does not circulate in the bag. They placed him on his belly and stretched the wire between his legs . . . And because his confessions were not to their satisfaction, the executioner sat on top of him and suffocated him . . . A few days after Junayd's murder, they tortured Sinūn. One of the soldiers disclosed that they placed his head in the sand, lifting it every now and then they to ask him to confess, but at some point his mouth and nose were full of sand; he suffocated and died . . . they buried him in the sand and wrote on his tomb: 'Deserter'. They took Fāḍil on a helicopter ride in the desert and threw him from above. They accused him of throwing himself from the

> aircraft in an act of suicide. They raped Ḥarrār and after that he committed suicide. General Balkhī became mad after they placed him in the disco. He lost his sanity and was seen running from one barrack to another and screaming, 'Music, containers . . . music . . . containers . . .' He ran away and fled, but they caught him and killed him with a bullet. (pp. 215–16)

Outside the novel, the real Camp Bucca was the site where death was sentenced secretly, without the law taking its due course. And like the stories of the seven generals, many other stories and voices will never be told or heard. We will never hear the voices of the true witnesses no matter how vivid the survivors' memories or how sincere and strong the attempts at reconstruction and testimony are. All those who died in the camp or were left neither alive nor dead are the *Muselmänner*, the true and absolute witnesses, but they cannot speak of what happened to them. Thus, the dual structure of testimony is as Agamben suggests: merely the act of an *auctor*.

Conclusion

Through the figure of the prisoner of war and the camp detainee, the *homo sacer*, the killable Iraqi, is shown entangled not only with the war in Iraq, but also with the terrorist attacks of 9/11 and the global war on terror. He is viewed with suspicion and subjected to torture and negation. Unlike the *homo sacer* as war deserter or as suicide bomber, who has some agency over his fate and can structure his actions, the camp detainee is a killable object who has no margin of action when his body betrays him under torture. The *homo sacer* as a camp inhabitant submits to his fate and loses all will inside the camp, becoming a *Muselmann*. But, as Shākir Nūrī shows in *The Madmen of Camp Bucca*, they do have one option: they can oppose torture and their inhuman condition. They can resist with words, poems and shared dreams, visions and stories. Those who survive can show their resistance with their testimonies for those who did not make it. It is these testimonies – like the ones we find in the novel – that can make a difference.

Notes

1. Giorgio Agamben, 'What Is a Camp?' in *Means without End: Notes on Politics*, trans. Vincenzo Binetti and Cesare Casarino (Minneapolis: University of Minnesota Press, 2000), p. 37.
2. Ibid.
3. Shākir Nūrī, *Majānīn Būkā* (The madmen of Camp Bucca) (Beirut: Sharikat al-maṭbūʿāt li al-tawzīʿ wa al-nashr, 2012), p. 28. Page references are given parenthetically in the text from this point; my translations throughout.
4. Mark Danner, 'Iraq: The War of the Imagination', *New York Review of Books*, 21 December 2006, pp. 81–8 and 94–6.
5. Andrew Hill, *Re-imagining the War on Terror: Seeing, Waiting, Travelling* (New York: Palgrave Macmillan, 2009).
6. Bob Woodward, *State of Denial: Bush at War, Part III* (New York: Simon & Schuster, 2006), p. 408, quoted in ibid., p. 46.
7. Alain Badiou, 'Fragments of a Public Diary on the American War against Iraq', *Contemporary French and Francophone Studies*, 8, 3, 2004, p. 234.
8. David Simpson, *9/11: The Culture of Commemoration* (Chicago: Chicago University Press, 2006), p. 145.
9. Jeremy Black, *War since 1945*, quoted in Hill, *Re-imagining the War on Terror*, p. 47.
10. Quoted in Hill, *Re-imagining the War on Terror*, p. 47.
11. Ibid., p., 106.
12. Ibid., p. 107.
13. Ibid., p. 108.
14. Giorgio Agamben, 'The Camp as the *Nomos* of the Modern', in *Means without End*, pp. 37–45.
15. Quoted in Giorgio Agamben, *Homo Sacer: Sovereign Power and Bare Life*, trans. Daniel Heller-Roazen (Stanford, CA: Stanford University Press, 1998), p. 11.
16. Agamben, 'What Is a Camp?', p. 39.
17. Ibid.
18. See Judith Butler, *Frames of War: When Is Life Grievable?* (London and New York: Verso, 2009).
19. Quoted in Agamben, *Homo Sacer*, p. 169, emphasis added.
20. Elaine Scarry, *The Body in Pain: The Making and Unmaking of the World* (New York: Oxford University Press, 1985), p. 61.

21. Michelle Brown, 'Setting the Conditions for Abu Ghraib', *American Quarterly*, 57, 3, September 2005, pp. 973–97.
22. Scarry, *The Body in Pain*, p. 44.
23. Scarry gives different examples whereby the naming of torture techniques is taken from different spheres of civilisation, and where the body's pain is claimed to be mimetic of a particular invention: for example the person's pain will be called the 'telephone' in Brazil. Taking this example, the chain of negation of human being and civilisation goes as follows: 'There is no human being in excruciating pain, that's only a telephone; there is no telephone; that is merely a means of destroying a human being who is not a human being, who is only a telephone, who is not a telephone, but merely a means of destroying a telephone.' (See Scarry, p. 44.)
24. Ibid., p. 44.
25. Ibid., pp. 44–5.
26. Ibid., p. 161.
27. Giorgio Agamben, *Remnants of Auschwitz: The Witness and the Archive*, trans. Daniel Heller-Roazen (Brooklyn, NY: Zone Books, 1999), p. 15.
28. Quoted in ibid., p. 34.
29. Quoted in ibid., pp. 33–4.
30. Ibid., p. 34.
31. Ibid., p. 120.
32. Ibid., p. 45.
33. Both expressions 'Mummy man' and 'Living dead' are quoted in *Remnants of Auschwitz*, p. 54.
34. Quoted in ibid., p. 55.

Conclusion

Whether in representations of more traditional wars such as the Iran–Iraq War (1980–8) or the Gulf War (1991) or the most recent American war of occupation (2003–11), the novels discussed in this book are focused on the centrality and vulnerability of human subjects in their relation to coercion, war and 'necropower', to use Achille Mbembe's term.[1] Re-endowing the war novel with depictions of the male war actor in his anti-war spirit, his desertion, and his utopian quest for freedom, with his vulnerability amid sectarian killings and suicide operations, Iraqi authors privilege and reveal these fundamental experiences and their corollary forms of living death and life in extremis.

The war experiences depicted today in Iraqi novels are not those of the heroes of battles or war martyrs sacrificed in the name of ideology and the homeland; they are the experiences of the 'other' war actor, a different kind of actor who refuses coercion, subjugation and humiliation. This 'other' war actor is also trying to reclaim some form of agency, whether through desertion, in suicide attack or through testimony as a prisoner of war. Novels examining old wars such as the Iran–Iraq War from the perspective of the 'other' soldier, the poet-deserter and the marginalised alienated artist-soldier shed light on an important aspect of the cultural and political landscape of the 1980s in Iraq, recovering the hidden memory of the war deserter and re-inscribing it into the history of the war and its literature. The 'other' war story of the Iran–Iraq War as it is surfacing today in the Iraqi novel is a story of rejection of violence, killing and the militarisation of life that was enforced during the years of the Baᶜath regime. By unearthing the story of the war deserter, *The Professor of Illusion*, *Khiḍr Qad and the Drab Olive Years* and *The Descent of the Angels* rehabilitate and humanise the war deserters by investigating their dreams, their fears, their experiences and their vulnerability as the living dead. All three novels dig deep into the deserters' singular and tragic fate and the spirit of insubordination and transgression that animates them under a totalitarian Iraq governed by fear and the rule of the exception.

The desertions of these alienated soldiers can be interpreted as liberating events and bids for agency, but at the same time we saw how they reduce the soldiers to sacred men, a category where nothing is left for them in the profane world except to be killed and where they end up bare before the law, which they experience in its most formal death-dealing capacity. They find in fiction, however, an ultimate salvation and redemption as they join the sacred and the mythical, as in the case of ᶜĪsā the poet and Khiḍr the alienated artist, who share prophetic names and are depicted as having prophetic destinies.

Three decades after the Iran–Iraq War and one decade after the fall of Saddam's regime, under the 'new' Iraq, it is rather extraordinary and perplexing to see in the post-occupation novel the persistence of the pattern of the deserter, with Iraqis still ending up in that category, fleeing the non-choice of death or death. This is one of the revelations of the post-occupation novel, most visible in the case of the narrator of Najm Wālī's *Baghdad Marlboro*, who is faced with this bewildering alternative in the context of the raging sectarian war, where the identities of the war actors are obscured, making it even more difficult to navigate and understand the complex landscape of war. Restlessly fleeing the fatality of killing in occupied and sectarian war-torn Iraq, the protagonist of *Baghdad Marlboro* is like a deserter who eventually has to leave the country altogether as Iraq becomes a place rife with death and unfit for life. The novel reveals how the occupation and the ensuing sectarian war that engulfed the country take us back full circle to strategies and war experiences of the past as if to signify that the awful face of the dictatorship is still living with the Iraqi people, connecting a dehumanised past with a present no less dehumanising. This continuum in the devaluation of human life exposes the false promises and the claims of a 'democratic' and peaceful Iraq.

In addition to the persistence of desertion as a strategy to escape violence and killing in the 'new' Iraq, the other strategy used to deal with war in the context of the American occupation is depicted in the figure of the suicide bomber, a new variable that emerged in force in post- Saddam Iraq, becoming a plague for the occupation and for the nascent 'democratic' Iraq. This espousal of violence and terror as a choice to resist occupation and dehumanisation is portrayed in Shākir Nūrī's *The Green Zone*. The portrayal of the suicide bomber in this novel and the maturation of the process and its motivations show the emergence of the private warrior and the privatisation of the business of war in occupied Iraq. The novel contextualises the phenomenon of suicide bombing as part of the political culture of death in modern Iraq and conceptualises it as a cumulative effect of the violence the Iraqi individual has been subjected to for decades. In the portrait the novel draws of Ibrāhīm the suicide bomber, there is no place for religious subjectivity, only for the political. Unlike the suicide bomber popularised as religious terrorist on the Internet, in media analyses and in the popular imagination at large, the suicide bomber in *The Green Zone* emerges as a secular subjectivity disturbing the prevailing stereotype of suicide bombing in the modern Middle East. Shākir Nūrī's novel frames the suicide act of Ibrāhīm in secular and political terms rather than in the vocabulary of martyrdom and Islamic militancy.

The narrator of *Baghdad Marlboro* and the protagonist of *The Green Zone* have different strategies to deal with violence in Iraq: the first rejects the vicious spiral of killing and ends up leaving the country altogether, perhaps forging a path of hope for the end of violence; the other claims killing and engages in perpetuating a cycle of violence. Does this grim choice suggest that post-occupation Iraqi novel finds itself at a dead end, unable to envision a more humane alternative to the prevailing death and violence?

As the preceding chapters have shown, the post-occupation novel is also keen in mapping the geography of the occupation, showing the pervasiveness of terror and abuse and investigating how with the occupation, the war on terror and the sectarian violence, the totality of space – whether the most hidden and remote (the desert) or the most guarded and walled (the Green Zone) or the most familiar and safe (the narrator's home in *Baghdad Marlboro*) becomes alienating and 'bare life'-producing. The two paradigmatic spaces, the city and the detention camp, are depicted as equally dehumanising sites of terror, humiliation, torture and abuse. In addition to this dichotomy, the lawless space of the Red Zone extends not just to the walled and cantoned areas of Baghdad but to the whole of Iraq, where live the disenfranchised local communities subjected to raid, terror and kidnapping.

All these spaces are in apparent opposition to one another, but, as I have shown, existence in all these realms is reduced to 'bare life'. Ostensibly, the city's Green Zone as the walled, safe haven of law, order and culture opposes the Red Zone and Camp Bucca in the Iraqi desert, where the 'evil of the terrorists' is contained and where lawlessness and barbarism reign.

Despite these apparent differences, these spaces converge because they are the sites of moral and legal transgressions by means of terror and torture. The lives of all of the occupants in all of these spaces are exposed, targeted and reduced to 'bare life'.

Giorgio Agamben finds in this paradigm that extends terror to all citizens 'the structuring principle of the camp' and 'the hidden matrix of the political space in which we live today'.[2] The extreme case of the materialisation of the camp into a dreadful reality is shown and discussed in *The Madmen of Camp Bucca*, one of the rare literary testimonies of the existence of American camps under the occupation, akin in its dehumanising practices to Nazi concentration camps. It is in the camp as practised by the American occupation and portrayed in the testimonies of the survivors that we can locate the most absolute realisation of bare life, where from a temporary suspension of the law the state of exception becomes indistinguishable from the norm itself, allowing for all kinds of torture and abuse of the detainees. According to Agamben, the paradigm of this bare life in the camp is the *Muselmann*, a point at which human beings cease to be human altogether.

Through the examination of different war experiences, whether under the rule of Saddam's regime or in the context of the American occupation and the war on terror, recent Iraqi novels portray the Iraqi individual – whether a soldier at the front or a fugitive war deserter who abhors ideology and politics or a humiliated individual under the occupier who blows himself up in a gesture of despair and revenge or a detention camp detainee – as a *homo sacer*, 'he who can be killed and not sacrificed'[3] without his killing becoming a murder. In these modalities of experiencing war and occupation, these four figures are revealed in their bareness, abandoned by the law, exposed and targeted, having only their given natural life, their *zoe*.

The novels identify two types of sacred man under the regime of Saddam Hussein and two new instances that emerged in the 'new Iraq', brought about by the American occupation and in the context of the sectarian war and the war on terror. The first two instances of the Iraqi *homo sacer* are the war deserter of the Iran–Iraq War and the soldier of the Gulf War who was buried alive in a mass grave or exterminated in the virtual camp on the Highway of Death. The new instances are the suicide bomber and the camp detainee. Under the new paradigm of the war on terror, anyone in Iraq can potentially become a *homo sacer* and a camp inhabitant. The novels used in this study show how from one war to another and from one decade to another, the *homo sacer* has proliferated in Iraq. The analysis has shown how we moved from individual cases of war desertion to end up in the camp and its population of thousands and thousands of detainees over a decade of war and occupation thanks to the use of the malleable trope of the state of emergency, becoming a state of exception where everything that is dehumanising becomes possible.

Notes

1. Achille Mbembe, 'Necropolitics', in *Foucault in an Age of Terror: Essays on Biopolitics and the Defence of Society*, ed. Stephen Morton and Stephen Bygrave (New York: Palgrave Macmillan, 2008), pp. 152–82.
2. Giorgio Agamben, 'What Is a Camp?' in *Means without End: Notes on Politics*, trans. Vincenzo Binetti and Cesare Casarino (Minneapolis: University of Minnesota Press, 2000), p. 37.
3. Giorgio Agamben, *Homo Sacer: Sovereign Power and Bare Life*, trans. Daniel Heller-Roazen (Stanford, CA: Stanford University Press, 1998), p. 83.

Bibliography

Primary Sources

ᶜAli, Jamāl Ḥusayn, *Amwāt Baghdad* (Beirut: Dār al-Farābī, 2008).

al-Anbārī, Shākir, *Najmat al-Battāwīn* (Damascus: Dār al-Madā li al-thaqāfa wa al-nashr, 2010).

al-Anbārī, Shākir, *Layālī al-kākā* (Damascus: Dār al-Madā li al-thaqāfa wa al-nashr, 2002).

Antūn, Sinān), *I 'jām: An Iraqi Rhapsody* (San Francisco: City Lights Books, 2007).

Antūn, Sinān, *The Corpse Washer* (New Haven, CT: Yale University Press, 2013).

ᶜAwwād, ᶜAli), *Halīb al-mārīnz* (Amman: Dāar faḍāʾāṭ, 2009).

Badr, ᶜAli, *Asātidhat al-wahm* (Beirut: al-Mu'assasa al-'arabiyya li-dirāsāt wa al-nashr, 2011).

Badr, ᶜAli, *Hāris al-tibgh* (Beirut: al-Mu'assasa al-'arabiyya li- al-dirāsāt wa al-nashr, 2009).

Badr, ᶜAli, *al-Jarīma, al-fann wa qāmūs Baghdad* (Beirut: al-Mu'assasa al-'arabiyya li- al-dirāsāt wa al-nashr, 2010).

Falak, Naṣīf, *Khiḍr Qad wa al-'asr al-zaytūnī* (Baghdad: Manshūrāt al-Jamal, 2006).

Ḥasan, Muḥammad, *Hubūṭ al-malā'ika* (Beirut: al-Tanwīr, li al-ṭibā'a wa al-nashar wa al-tawzīᶜ, 2013).

Ḥillāwī, Jinān J., *Layl al-bilād* (Beirut: Dār al-Ādāb, 2002).

Hussein, Hadiya, *Mā baᶜd al-hubb* (Beirut: al-Mu'assasa al-'arabiyya li- al-dirāsāt wa al- nashr, 2003; translated into English by Ikram Masmoudi as *Beyond Love*, Syracuse, NY: Syracuse University Press, 2012).

Kachāchī, Inaᶜām, *al-Ḥafīda al-Amrīkiyya* (Beirut: Dar al-Jadīd, 2009; translated into English by Nariman Youssef as *The American Granddaughter* (Doha, Qatar: Bloomsbury Qatar Foundation, 2012).

Kāẓim, Lamīs, *ᶜAqīq al-nawāris* (Beirut: al-Mu'assasa al-'arabiyya li- al-dirāsāt wa al-nashr, 2009).

Al-Khālidī, Ḍiyā', *Qatala* (Beirut: al-Tanwīr, li al-ṭibā'a wa al-nashar wa al-tawzī', , 2012).

Nūrī, Shākir, *Majānīn būkā* (Beirut: Sharikat al-maṭbū'āt li al-tawzī' wa al-nashr, 2012).

Nūrī, Shākir, *al-Minṭaqa al-Khaḍrā'* (Dubai: Thaqāfa li al-nashr wa al-tawzī', 2009).

al-Ramlī, Muḥsin, *Ḥadā'iq al-ra'īs* (Dubai: Thaqāfa li al-nashr wa al-tawzī', 2012).

al-Raṣīf, Jāsim, *Ru'ūs al-ḥurriya al-mukayyasa* (Beirut: al-Mu'assasa al-'arabiyya li-al-dirāsāt wa al-nashr, 2007).

Al-Rikābī, 'Abd al-khāliq, *Layl 'Ali bābā al-ḥazīn* (Beirut: al-Mu'assasa al-'arabiyya li-al-dirāsāt wa al-nashr, 2013).

Al-Sa'dāwī, Aḥmad, *Frānkinshtāyn fī Baghdad* (Beirut: Manshūrāt al-Jamal, 2013).

Al-Sālim, Wārid Badr, *'Ajā'ib Baghdad* (Beirut: Manshūrāt al-Jamal, 2012).

Shāwī, Burhān), *Mashrahat Baghdād* (Beirut: al-Dār al-'arabiyya li al-'ulūm nāshirūn, 2012).

al-'Ubaydī, 'Abd al-Karīm, *Ḍayā' fī Ḥafr al-Bāṭin* (Baghdad: Manshūrāt masārāt, 2009).

Wālī, Najm, *Baghdad mālbūrū* (Beirut: al-Mu'assasa al-'arabiyya li-al-dirāsāt wa al-nashr, 2012).

Secondary Sources

'Abbūd, Salām, *Thaqāfat al-'unf fī al-'Irāq* (Cologne: Manshūrāt al-Jamal / Al-Kamel Verlag, 2002).

Adūnis, *An Introduction to Arab Poetics*, trans. Catherine Cobham (Cairo: American University in Cairo Press, 1992).

Agamben, Giorgio, *Homo Sacer: Sovereign Power and Bare Life*. trans. Daniel Heller-Roazen (Stanford, CA: Stanford University Press, 1998).

Agamben, Giorgio, *Language and Death: The Place of Negativity*, trans. Karen E. Pinkus with Michael Hardt (Minneapolis: University of Minnesota Press, 2006).

Agamben, Giorgio, *Means without End: Notes on Politics*, trans. Vincenzo Binetti and Cesare Casarino (Minneapolis: University of Minnesota Press, 2000).

Agamben, Giorgio, *Remnants of Auschwitz: The Witness and the Archive*, trans. D. Heller-Roazen (Brooklyn, NY: Zone Books, 1999).

Al-Ali, Nadje, and Deborah al-Najjar (eds), *We Are Iraqis: Aesthetics and Politics in a Time of War* (Syracuse, NY: Syracuse University Press, 2013).

Allen, Roger, *The Arabic Novel: An Historical and Critical Introduction* (Syracuse, NY: Syracuse University Press, 1995).

Allen, Roger, *An Introduction to Arabic Literature* (Cambridge: Cambridge University Press, 2000).

Altoma, Salih, *Iraq's Modern Arabic Literature: A Guide to English Translation since 1950* (Lanham, MD: Scarecrow Press, 2010).

Arendt, Hannah, *The Origins of Totalitarianism* (New York: Harcourt, 1973).

Asad, Talal, *On Suicide Bombing* (New York: Columbia University Press, 2007).

Badini, Dounia A., 'La vie littéraire autour de la revue libanaise *Shi*ᶜ*r* (1957–1970)', *Middle Eastern Literatures*, 13, 1 (April 2010), pp. 69–89.

Badini, Dounia A., *La revue* Shiᶜr / *Poésie et la modernité poétique arabe, Beyrouth (1957–1970)* (Paris: Actes Sud Sindbad, 2009).

Badiou, Alain, 'Fragments of a Public Diary on the American War Against Iraq', *Contemporary French and Francophone Studies*, 8, 3 (2004).

Baudrillard, Jean, *The Gulf War Did Not Take Place*, trans. Paul Patton (Bloomington: Indiana University Press, 1995).

Baudrillard, Jean, *The Spirit of Terrorism and Other Essays*, trans. Chris Turner (London: Verso, 2002).

Bauman, Zygmunt, *Society under Siege* (Cambridge: Polity Press, 2002).

Bauman, Zygmunt, 'Wars of the Globalization Era', *European Journal of Social Theory*, 4, 1 (2001), pp. 11–28.

Bennett, Harold, 'Sacer Esto', *Transactions of the American Philological Association*, 61 (1930), pp. 5–18.

Bennis, Phyllis, and Michel Moushabeck (eds), *Beyond the Storm: A Gulf Crisis Reader* (Northampton, MA: Interlink, 1998).

Bin, Alberto, Richard Hill and Archer Jones, *Desert Storm: A Forgotten War* (Westport, CT: Praeger, 1998).

Braudy, Leo, *From Chivalry to Terrorism: War and the Changing Nature of Masculinity* (New York: Knopf, 2003).

Briemberg, Mordecai (ed.), *It Was, It Was Not: Essays & Art on the War against Iraq* (Vancouver: New Star Books, 1992).

Brown, Michelle, 'Setting the Conditions for Abu Ghraib', *American Quarterly*, 57, 3 (September 2003).

Butler, Judith, *Frames of War: When Is Life Grievable?* (London and New York: Verso, 2009).

Caiani, Fabio, and Catherine Cobham, *The Iraqi Novel: Key Writers, Key Texts* (Edinburgh: Edinburgh University Press, 2013).

Chandrasekaran, Rajiv, *Imperial Life in the Emerald City: Inside Iraq's Green Zone* (New York: Knopf Publishing Group, 2006).

Clausewitz, Carl von, *On War*, trans. James John Graham (Baltimore: Penguin, 1962).

Coker, Christopher, *The Future of War: The Re-enchantment of War in the Twenty-First Century* (Malden, MA: Blackwell, 2004).

Coker, Christopher, *Waging War without Warriors? The Changing Culture of Military Conflict* (Boulder, CO: Lynne Rienner, 2002).

cooke, miriam, 'Death and Desire in Iraqi War Literature', in *Love and Sexuality in Modern Arabic Literature*, ed. Roger Allen, Hillary Kilpatrick and Ed de Moor, pp. 184–99 (London: Saqi, 1995).

cooke, miriam, *Women and the War Story* (Berkeley: University of California Press, 1996).

Cordesman, Anthony H., *The Iraq War: Strategy, Tactics, and Military Lessons* (Westport, CT: Praeger, 2003).

Cordesman, Anthony H., and Ahmed Hashim, *Iraq, Sanctions and Beyond* (Boulder, CO: Westview Press, 1997).

Davis, Eric, *Memories of State: Politics, History, and Collective Identity in Modern Iraq* (Berkeley: University of California Press, 2005).

De Landa, Manuel, *War in the Age of Intelligent Machines* (New York: Zone Books, 1991).

De Moor, Ed, 'The Rise and Fall of the Review *Shi'r*', *Qaderni di Studi Arabi*, 18 (2000), pp. 85–96.

Dean, Michel, *The New Police Science* (Stanford, CA: Stanford University Press, 2006).

Diken, Bulent, and Carsten Bagge Lausten, 'The Camp', *Geografiska Annaler, Series B, Human Geography*, 88, 4 (2006), pp. 443–52.

Dudziak, Mary L., *War.Time: An Idea, Its History, Its Consequences* (Oxford: Oxford University Press, 2012).

Edkins, Jenny, 'Sovereign Power, Zones of Indistinction, and the Camp', *Alternatives*, 25 (2000), pp. 3–25.

Ek, Richard, 'Giorgio Agamben and the Spacialities of the Camp: An Introduction', *Georgrafiska Annaler. Series B, Human Geography*, 88, 4 (2006), pp. 363–86.

Esmeir, Samera, 'The Violence of Non-violence: Law and War in Iraq', *Journal of Law and Society*, 34 (2007), pp. 99–115.

Fanon, Frantz, *Black Skin, White Mask*, trans. Richard Philcox (New York: Grove Press, 1967).

Fanon, Frantz, *The Wretched of the Earth*, trans. Richard Philcox (New York: Grove Press, 1963).

Fitzpatrick, Peter, 'Bare Sovereignty: *Homo Sacer* and the Insistence of the Law', *Theory & Event*, 5, 2 (2001).

Foucault, Michel, *Il faut défendre la société* (Paris: Seuil/Gallimard, 1997).

Foucault, Michel, *The History of Sexuality*, trans. Robert Hurley (New York: Random House, 1978).

Foucault, Michel, *Power/Knowledge: Selected Interviews and Other Writings, 1972–1977* (New York: Pantheon Books, 1980).

Foucault, Michel, *Society Must Be Defended: Lectures at the College de France*, ed. Mauro Bertani and Alessandro Fontana, trans. David Macey (New York: Picador, 2003).

Fowler, W. Ward, 'The Original Meaning of the Word Sacer', *Journal of Roman Studies*, 1 (1911), pp. 57–63.

Glosson, General Buster, *War with Iraq: Critical Lessons* (Charlotte, NC Glosson Family Foundation, 2003).

Gray, Chris Hables, *Postmodern War: The New Politics of Conflict* (New York: Guilford Press, 1997).

Gregory, Derek, 'The Black Flag: Guantanamo Bay and the Space of Exception', *Geografiska Annaler, Series B, Human Geography*, 88 (2006), pp. 405–27.

Gregory, Derek, *The Colonial Present: Afghanistan, Palestine, Iraq* (Malden, MA: Blackwell, 2004).

Gupta, Suman, *Imagining Iraq: Literature in English and the Iraq Invasion* (New York: Palgrave Macmillan, 2011).

al-Ḥamdānī, Raᶜd, *Qabla an yughādiranā al-tārīkh* (Before history leaves us) (Beirut: al-Dār al-ᶜarabiyya li al-ᶜulūm, 2007).

Hardt, Michael, and Antonio Negri, *Multitude: War and Democracy in the Age of Empire* (London: Penguin, 2004).

Hill, Andrew, *Re-imagining the War on Terror: Seeing, Waiting, Travelling*, (New York: Palgrave Macmillan, 2009).

Hussain, Nasser, and Melissa Ptacek, 'Thresholds: Sovereignty and the Scared' (book review), *Law and Society Review*, 34, 2 (2000), pp. 495–515.

Hynes, Samuel, *The Soldier's Tale: Bearing Witness to Modern War* (New York: Penguin, 1997).

Ibrāhīm, ᶜAbdallāh, *al-Binā᾿ al-fannī li riwāyat al-ḥarb fī alᶜIrāq: Dirāsa li naẓm al-sard wa al-binā᾿ fī al-riwāya al-ᶜirāqiyya al-muᶜāṣira* (Baghdad: Dar al-shu'ūn al-thaqāfiyya alᶜāmma, 1988).

Ibrāhīm, ᶜAbdallāh, *al-Takhayyul al-tārīkhī: al-Sard wa al-ᵓimbrāṭūriyya wa al-tajriba al-ᵓistiᶜmāriyya* (Beirut: al-Mu'assasa al-'arabiyya li al-dirāsāt wa al-nashr, 2011).

Ibrāhīm, Salām, 'al-Riwāya al-ᶜIrāqiyya: Raṣd al-kharāb', *Tabayyun*, 2 (December 2012), pp. 175–98.

Jabrā, Ibrāhīm Jabrā, *al-Fann wa al-ḥulm wa al-fiᶜl* (Baghdad: Dār al-shuᵓūn al-thaqāfiyya al-ᶜāmma, 1986).

Jayyūsī, Salma Khaḍra, *Trends and Movements in Modern Arabic Poetry* (Leiden: Brill, 1977).

Jayyūsī, Salma Khaḍra, 'Modernist Poetry in Arabic', in M. M. Badawi (ed.), *Modern Arabic Literature*, The Cambridge History of Arabic Literature (Cambridge: Cambridge University Press,1993), pp. 132–79.

Johnson, Rob, *The Iran–Iraq War* (New York: Palgrave Macmillan, 2010).

Kachāchī, Inaᶜām, *Paroles d'Irakiennes: Le drame Irakien écrit par des femmes* (Paris: Le serpent à plumes, 2003).

Kaldor, Mary, *New and Old Wars: Organized Violence in a Global Era* (Oxford: Polity Press, 1999).

Khudayrī, Batūl, *Kam badat al-samāᵓ qarība* (A sky so close) (Beirut: Arab Institute for Research and Publishing, 1999), translated as Betool Khedairi, *A Sky so Close* (New York: Anchor Books, 2001).

Kukis, Mark, *Voices from Iraq: A People's History, 2003–2009* (New York: Columbia University Press, 2011).

Lapham, Lewis H., 'Trained Seals and Sitting Ducks', http://harpers.org/archive/1991/05/trained-seals-and-sitting-ducks/.

Makiya, Kanan, *Cruelty and Silence: War, Tyranny, Uprising and the Arab World* (New York: Norton, 1993).

Masmoudi, Ikram, 'Portraits of Iraqi Women: Between Testimony and Fiction', *International Journal of Contemporary Iraqi Studies*, 4, 1–2 (2010).

Maṭlūb, Aḥmad, *al-Shiᶜr fī zaman al-ḥarb* (Poetry in times of war) (Baghdad: Dār al-shᵓūn al-thaqāfiyya al-ᵓāmma, 1987).

Mbembe, Achille, 'Necropolitics', in Stephen Morton and Stephen Bygrave (eds), *Foucault in an Age of Terror: Essays on Biopolitics and the Defense of Society*, pp. 152–82 (New York: Palgrave Macmillan, 2008).

Milich, Stephan, Friederike Pannewick and Leslie Tramontini (eds), *Conflicting Narratives: War, Violence and Memory in Iraqi Culture* (Wiesbaden: Reichert, 2012).

Mukhīf, ᶜAlī (ᶜAbd al-Ḥusayn), *Fī Qiṣṣat al-ḥarb: Dirāsa naqdiyya* (Baghdad: Dar al- shu'ūn al-thaqāfiyya wa al-nashr, manshūrāt wizārat al-thaqāfa wa al-iᶜlām, silsilat dirāsāt, 1984).

al-Musāwī, Muḥsin J., *al-Mar'ī wa al-mutakhayyal: Adab al-ḥarb al-qaṣaṣī fī al-ᶜIrāq* (Baghdad: Dār al-shu'ūn al-thaqāfiyya al-ᶜāmma, 1986).

al-Musāwī, Muhsin J., *Arabic Potery: Trajectories of Modernity and Tradition* (New York: Routledge, 2006).

al-Musāwī, Muḥsin J., *The Postcolonial Arabic Novel: Debating Ambivalence* (Leiden: Brill, 2003).

al-Musāwī, Muhsin J., *Reading Iraq: Culture and Power in Conflict* (London: I. B. Tauris, 2006).

Norris, Andrew, 'Giorgio Agamben and the Politics of the Living Dead', *Diacritics*, 30, 4 (2000), pp. 38–58.

Norris, Andrew (ed.), *Politics, Metaphysics, and Death: Essays on Giorgio Agamben's* Homo Sacer (Durham, NC: Duke University Press, 2005).

Norris, Christopher, *Uncritical Theory: Postmodernism, Intellectuals, and the Gulf War* (London: Lawrence and Wishart, 1992).

Norris, Margot, 'Military Censorship and the Body Count in the Persian Gulf War', *Cultural Critique*, 19 (Autumn 1991), pp. 223–45.

Norris, Margot, *Writing War in the Twentieth Century* (Charlottesville: University of Virginia Press, 2000). Pape, Robert, *Dying to Win: The Strategic Logic of Suicide Terrorism* (New York: Random House, 2005).

Pinault, David, 'Images of Christ in Arabic Literature', *Die Welt des Islam*, New Series, 27, 1–3 (1987), pp. 103–25.

al-Radi, Nuha, *Baghdad Diaries: A Woman's Chronicle of War and Exile* (New York: Vintage Books, 1998).

Rohde, Ashim, *State–Society Relations in Baᶜthist Iraq: Facing Dictatorship* (New York: Routledge, 2010).

Saeed, Mahmoud, *Saddam City*, trans. Ahmad Sadri (London: Saqi Books, 2004).

Sartre, Jean-Paul, *Baudelaire* (Paris: Gallimard, 1947).

Sartre, Jean-Paul, *What Is Literature? And Other Essays* (Cambridge, MA: Harvard University Press, 1988).

Sassoon, Joseph, *Saddam Hussein's Baᶜth Party: Inside an Authoritarian Regime* (Cambridge: Cambridge University Press, 2011).

Scarry, Elaine, *The Body in Pain: The Making and Unmaking of the World* (New York: Oxford University Press, 1985).

Schmitt, Carl, *The Nomos of the Earth in the International Law of the Jus Publicum Europaeum* (New York: Telos Press Publishing, 2003).

Shabbout, Nada, 'The Free Art of Occupation: Images for a New Iraq', *Arab Studies Quarterly*, 28, 3–4 (2006), pp. 41–55.

Simpson, David, *9/11: The Culture of Commemoration* (Chicago: Chicago University Press, 2006).

Tagma, Halit Mustafa, 'Homo Sacer vs. Homo Soccer Mom: Reading Agamben and Foucault in the War on Terror', *Alternatives: Global, Local, Political*, 34, 4 (2009), pp. 407–35.

Tramontini, Leslie, ' "Speaking Truth to Power" Intellectuals in Iraqi Baathist Cultural Production', *Middle East-Topics & Arguments*, 1 (2013), pp. 53–61.

Virilio, Paul, *Desert Screen: War at the Speed of Light*, trans. Michael Degener (London: Bloomsbury Academic, 2005).

Walther, Wiebke, 'Between Heroism, Hesitancy, Resignation and New Hope: The Iran–Iraq War 1980–1988 in Iraqi Poetry', in Stephan Milich, Friedrike Pannewick and Leslie Tramontini (eds), *Conflicting Narratives: War, Trauma and Memory in Iraqi Culture*, pp. 75–107 (Wiesbaden: Reichert Verlag, 2012).

Wilson, Colin, *The Outsider* (Boston: Houghton Mifflin, 1956).

Wissbort, Daniel (ed.), *Iraqi Poetry Today* (London: King's College London, University of London, 2002).

Zeidan, Joseph, 'Myth and Symbol in the Poetry of Adūnis and Yūsuf al-Khāl', *Journal of Arabic Literature*, 10 (1979), pp. 70–94.

Index

^{c}Abbās, Luʾay Ḥamza, 18
Al-^{c}Abbās, 131n
^{c}Abbūd, Salām, 11, 35
^{c}Abd al-Amīr, ^{c}Ali, 115–16, 117–20, 123
^{c}Abd al-Amīr, Khuḍayyir, 34
^{c}Abd al-Ḥusayn, Fayṣal, 11
^{c}Abdallah, Ibtisām, 88
^{c}Abd al-Wāḥid, ^{c}Abd al-Razzāq, 34–5
Abode of Peace *see* Dār al-Salām
Abode of War *see* Dār al-Ḥarb
Absent (*Ghāʾib*) (Khudayrī), 19
Abū Ghraib prison, 78, 79, 185, 191, 193
Achille, Louis T., 151–2
Adūnīs, 53
Afghanistan, 188, 190, 194
Agamben, Giorgio
  bare life and, 63
  on camp space, 192–3, 218
  friedlos and, 70
  on Hobbesian state of nature, 84n
  homo sacer and, 3–7, 20, 30, 177, 184
  on nature and exception, 61
  police and, 121–2
  survival and testimony, 206–9, 212
  werewolf and, 72
Ahmad, Eqbal, 112
Akhmatova, Anna, 41, 51, 83n
alcohol, 155, 168–9, 176
Alexander the Great, 75
Ali, Jamāl Ḥusayn, 2
^{c}Ali, ^{c}Awwād, 16, 18
^{c}Ali Bābā (fictional character), 146, 147
alienation
  desertion and, 66–71
  Green Zone and, 143
  of poet-soldiers, 43–6, 80–1
Allen, Roger, 82n
The American Granddaughter (*al-Ḥafida al-Amrīkiyya*) (Kachāchī), 19
  occupation and, 21, 23, 135–6
  war on terror and, 159–61
Amity Line, 139
Amputation Workshops, 65
Amwāt Baghdad (The dead of Baghdad) (Ali, J. Ḥ.), 2
al-Anbārī, Shākir, 11, 16
animals
  sexual abuse of, 107
  soldiers as, 96, 110
Antūn, Sinān, 11, 17
Appelfeld, Aharon, 95
Arabic Booker *see* International Prize for Arabic Fiction
Arabs, 195
Arḍ al-layālī (The land of the nights) (al-^{c}Ubaydī, N.), 18
Arḍ al-Sawād (Land of Blackness), 65–6
Aristotle, 4
art, poets with war and, 51–2
Asātidhat al-wahm (The professors of illusion) *see The Professors of Illusion*
Auschwitz, 208–9
awards, literary *see* ^{c}Qādisiyyat Saddam
al^{c}-Azzāwī, Fāḍil, 10, 11

Ba^{c}ath party, 195
  facial hair and, 64
  fiction writers under, 10–14, 35
  Hussein, Saddam, and, 2, 9, 10–14, 35, 59
  identity and, 62
  with *Khiḍr Qad and the Drab Olive Years*, 61–6, 126–7
  with Palestine, 64
  propaganda, 107
Badini, Dounia, 54
Badiou, Alain, 188
Badr, ^{c}Ali
  in exile, 11, 12, 36
  on poet-soldiers, 83n
  war literature and, 15–16, 20, 22
  see also The Professors of Illusion

Baghdad
  death as all-pervasive in, 2
  Green Zone in, 23, 135, 139–40, 145
  historical occupations of, 137–9, 141
  looting of, 145, 146
  Red Zone in, 23, 135, 143–4, 159, 178, 217–18
  walls in, 141–2
Baghdad Diaries (al-Radi), 88
Baghdad Marlboro (*Baghdad mālbūru*) (Wālī)
  Green Zone in, 144
  Gulf War in, 111–12
  individual choice with occupation and, 165
  live burials in, 86, 111–12
  occupation and, 16, 23, 135–6, 137, 157–9
  Red Zone in, 144, 159
  silence about Gulf War in, 87–8
  soldiers as *homo sacer* in, 85
  war deserters in, 179–82, 216
  war on terror and, 164
Baghdad Radio, 115
Bahiyya Group (fictional group), 38–9, 56
bare (naked) life
  in Camp Bucca, 23–4, 185, 218
  homines sacri and, 6–7, 20, 56
  homo sacer with, 3, 4, 5, 20, 30, 56–8
  in *Khiḍr Qad and the Drab Olive Years*, 63
  political power with, 6
  in *The Professors of Illusion*, 37, 39–40, 54–8
  sacer esto and, 5
  with sovereign exception, 3, 4, 6–7, 20
  violence and, 4
  of war deserters and poet-soldiers, 37, 39–40
Baṣrayātha (*Baṣrayātha: Portrait of a City*) (Khuḍayyir), 14
Baudelaire, Charles, 46, 47, 51, 52
Baudrillard, Jean, 1, 91, 93, 101–2, 129
Bauman, Zygmunt, 137
Bayt ʿalā nahr Dijla (A house on the Tigris) (al-ṣaqr), 13
Benjamin, Walter, 3
Bennett, Harold, 5
Bennis, Phyllis, 112
Beyond Love (*Mā baʾd al-ḥubb*) (Hussein, H.), 19, 86
  Gulf War and, 116–21, 124, 127–8
  soldiers as *homo sacer* in, 85, 87
  war literature and, 20
Beyond the Storm: A Gulf Crisis Reader (Bennis and Moushabeck), 112
Bin, Alberto, 93
Bin Laden, Osama, 189
biographical novel, 10, 15
biological life *see zoe*
biopolitics, 3, 4, 5, 47
bios (qualified life), 4
biotechnological revolution, 93
Black, Jeremy, 189
Black Skin, White Masks (Fanon), 151
Black Water, 155
Blāsim, Ḥasan, 18
blind ones (*al-ʿimyān*), 152
bodies
  with pain and torture, 203–6, 214n
  warfare and, 120–1, 162–4
The Body in Pain: The Making and Unmaking of the World (Scarry), 96–7, 99–100, 120–1, 199
Boers, 193
Breton, André, 51, 52
Briemberg, Mordecai, 90
Brown, Michelle, 200
burials, mass graves, 86, 89, 111–24
Bush, George H. W., 102, 111, 146
  vengeance with 9/11 and Iraq, 186–90
  with war on terror, 159, 164, 191–2, 194

Caiani, Fabio, 8, 11
Camp Bucca, 123
  background, 184–5
  bare life in, 23–4, 185, 218
  Cuba and, 190, 193
  identity at, 196, 198
  as incubator for extremists, 198
  inside, 193–202
  as lawless space, 192–3, 194
  names and, 187–8, 196, 198
  survival and testimony, 205–12
  torture: with music, 199–201; resisting, 202–5; shame and, 198; with sunlight, 199–200
  see also The Madmen of Camp Bucca
camp space
  Agamben on, 192–3, 218
  detainee, 2
  with *homines sacri* and sovereign power, 193
  homo sacer and, 19–20, 212, 218–19
  as lawless, 192–3, 194
  virtual camp and exception, 87, 121–4, 219
'The Camp as the *Nomos* of the Modern' (Agamben), 192–3
censorship
  Gulf War and media, 111–12, 114
  influence, 35
  self-imposed, 13–14
Central Intelligence Agency (CIA), 189–90
Chandrasekaran, Rajiv, 139
checkmate
  in Gulf War: buried alive, 124–9; human moments, 109–12
  origins, 131n
Chediac, Joyce, 115

Cheney, Dick, 111
children, 40–1
Christ figure, 57–8, 83n
CIA *see* Central Intelligence Agency
Cobham, Catherine, 8, 11
Coker, Christopher, 93–4
contest
  with sitting ducks, 106–7
  warfare as, 99–109
cooke, miriam, 32–3, 88, 92
co-optation, silence and, 10–14
Cordesman, Anthony, 28–9, 125, 128–9
The Corpse Washer (Antūn), 17
Cruelty and Silence: War, Tyranny, Uprising, and the Arab World (Makkiya), 88
Cuba, 190, 193
curse, *sacer esto* as, 5

dance
  tango as occupation, 148–9, 174–5, 177
  Zīrān, 173–4
Danner, Mark, 181
Dār al-Ḥarb (the Abode of War), 144–5, 147
Dār al-Islam, 144–5
Dār al-Salām (the Abode of Peace), 144, 147
Daᶜwa Party, 125
Ḍayā fī Ḥafr al-Bāṭin (Loss in Ḥafr al-Bāṭin) *see Loss in Ḥafr al-Bāṭin*
Dean, Michel, 122
death
  as all-pervasive, 2, 14, 54–5, 78–9
  genocide, 3, 65–6, 88
  Highway of Death, 86, 111–12, 113, 115–16, 219
  killing and, 2–6, 65–6, 198
  Killing Box, 87, 114–16, 123–4, 184
  of language and men, 54–8
  squads, 35
  symbiosis with, 54
defeat *see* checkmate
dehumanisation, of soldiers, 86–7, 218
deployment, moral conditions for, 95–8
desaparecidos (disappeared ones), 19, 67
The Descent of the Angels (*Hubūṭ al-malāʾika*) (Ḥasan), 16
  with Iran–Iraq War, 77–9
  torture in, 78
  war deserters in, 29–30, 78–9, 180, 215–16
  war literature and, 20, 22
desertion
  alienation and, 66–71
  in Gulf War, 28, 97–8, 103–4, 108
  in Iran–Iraq War, 28
  as liberating event, 72–6, 81
  war deserters, 2, 7, 16, 19–21, 29, 37, 39–40, 69–72, 76, 78–9, 179–82, 215–16
  werewolf and topography of, 71–2
  see also The Descent of the Angels; *Khiḍr Qad and the Drab Olive Years*; *Loss in Ḥafr al-Bāṭin*; *The Professors of Illusion*
Desert Storm (Bin), 93
detainee, 2, 7, 11; *see also* Abū Ghraib prison; Camp Bucca; Guantánamo Bay; *The Madmen of Camp Bucca*
diary, of poet-soldier, 115–20, 123, 124
Diary of a Solder Returning from the Defeat (ᶜAbd al-Amīr, ᶜA.), 117–20, 123, 124
dictatorship, novels written under, 7, 12
Diken, Bulent, 145
Dini Group, 155–6
disappeared ones (*desaparecidos*), 19, 67
disco, 200–2, 210
Dog War, 64–5, 69; *see also* Iran–Iraq War
draft, 65, 96
al-Duktūr Ibrāhim (al-Nūn Ayyūb), 8
al-Dulaymī, Luṭfiyya, 14, 19

Egypt, 31
Eliot, T. S., 52, 56
enemies, war on terror, 190–2
Etienne, Bruno, 178
exception (exclusion)
  bare life with sovereign, 3, 4, 6–7, 20
  homo sacer and double, 5–6
  in *Khiḍr Qad and the Drab Olive Years*, 61–6
  sacratio and, 4
  with setting apart, 4–5
  sovereign power and, 3–7, 20
  of violence and unsanctionable killing, 5–6
  virtual camp as space of, 87, 121–4, 219
exile
  fiction writers in, 7, 9–10, 11–12, 14–21, 36, 59
  novels written in, 7, 12; identity and life in exile, 17–18; occupation, 16–17, 21; war literature, 14–16, 20; women writers, 18–19
extermination, 124; *see also* genocide; Highway of Death; Killing Box
extraordinary-rendition program, CIA and, 189–90
extremists, incubator for, 198

facial hair, 64
Falak, Naṣīf, 15, 18, 59, 66, 125
  poet-soldiers and, 83n
  war literature and, 20, 22
  see also Khiḍr Qad and the Drab Olive Years
Fanon, Frantz, 139, 143–4, 151
al-Farīsa (The prey) (ᶜAbbās), 18

Farmān, Ghā'ib Tu'ma, 8–9, 10, 46
Fayḍī, Sulaymān, 8
al-Faytūrī, Muḥammad, 82n
fiction
IPAF, 17
reality and, 67–9
theoretical framework, 2–7
fiction writers
under Ba'ath party, 10–14, 35
in exile, 7, 9–10, 11–12, 21, 36, 59; with freedom, 14–20
with literature and Iran–Iraq War, 12–13, 32–5
migration of, 11–12
under oppression, 13–14
as prisoner of war, 11
as soldiers, 11, 21, 32
as war deserters, 21
women, 18–19, 21
Fisher, Fritz, 31
Fitzpatrick, Peter, 4, 57
'Flames of Fire in Qādisiya' (cooke), 32–3, 88
forgotten war, 65; *see also* Gulf War; Iran–Iraq War
form-of-life, 4
Foucault, Michel, 3, 4, 20, 30
Fowler, W. Warde, 5
Frānkinshtāyn fī Baghdad (Frankenstein in Baghdad) (Sa'dāwī), 2, 16
freedom
desertion as, 72–6, 81
fiction writers in exile with, 14–20
language of, 74–5
in poetry, 46–8, 55
today, 32
see also The Madman of Freedom Square
Freedom Memorial, 60
The freedom of the bagged heads (*Ru' ūs al-ḥurriya al-mukayyasa*) (al-Raṣīf), 21, 135, 152
friedlos (without peace), 70, 72
Friedman, Thomas, 146
The Future of War (Coker), 93

Garner, Jay, 147
Geneva Conventions, 124, 185, 194, 207
genocide, 3, 65–6, 88; *see also* Holocaust, Jews and
Germanic laws, 70
Ghā'ib see *Absent*
Gilgamesh, 75
glorification, of killing, 113
Glosson, Buster (General), 114–15, 132n
graves, live burial in mass, 86, 89, 111–24
Gray, Chris, 90
The Green Zone (*al-Minṭaqa al-Khaḍrā*) (Nūrī), 2
alcohol in, 155, 168–9, 176
American occupiers characterised in, 152–6
homo sacer in, 169–70, 176–7, 184
identity in, 167–8
individual choice with occupation and, 165
masks in, 166–7
music and, 154–5, 162
occupation and, 21, 23, 135–7, 156; occupier and occupied, 149–52; tango as dance of, 148–9, 174–5, 177
Red Zone and, 159, 178
suicide bomber in, 137, 165–78, 217
war on terror and, 160–5
Zīrān dance in, 173–4
Green Zone *see* occupation, US in Iraq
Gregory, Derek, 146, 159
Guantánamo Bay, 123, 185, 190, 191, 193–4
The Gulf War Did Not Take Place (Baudrillard), 101–2
Gulf War (1991)
in *Baghdad Marlboro*, 111–12
Beyond Love and, 116–21, 124, 127–8
checkmate and buried alive, 124–9
deployment with moral conditions, 95–8
desertion in, 28, 97–8, 103–4, 108
Highway of Death in, 86, 111–12, 113, 115–16, 219
holocaust of, 106, 112
human moments in, 109–12
Hussein, Saddam, and, 87–8, 102, 114, 116–17
influence, 32
Khiḍr Qad and the Drab Olive Years and, 125–7
Killing Box and, 87, 114–16, 123–4, 184
killing in, 65–6
with live burials in mass graves, 86, 89, 111–24
Loss in Ḥafr al-Bāṭin and, 95–8, 100–11
media censorship in, 111–12, 114
migration and, 11
mythologised and forgotten, 87–93
as postmodern war, 22, 89–93, 100–3
Shi'a population and, 125
silence about, 87–8
with sitting ducks, 106–7, 112
sons of new war and short contest, 99–109
turkey shoot and mass killing in: explanation of, 112–14; history, 114–16; massacre, 116–21; as police operation and virtual camp, 121–4
warfare changes, 93–5, 101
war literature and, 18, 20, 88–9
as world war, 89–90, 113, 121

re-examination of, 28, 32, 88, 215
war literature and, 12–16, 20, 22, 30–5, 77–9
as war of identity, 31
Iraq, 2, 9, 41
today, 134
vengeance with 9/11 and, 186–90
see also occupation, US in Iraq
'Iraq: The War of the Imagination' (Danner), 181
Iraqi Governing Council, 159
Iraqi Ministry of Culture and Information, 12, 34, 88
The Iraqi Christ (*al-Masīḥ al-ʿirāqī*) (Blāsim), 18
Islam, 144–5, 188, 197

Jabrā, Jabrā Ibrāhīm, 13, 33, 34
Jaʿfar, Ḥasab al-Shaykh, 51, 83n
Jalāl Khālid (al-Sayyid), 8
Jandārī, Maḫmūd, 14
Jayyusi, May, 177
al-Jazāʾirī, Zuhayr, 11
Jews *see* Holocaust, Jews and
jihād, 145
al-Jubaylī, Ḍiyā, 18

Kachāchī, Inaʿām, 18, 19, 21; *see also The American Granddaughter*
Kafka, Franz, 113, 131n, 179
Kam badat al-samāʾ qarība see *A Sky so Close*
Karbalā, 128, 133n
Karrādat Maryam (Republican Palace), 140–1, 147
al-Khāl, Yūsuf, 53, 54
al-Khālidī, Ḍiyāʾ, 2, 18
Khamsat aṣwāt (Five voices) (Farmān), 9, 46
Khaṭṭ aḥmar (Red line) (al-Raṣīf), 13
Khayyūn, Ali, 34
al-Khiḍr (spiritual guide), 59, 83n
Khiḍr Qad and the Drab Olive Years (*Khiḍr Qad wa al-ʿaṣr al-zaytūnī*) (Falak), 15
alienation and desertion, 66–71
Baʿath party and, 61–6, 126–7
bare life in, 63
burials in, 86
desertion as liberating event, 72–6, 81
exception and Baʿath in, 61–6
friedlos in, 70, 72
genocide in, 65–6
Gulf War and, 125–7
homines sacri and, 65–6, 126
homo sacer in, 60–1, 69–71, 76, 85
with Iran–Iraq War, 58–76
Moses figure in, 74–5, 84n
nature in, 61–6, 73
plot, 58–61
publishing history, 59
reality and fiction in, 67–9
silence in, 72–3
torture in, 63
war deserter in, 29–30, 180, 215–16
war literature and, 20, 22
werewolf and topography of desertion, 71–2
Khomeini, Ruḥullah (Ayatollah), 31
Khudayrī, Batūl, 19
Khuḍayyir, Muḥammad, 14
Khuzestan, 30
killing, 18
as all-pervasive, 2
as exception with violence and unsanctionable, 5–6
by extremists, 198
genocide, 3, 65–6, 88
glorification of, 113
in Gulf War, 65–6, 112–24
sacratio and, 4
see also death; *homines sacri*; *homo sacer*
Killing Box, 87, 114–16, 123–4, 184; *see also* Highway of Death
the king is dead (*al-shaykh maat*), 131
Kissinger, Henry, 188
knowledge
subjugated, 20, 30
warfare and practical, 95
Kurds, 65, 77, 84n, 88, 151
Kuwait, 30–1
invasion of 1990, 11, 82n, 88
withdrawal from, 114–16

Land of Blackness (Arḍ al-Sawād), 65–6
language
death of men and, 54–8
of freedom, 74–5
Lapham, Lewis H., 112
Lausten, Carsten Bagge, 145
lawless
camp space as, 192–3, 194
Dār al-Ḥarb as, 144–5
Red Zone as, 23, 143–4, 159, 217–18
laws
friedlos and Germanic, 70
homo sacer and Roman, 3, 5, 81
sovereign power and, 132n
Layl al-bilād (The country's long night) (Hillāwī), 15
Levi, Primo, 208–9
life
categories: bare life, 3–7, 20, 23–4, 30, 37, 39–40, 54–8, 63, 185, 218; *bios*, 4; form-of-life, 4; *zoe*, 3, 4, 47

life (*cont.*)
homines sacri, 6–7, 20, 56
homo sacer and, 3–6
as sacred, 4–5
literature
awards, 12, 13, 26n, 32–3, 80
homo sacer in, 19–20
Iran–Iraq War background and, 30–5
see also war literature
Locke, John, 142
The Long Way Back (*al-Raj*ᶜ *al-ba*ᶜ*īd*) (al-Takarlī), 10
looting, of Baghdad, 145, 146
loss *see* checkmate
Loss in Ḥafr al-Bāṭin (*Ḍayā fī Ḥafr al-Bāṭin*) (al-ᶜUbaydī, A.), 2, 18
checkmate in, 109–12
desertion in, 97–8, 103–4, 108
Gulf War and, 95–8, 100–11
with moral conditions of deployment, 95–8
soldiers as animals and insects in, 96, 110
soldiers as *homo sacer* in, 85–6
war literature and, 20

*Mā ba*ᵓ*d al-ḥubb* see *Beyond Love*
machine, torture, 131n
Mackey, Sandra, 31
MacLeish, Archibald, 53
Madīnat al-ṣuwar (City of pictures) (ᶜAbbās), 18
The Madman of Freedom Square (*Majnūn sāḥat al-ḥurriya*) (Blāsim), 18
The Madmen of Camp Bucca (*Majānīn Būkā*) (Nūrī), 2
camp conditions, 185–6, 192–202, 218
with enemy imagined, 191–2
occupation and, 21, 23
prayer to transcend pain, 203–6
survival and testimony, 205–12
torture: *Muselmann* and, 211; music as, 201–3, 210–12; resisting, 202–5; with sunlight, 210
vengeance with Iraq and 9/11, 186–90
madness, 2, 11, 196, 200, 212
al-Maḥbūbāt (The beloved ladies) (Mamdūḥ), 19
Majānīn Būkā (The madmen of Camp Bucca) *see The Madmen of Camp Bucca*
Majnūn sāḥat al-ḥurriya see *The Madman of Freedom Square*
Makkiya, Kanan, 88
Mallarmé, Stéphane, 46
Mamarrāt al-sukūn see *Zubaida's Window*
Mamdūḥ, ᶜĀliya, 11, 19
Mandelstam, Osip, 41
Man yaftaḥ bāb al-ṭalṣam (Who opens the talisman's door) (al-Rukābī), 14
Man yarith al-firdaws (Who inherits paradise) (al-Dulaymī), 14
Marbid Festival, 82n
*al-Mar*ᵓ*ī wa al-mutakhayyal* (The seen and the imagined) (al-Mūsawī), 12
al-Markab (The boat) (Farmān), 8
martyrs, suicide bombers as, 177
Marxism, 8
*al-Masarrāt wa al-awjā*ᶜ (Joys and sorrow) (al-Takarlī), 10
Mashraḥat Baghdad (The morgue of Baghdad) (Shāwī), 2, 17
*al-Masīḥ al-*ᶜ*irāqī* see *The Iraqi Christ*
masks, 166–7
massacre, 116–21, 128, 133n; *see also* genocide; Highway of Death; Killing Box
Maṭar aswad ... maṭar aḥmar (Black rain ... red rain) (ᶜAbdallah), 88
Maṭlūb, Aḥmad, 34
Mayakovsky, Vladimir, 41, 83n
Mbembe, Achille, 215
media
Abū Ghraib and, 185
Gulf War and censorship of, 111–12, 114
men
death of language and, 54–8
as wolf to men, 71–2
see also homines sacri; *homo sacer*; *Muselmann*
metal music, 200, 203
migration, of intellectuals, 7, 11–12
Mīkhāᵓīl, Dunyā, 88
al-Minṭaqa al-Khaḍrā (The Green Zone) *see The Green Zone*
Mīrī, Khuḍayyir, 11
Mongols, 141
Monroe Doctrine, 122
moral conditions, deployment, 95–8
Moses (biblical figure), 74–5, 84n
Moushabeck, Michel, 112
al-Mūsawī, Muḥsin, 12, 41, 51
Muselmann (sacred man), 23, 208–10, 211, 212, 218
music
in *The Green Zone*, 154–5, 162
as torture, 199–203, 210–12
Muṭaq, Ḥasan, 14
myths
Gulf War as, 87–93
People of the Cave or Seven Sleepers, 40–1

Najmat al-Battāwīn (The star of al-Battāwīn) (al-Anbārī), 16
naked life *see* bare life
al-Nakhla wa al-jīrān (The palm tree and the neighbours) (Farmān), 8–9
names, Camp Bucca and, 187–8, 196, 198

Nāṣir, ᶜAbd al-Sattār, 11, 33–5
natural life *see zoe*
nature
Amity Line and, 139
Hobbesian state of, 84n
in *Khiḍr Qad and the Drab Olive Years*, 61–6, 73
nausea *see The Professors of Illusion*
Nazis, 193, 195, 208, 218
Nebuchadnezzar (King), 32
9/11, 185–90
Nisāᶜ ʾalā safar (*Women on a Journey*) (Zangana), 19
Noah (biblical figure), 204–5
The Nomos of the Earth (Schmitt), 121, 139
Norris, Christopher, 91
Norris, Margot, 113
novels
biographical, 10, 15
development of, 7–10
influential, 7–8, 10
occupation, 16–17, 21
theoretical framework, 2–7
war literature, 12–16, 20, 88–9
written in exile, 7, 12, 14–21
written under dictatorship, 7, 12
see also specific titles
al-Nūn Ayyūb, Dhū, 8
Nūrī, Shākir, 2, 176
on Camp Bucca, 192
on occupation, 21, 137, 139, 156
see also The Green Zone; *The Madmen of Camp Bucca*

occupation, US in Iraq
as eternal return: with American occupiers characterised, 152–6; Baghdad and historical occupation, 137–9; inside/outside divide, 136–7, 139–48; occupier and occupied, 149–52; tango as dance of occupation, 148–9, 174–5, 177
Green Zone: alienation and, 143; *homer sacer* and, 135; Karrādat Maryam in, 140–1, 147; Red Zone and, 159, 178; as safe space, 23, 139–41, 144–5, 147, 218; violence in, 142
individual choice in response to, 165
novels about, 16–17, 21
Red Zone, 178; *homer sacer* and, 135; as lawless space, 23, 143–4, 159, 217–18
re-examination of, 88
terror: full circle, 178–82; individual choices with, 165; sectarianism and, 156–65; suicide bomber in making, 165–78, 217
see also The American Granddaughter; *Baghdad Marlboro*; Camp Bucca; *The freedom of the bagged heads*; *The Green Zone*; *The Madmen of Camp Bucca*
Operation Desert Storm *see* Gulf War
oppression, fiction writers under, 13–14
The Outsider (Wilson), 44

pain
Amputation Workshops and, 65
prayer to transcend, 203–6
psychological and physical, 62–3
torture and, 203–6, 214n
see also The Body in Pain: The Making and Unmaking of the World
Palestine, 64, 97
Pape, Robert, 178
peace *see* Dār al-Salām; *friedlos*
People of the Cave (al-Ḥakīm), 82n
People of the Cave myth, 40–1
Persian Gulf War *see* Gulf War
Peshmerga, 77, 84n
physical pain, psychological and, 62–3
poetry
freedom in, 46–8, 55
Hussein, Saddam, in, 34–5, 82n
poetic vision, with *The Professors of Illusion*, 50–4
politics and, 51
Shiᶜr poetry group, 53–4
poets
with art and war, 51–2
poet-soldiers: alienation of, 43–6, 80–1; bare life of, 37, 39–40; diary, 115–20, 123, 124; existence of, 83n
Russian, 41
with survival and testimony, 207–8
see also The Professors of Illusion
Poets of Five O'Clock (fictional group), 38–9
police operation, 121–4, 132n
political power
with bare life, 6
homo sacer with, 6–7
violence of, 3, 9
politics
biopolitics, 3, 4, 5, 47
poetry and, 51
with *zoe* politicised, 4, 47
postmodern war *see* Gulf War
Powell, Colin, 111
power *see* political power; sovereign power
prayer, pain and, 203–6
prisoners of war, 2, 7, 11; *see also* Abū Ghraib prison; Camp Bucca; Guantánamo Bay; *The Madmen of Camp Bucca*
production, of war literature, 12–13, 32–4

The Professors of Illusion (*Asātidhat al-wahm*) (Badr), 15–16
  bare life in, 37, 39–40, 54–8
  Christ figure in, 57–8, 83n
  desertion in, 36–58
  explanation of, 36–43
  with Iran–Iraq War, 36–58
  nausea of experience and purity in, 47–50
  poetic vision, 50–4
  with poetry as freedom, 46–8, 55
  poet-soldiers, 37, 39–40, 43–6, 80–1, 83n
  war deserter in, 29–30, 180, 215–16
  war literature and, 20, 22
propaganda
  Ba^c^ath party, 107
  recruitment of soldiers with, 96–7
  war literature as, 33–4
psychological pain, physical and, 62–3
punishments, for war deserters, 29, 39, 70, 76, 78–9
purity, 47–50

Qabbānī, Nizār, 82n
Qabla an yughādiranā al-tārīkh (Before history leaves us) (al-Ḥamdānī), 88
Qādisiyyat Saddam, Qiṣaṣ taḥta lahīb al-nār (Saddam's Qādisiyya, stories under fire) (Iraqi Ministry of Culture and Information), 12, 34
^c^Qādisiyyat Saddam, 12, 13, 26n, 32–3, 80
al-Qaeda, 189, 196, 199
al-Qal^c^ a al-khāmisa (The fifth fortress) (al^c^-Azzāwī), 10
Qatala (Killers) (al-Khālidī), 2, 18
al-Qazwīnī, Iqbāl, 19
qualified life *see bios*
Qur^ɔ^ān, 83n
al-Qurbān (The offering) (Farmān), 8

race, 151–2, 192
al-Radi, Nuha, 88
al-Raj^c^ al-ba^c^īd see *The Long Way Back*
al-Raṣīf, Jāsim, 13, 21, 135, 152
reality, fiction and, 67–9
Red Zone *see* occupation, US in Iraq
Re-imagining the War on Terror (Hill), 190
Remnants of Auschwitz (Levi), 208–9
Republican Palace *see* Karrādat Maryam
resistance, torture, 202–5
Rilke, Rainer Maria, 51
Rimbaud, Arthur, 47
al-Riwāya al-īqāẓiyya (Fayḍī), 8
Roman law
  biopolitics and, 3, 5
  homo sacer, 3, 5, 81
  with *sacer esto* as penalty, 5
Roosevelt Corollary, 122
al-Rubay^c^ī, Abd al-Raḥmān Majīd, 10
al-Rukābī, Abd al-Khāliq, 14
Russia, 40–2
Ru^ɔ^ ūs al-ḥurriya al-mukayyasa see *The freedom of the bagged heads*

al-Sabāh^ɔ^, Su^c^ād, 82n
sacer esto, 5
sacratio, 4
sacred, 4–6
sacred man *see homo sacer*; *Muselmann*
sacred people *see homines sacri*
ṣadāqat al-nimr (The tiger's friendship) (^c^Abbās), 18
Sa^c^dāwī, Aḥmad, 2, 16–18
ṣaḥwa groups, 196
ṣalāḥ, ṣalāḥ, 18
Salīm, Jawād, 60
al-Sālim, Wārid Badr, 34
Sandline International, 156
al-ṣaqr, Mahdī ^c^Īsā, 13
Sartre, Jean-Paul, 49
Saudi Arabia, 30–1
al-ṣāyigh, ^c^Adnān, 34
al-Sayyāb, Badr Shākir, 51, 53
al-Sayyid, Maḥmūd Aḥmad, 8
Scarry, Elaine, 62–3, 96–7
  on bodies and warfare, 120–1
  on torture, 199, 200–1, 204, 214n
  on warfare as contest, 99–100
Scheherazade (fictional character), 147, 206
Schmitt, Carl, 3, 121, 139, 193
Schwarzkopf, Norman (General), 90, 105, 111
sectarianism *see* occupation, US in Iraq
self-imposed censorship, 13–14
Seven Sleepers myth, 40–1
sexual abuse, of animals, 107
shame, torture, 198
Shaṭṭ al-^c^Arab waterway, 31
Shāwī, Burhān, 2, 17
al-shaykh maat (the king is dead), 131
Shi^c^a population, 131n, 195–6
  Gulf War and, 125
  Iran–Iraq War and, 30–1
  uprising, 88, 89
Shi^c^r poetry group, 53–4
silence
  co-optation and, 10–14
  about Gulf War, 87–8
  in *Khiḍr Qad and the Drab Olive Years*, 72–3
Simpson, David, 189
sitting ducks, 106–7, 112

A Sky so Close (*Kam badat al-samā' qarība*) (Khudayrī), 19
soldiers
as animals and insects, 96, 110
buried alive, 86, 89, 111–24
dehumanisation of, 86–7, 218
fiction writers as, 11, 21, 32
as *homines sacri*, 86–7, 110
as *homo sacer*, 85–7
moral conditions and deployment of, 95–8
poet-soldiers, 37, 39–40, 43–6, 80–1, 83n, 115–20, 123, 124
recruitment with propaganda, 96–7
warriors, 2, 7, 19–20, 34, 94–5, 101
see also Loss in Ḥafr al-Bāṭin; war deserters
The Soldier's Tale (Hynes), 95
South Africa, 193
'Sovereign Police' (Agamben), 121
sovereign power
biopolitics and, 3
camp space and, 193
exception: bare life produced from, 3–4, 6–7, 20; *sacratio*, 4; with setting apart, 4–5
homo sacer with, 6–7
with killing, 5–6
law and, 132n
role of, 2–3
violence of, 3–4, 132n
spiritual guide (al-Khiḍr), 59, 83n
Stalin, Joseph, 37, 41
State of Denial (Woodward), 188
subjugated knowledge, 20, 30
suicide bombers, 2, 137
with geography of occupation and war on terror, 23
as *homo sacer*, 19–20
making of, 165–78, 217
as martyrs, 177
see also The Green Zone
sunlight, torture, 199–200, 210
Sunni population, 195–6
Sunni Triangle, 159
Ṣurākh al-nawāris (The cry of the seagulls) (al-ṣaqr), 13
surrender *see* checkmate
survival, Camp Bucca testimony and, 205–12
symbiosis, with death, 54

al-Takarlī, Fu'ād, 10, 13
Takfīrī population, 195, 196, 197–8
Ṭālib, ʿAli ibn Abī, 131n
Tamil Tigers, 178
tango, as dance of occupation, 148–9, 174–5, 177
technology, 93, 113, 157
terror *see* occupation, US in Iraq; war on terror
testimony, with Camp Bucca survival, 205–12
Thaqāfat al ʿunf fī al-ʿIrāq (The culture of violence in Iraq) (ʿAbbūd), 35
theoretical framework, novels and fiction
death and killing, 2
power, with exception, 3–7
A Thousand and One Nights, 146–7, 151, 206
torture
at Camp Bucca, 198–205
in *The Descent of the Angels*, 78
in *Khiḍr Qad and the Drab Olive Years*, 63
machine, 131n
in *The Madmen of Camp Bucca*, 201–5, 210–12
madness from, 196, 200, 212
pain and, 203–6, 214n
'Trained Seals and Sitting Ducks' (Lapham), 112
Trier, Jost, 139
turkey shoot *see* Gulf War

al-ʿUbaydī, ʿAbd al-Karīm, 18, 20; *see also Loss in Ḥafr al-Bāṭin*
al-ʿUbaydī, Nāẓum, 18
United Nations (UN), 115, 129, 194
United States (US)
Bush and, 102, 111, 146, 159, 164, 186–92, 194
CIA, 189–90
with jihād and war on terror, 145
Killing Box and, 87, 114–16, 123–4, 184
as occupier, 152–6
virtual camp and, 87, 121–4, 219
see also Camp Bucca; occupation, US in Iraq
al-ʿUqābī, Ḥamīd, 15
'Uṣghī ilā Ramādī (I listen to my ashes) (al-ʿUqābī), 15

vengeance, 9/11 and Iraq, 186–90
violence
as all-pervasive, 2, 5, 9, 35, 62, 142, 217
Amputation Workshops and, 65
bare life and, 4
as exception with unsanctionable killing, 5–6
of political power, 3, 9
of sovereign power, 3–4, 132n
Virilio, Paul, 89–90, 92
virtual camp, 87, 121–4, 219
virtual warriors, 94–5, 101

Waging War without Warriors? (Coker), 94
Wahhābī population, 195–6
Wālī, Najm, 137, 178
in exile, 11, 14–15

Wālī, Najm (*cont.*)
occupation and, 21
with war literature, 14–16
see also Baghdad Marlboro
walls, history of, 141–2
war *see* Dār al-Ḥarb; Gulf War; Iran–Iraq War
war deserters, 2, 7, 16, 215
in *Baghdad Marlboro*, 179–82, 216
bare life of, 37, 39–40
fiction writers as, 21
full circle with, 180–1
as *homo sacer*, 19–20, 69–71
punishment for, 29, 39, 70, 76, 78–9
as werewolf, 71–2
see also The Descent of the Angels; desertion; *Khiḍr Qad and the Drab Olive Years*; *Loss in Ḥafr al-Bāṭin*; *The Professors of Illusion*
warfare
bodies and, 120–1, 162–4
changes in, 93–5, 101
as contest, 99–109
postmodern, 22, 89–93, 100–3
practical knowledge of, 95
technology of, 113
torture and, 199
war literature
Gulf War and, 18, 20, 88–9
Iran–Iraq War and, 12–16, 20, 22, 30–5, 77–9
production of, 12–13, 32–4
as propaganda, 33–4
see also specific titles
war on terror
in *The American Granddaughter*, 159–61
Baghdad Marlboro and, 164
beginnings, 159
Bush and, 159, 164, 191–2, 194
CIA with terror suspects, 189–90
with enemy imagined, 190–2
in *The Green Zone*, 160–5
jihād and, 145
with 9/11, 185
suicide bombers and, 2, 19–20, 23, 137, 165–78, 217
vengeance with 9/11 and Iraq, 186–90
see also Camp Bucca
warriors, 2, 7
as *homo sacer*, 19–20
as literary figure, 34
warfare changes and virtual, 94–5, 101
see also soldiers
War with Iraq (Glosson), 115
al-Washm (al-Rubayʿī), 10
The Waste Land (Eliot), 56
werewolf
desertion and, 71–2
as enemy in war on terror, 191–2
Wilson, Colin, 44, 46
without peace (*friedlos*), 70, 72
witnesses *see* testimony, with Camp Bucca survival
wolf *see* werewolf
women, 18–19, 21
Women and the War Story (cooke), 32–3, 88
Women on a Journey see Nisāʿ ʾalā safar
Woodward, Bob, 188
world war, Gulf War as, 89–90, 113, 121
The Wretched of the Earth (Fanon), 139
writers *see* fiction writers

Yawmiyyāt mawja khārij al-baḥr (The journal of a wave outside the sea) (Mīkhāʾīl), 88
Yazīd (Umayyad caliph), 133n
Yūsuf, Saʿdi, 51

Zangana, Hayfāʾ, 11, 19
Zīrān dance, 173–4
zoe (biological or natural life), 3, 4, 47
Zubaida's Window (*Mamarrāt al-sukūn*) (al-Qazwīnī), 19